THE
DINOSAUR
HANDBOOK

THE
DINOSAUR
HANDBOOK

Maria Costantino

Published by SILVERDALE BOOKS
An imprint of Bookmart Ltd
Registered number 2372865
Trading as Bookmart Ltd
Blaby Road
Wigston
Leicester
LE18 4SE
©2004 D&S Books Ltd

D&S Books Ltd
Kerswell,
Parkham Ash, Bideford
Devon, England
EX39 5PR

e-mail us at:-
enquiries.dspublishing@care4free.net

This edition printed 2004

ISBN 1-845090-00-4

DS0083. The Dinosaur Handbook.

Creative Director: Sarah King
Project editor: Judith Millidge
Designer: 2H Design
Illustrator: Ronald Swanwick

Typeset in Sabon

Printed in China
1 3 5 7 9 10 8 6 4 2

Contents

What is a dinosaur?

In 1841, the British anatomist Richard – later Sir Richard – Owen (1804-92), addressed the annual meeting of the British Association for the Advancement of Science, in Plymouth, England. Owen's presentation at the meeting was a review of all the fossil-reptiles that had been found in the British Isles to that date.

With his training in anatomy, Owen was able to recognise that from the remains of three fossil reptiles – *megalosaurus, iguanodon,* and *hylaeosaurus* – that these were completely different to any other fossilised or living creature. Owen described how these three fossil-reptiles were all extremely large – about the size of a full-grown elephant – that they all lived on land, and, that they all had distinctive 'pillar-like' legs that were 'tucked in' underneath their body. Owen noticed that this position of the legs was totally different to the 'splayed' leg position- where the upper leg joins the body at the sides- that is typical of other reptiles, and he named these strange reptiles *dinosaurs*, which is derived from the Greek words *deinos* and *saurus* which mean 'terrible reptiles'.

Iguanodon skeleton.

To be precise, dinosaurs were members of a particular group of reptiles: they were all creatures that had four limbs (although some did walk 'upright' on their two hind legs) and they lived on land. While a few may have waded into shallow, swampy water, dinosaurs were not 'designed' to be efficient swimmers and they didn't live in the sea. The gigantic sea reptiles mentioned later in this book- such as plesiosaurs, mosasaurs and ichthyosaurs, were not, in fact, dinosaurs at all. In the same way, dinosaurs did not fly. The 'flying reptiles' of the 'age of the dinosaurs' like the pterosaurs, were strictly speaking not dinosaurs!

Not a dinosaur, but a marine reptile.

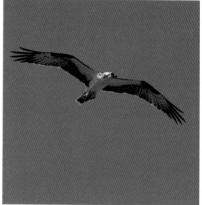

Not a dinosaur, but a 'flying reptile.

Dinosaurs belonged to the group of reptiles known as *archosaurs*, which means 'ruling reptiles'. The archosaur group includes some now extinct creatures, such as the theocodonts, as well as some very well known extant (or, still living) creatures such as crocodiles, and some very familiar living descendants – birds!

The Crocodile is an extant member of the dinosaurs.

Birds are living descendants of dinosaurs.

Fossils

Everything we know about dinosaurs is based on their fossilised remains. The most common fossils are the naturally preserved remains of once living organisms which have become 'entombed' in sediments – layers of sand, silt, mud and rock. Gradually, the organism's original tissues decomposed and was replaced by minerals. In other fossils, the soft tissue of the original organism or object was destroyed by the acidic effects of groundwater, and minerals later formed a replica of it. These fossils are therefore composed of new 'replacement' minerals that are harder and heavier versions of the original 'material'. Not only can fossils often be very different in colour to the object that originally formed them, but because of pressure inside the rocks in which they are found, fossils can also be distorted in shape. It is also important to remember that over millions of years, the shifting of the continental plates means that the sediments containing fossil remains may have moved far away from their original 'resting place'.

BODY FOSSILS

The remains of plants and animals, such as shells and teeth, bones and leaves, are among the best known fossil remains. These are called body fossils. The soft parts of organisms – such as flesh, skin, and internal organs- are usually lost

before the fossilisation process begins, having been broken down by bacteria or even eaten by scavengers. Consequently, the fossil remains of soft-bodied animals like jellyfish are extremely rare. Sometimes though, a very rapid burial in soft sediment combined with the presence of certain types of bacteria mean that the soft parts of bodies are retained and fossilised. In these exceptional circumstances, palaeontologists have the opportunity to study not only the fossilised remains of hard body parts like bones and teeth, but the skin and internal organs too.

T-Rex teeth: the 'hard' remains such as teeth, bones and claws are among the most common finds.

TRACE FOSSILS

Traces – the 'things left behind' by organisms – such as egg shells, footprints, marks made by claws, nests, and even droppings, can also become fossilised. These are called trace fossils. Trace fossils are the most numerous type of fossil, but because these traces are not always found next to the organism which made them, they are very difficult to identify precisely. Fossils can also be preserved in materials such as amber, tar, peat and ice. Dinosaur fossils however, are all found in rock, but of the millions of dinosaurs that must have died, a mere handful became fossilised.

The discovery of dinosaurs

More than 2,400 years ago, the ancient Greek scholars were collecting and describing fossil seashells, but, it was only in the past 300 years or so, that the mystery of what fossils were and how they were formed was unravelled. By the late 18th century, most educated people recognised that fossil seashells were parts of animals that lived beneath the seas, but they had a problem working out how these fossils came to be embedded in rocks on land high up the side of cliffs at the shore line and even in mountains way inland from the sea. The most common reason was taken from the Bible: these animals had been stranded by the great flood that had been sent by God as a punishment for man's misbehaviour. For the most part, early fossil discoveries were regarded as dead members of species that still existed. This fitted in the religious concept known as the *plenum*, which supposed that God had created and populated the Earth with every conceivable type of living thing. With this in mind, it was beyond belief that God would have allowed any of his creations to become extinct.

It was only around 200 years ago that scientists began to posit a new theory to explain the appearance of these fossils: that the rocks beneath our feet had once been mud or sand on the sea floor. These sediments had been subjected to great pressure – literally squashed – and hardened into rock and the movement in the earth had raised the rock above the level of the sea, with the fossils embedded in it. In some instances, wind, rain, sun, frost and running water wore away at the rock leaving the fossil exposed.

In 1770, deep in a chalk mine near Maastricht in Holland, the important discovery of the jaws of a huge fossil animal was made. The discovery provoked a great deal of interest- and controversy. Baron Georges Cuvier (1769-1832), the father of modern palaeontology and comparative anatomy, described the jaws and recognised them as belonging to a gigantic marine lizard which he called *Mosasaurus*, meaning 'Meuse reptile', after the river which flows through the region. To Cuvier, the jaws were clearly an example of his long held belief that there had in fact been extinctions of animals in earlier times. Cuvier paved the way for the scientific acceptance of extinction so that by the beginning of the 19th century, many people began to accept

Ammonites are the fossilised remains of cephalopod molluscs.

A new theory to explain the appearance of fossils was formed only 200 years ago.

that many of the fossils they were finding represented creatures that were not like any that were alive.

AMATEURS AND ENTHUSIASTS

By 1800, there were a number of very keen fossil hunters who began collecting specimens. Not all were scientists though: one of the first and greatest discoveries was in fact made by an 11-year-old girl called Mary Anning (1799-1847). In 1811 Mary discovered a complete Jurassic age *Ichthyosaur* fossil skeleton in the sea cliffs at Lyme Regis, in Dorset on England's south coast. She became the first person to make a living from fossil hunting! Mary went on to discover the first plesiosaur in 1821 and the first *Pterodactyl* in 1828. Most of her finds she sold to collectors and institutions: Mary's fossilised ichthyosaur skeleton can be seen today in London's Natural

History Museum. While the rocks of Lyme Regis that Mary was searching did come from the age of the dinosaur, the discoveries of dinosaurs themselves came from further east in England.

Ichthyosaur: *one of the best-known marine reptiles. The first complete fossilised skeleton was found in 1811 in England.*

THE IGUANODON AT THE SIDE OF THE ROAD

In 1822, Gideon Algernon Mantell, a family doctor from Lewes in Sussex and an enthusiastic amateur geologist and fossil hunter, set off with his wife, Mary Ann, in their horse and carriage to visit a patient. While Dr Mantell administered to his patient, Mrs Mantell, took a short stroll to stretch her legs. Walking along the country road she noticed a pile of stones and gravel used for filling in ruts and potholes. Among the rubble, Mrs Mantell noticed some teeth. Informing her husband, Dr Mantell traced the stones and gravel back to the quarries in the Tilgate Forest near Cuckfield where he soon discovered more remains.

At first Dr Mantell had trouble identifying the teeth and so they were shown to the eminent anatomists of the time- Georges Cuvier in Paris, and William Buckland in Oxford- but these two were in fact sceptical about Dr Mantell's information about the age of the rocks in the quarries and disregarded his 'dental finds'. Dr Mantell however firmly believed that the teeth were from 'secondary' or Mesozoic rocks, and were reptilian. With further comparisons

he finally revealed that the teeth he (and his
wife) had discovered were very similar to those
of the South American lizard, the iguana. In
1825 Mantell published his findings: the teeth
he claimed belonged to a giant, 12m (40 ft) long
herbivorous fossil lizard he called *Iguanodon*
("Iguana-tooth") an extinct relative of the living
iguana. After so much research, even Baron
Cuvier was forced to admit that he had made a
mistake and Mantell's article published Cuvier's
'apology'!

*Teeth discovered by
a Sussex roadside in
1822 once belonged
the giant herbivore
Iguanodon.*

Megalosaurus

A year earlier in 1824, William Buckland (1784-1856) had also described
the partial remains of a large reptile, but this time, a carnivorous one. The
remains had been found in Stonesfield in north Oxfordshire, and were named
by Buckland as *Megalosaurus* (big reptile). The remains are still on view
today at the University Museum, Oxford. Both *Megalosaurus* and *Iguanodon*
seemed to belong to the *Mosasaurus* category of fossil reptiles, except that
both were land rather than marine dwellers. Despite the fact that they were
major discoveries, the true significance of these fossil remains – along with
the partial fossil skeleton of the 'armoured reptile' named *Hylaeosaurus*
which was also described by Dr Mantell in 1833 – were unrecognised until
Sir Richard Owen revealed that these three fossil reptiles were truly unlike
any living lizards with which they had been compared. Owen recognised
Iguanodon, *Megalosaurus*, and *Hylaeosaurus* as a separate suborder – the
Dinosauria.

Owen's conception of dinosaurs as 'elephantine reptiles' gained a great deal
of prominence in the mid 1850s, particularly after he asked the sculptor
Waterhouse Hawkins to make a complete 'zoo' of life sized concrete models
which were placed in the gardens surrounding the reconstructed Crystal
Palace at Sydenham in south-east London.

Hugely popular at the time, we now know that they are inaccurate- his
Iguanodon sported a horn on its nose - but they can still be seen in the park
today, and are worth visiting by any dinosaur hunter.

Megalosaurus' or 'big reptile', was a carnivorous dinosaur.

New discoveries, new insights

Throughout the 19th century, it seemed that everyone, everywhere, had caught 'dinosaur fever'. More and more remains were being unearthed in Britain and in Europe, but it was in America that the most exciting finds were to be made. In fact, Americans had been finding fossil dinosaur bones and footprints long before anyone else – they just didn't realise it! In 1800, Pliny Moody found huge fossil footprints in the Connecticut Valley: the 'birdlike' shape of the prints led many to believe that they were the very footprints of the raven sent by Noah from the Ark to find dry land. In fact, what Moody had discovered were the tracks left by a dinosaur in the Triassic age as the creature had crossed mud flats.

1855 marked the real beginning of American dinosaur discoveries. Ferdinand Hayden (1829-87) was a young geologist conducting surveys of the western territories for the US government who collected fossils and recorded the geological composition of the land in which they were found. In 1855 Hayden was surveying the Upper Missouri and while in Montana, found some scattered teeth which seemed to resemble those of *Iguanodon* and *Megalosaurus* found in Britain. In 1858, these teeth were examined by Joseph Leidy (1823-91), professor of anatomy at the University of Pennsylvania who identified some of the teeth as belonging to a herbivorous dinosaur he called *Trachodon*, or rugged-tooth (today we know this dinosaur as the duckbilled *Anatosaurus*), and to a ferocious *Megalosaurus* which he named *Deinodon horridus*, which translates as 'the most horrible of the terror-teeth'!

The Megolosaurus *jaw housed sharp teeth designed for a meat-eating diet.*

In the same year, 1858, Leidy also examined a partial skeleton found in Haddonfield, New Jersey. This creature, named *Hadrosaurus*, once again had teeth like *Iguanodon*, but also had its fore and hind legs preserved intact. Leidy discovered that unlike Owen's 'vision' of a large elephantine creature, his *Hadrosaurus* had a posture that was more like a kangaroo! Leidy's discovery would take us closer to a greater and more accurate understanding of this type of dinosaur than anyone so far, and once again the sculptor Waterhouse Hawkins was called upon to build models of the dinosaurs Leidy described.

Leidy's views on dinosaurs – rather than
Owen's- were finally confirmed in the 1880s
following the discovery by coal miners in
1878 in the village of Bernissart in south-west
Belgium of no fewer than 40 complete and
partial *Iguanodon* skeletons. The scientific
description of the remains was done by Louis
Dollo (1857-1891) and for the first time, Owen's *Iguanodon*- which he 'knew'
only from its teeth- could be accurately reconstructed.

*Discovered by
Joseph Leidy
in 1858, the
Hadrosaurus
skeleton shows the
'kangaroo'-type
posture.*

COPE AND MARSH: RIVALS IN THE RACE FOR KNOWLEDGE

In 1877, just before the the significant finds in Bernissart
were uncovered, even richer deposits were discovered
in Colorado, USA by two schoolmasters working
independently of each other. One of the teachers, Arthur
Lakes, discovered bones at Morrison, Colorado which he
sent for examination to Orthniel Charles Marsh (1831-
99), a professor at Yale College, later Yale University.
One of the great pioneers of dinosaur studies, Marsh
built up one of the most extensive fossil collections in the
world, and later persuaded his uncle, George Peabody
to establish the Peabody Museum of Natural History at
Yale. Marsh's own teams had already made a number of
important discoveries: in 1871 they had found the first American *Pterodactyl*
fossils, as well as the remains of the earliest horses in North America.

*Pterodactyl: a
reptile of the air.
Many species
of 'wing-finger'
reptiles have now
been discovered.*

Marsh's great rival in the quest for knowledge of dinosaurs was Edward
Drinker Cope (1840-97). The son of a Quaker family, Cope would discover
more than 1,000 species of extinct vertebrates (animals with backbones)
in the USA, and publish more than 1,200 books and papers adding to our
knowledge of evolutionary history. In 1877, schoolmaster O.W. Lucas had
been exploring rocks near Canyon City, Colorado where he found fossils
which he sent to Cope for analysis.

The discoveries by the two schoolmasters fuelled the rivalry between Cope
and Marsh which had begun in 1870 when Cope had shown Marsh the
skeleton of *Elasmosaurus*, a plesiosaur found in Kansas. Marsh quickly

pointed out a dramatic error in Cope's study: the head of the animal had been placed on the wrong end! Cope would never forgive Marsh for pointing this out, and the bitter battle between the two was on! Soon teams hired by Cope and Marsh extended their excavations beyond Colorado to Wyoming at Como Bluff, to Montana, to the Connecticut Valley and into New Mexico.

The teams spied on each other and the rivalry even encouraged acts of vandalism – smashing each other's fossils with hammers, and even damaging the food, water and tents at each other's camps! Despite the intense competition, between 1877 and the late 1890s, Cope and Marsh between them described about 130 new species of dinosaurs with many of the fossil remains finding their way into museums in America, in particular, the Peabody Museum at Yale University, the Smithsonian Institution in Washington D.C, and the American Museum of Natural History in New York.

One of the richest finds of dinosaur bones – 350 tons – was made in 1909 in Utah by Earl Douglass.

BONE CABIN QUARRY AND DINOSAUR NATIONAL MONUMENT

Following Cope's and Marsh's deaths a much more co-ordinated – and less violent- exploration of regions of North America was instituted by the American Museum of Natural History. In 1898, a small cabin, built as a shelter by a shepherd was discovered in Wyoming. Called 'Bone Cabin' the shelter had been made out of some of the hundreds of dinosaur bones that were to be found scattered across the area!

But by far the richest finds of dinosaur skeletons that the world has ever known was discovered near Vernal, in the Uinta mountains of Utah in 1909 by Earl Douglass (1862-1931). Working for the Carnegie Museum in Pittsburgh, in Utah between 1909 and 1923, Douglass discovered 350 tonnes (350 tons) of fossilised dinosaur remains in the Carnegie Quarry including *Allosaurus, Diplodocus, Apatosaurus, Camarasaurus,* and *Stegosaurus.* So vast were the finds that in 1915, by Presidential decree, the site was named Dinosaur National Monument, and today a working museum stands on the site surrounded by fossil bearing rocks- with fossils still in place and clearly visible! In honour of his work, the quarry itself was also renamed as the Douglass Quarry.

World-wide finds

While the end of the 19th century marked the end of the great pioneering age of dinosaur discoveries, there were still plenty of dinosaur remains to be discovered across the world.

In Europe, in spite of a long tradition of dinosaur discovery and excavation, finds in the 20th century were to be greatly outshone by huge discoveries elsewhere in the world. Nevertheless, in the sandstone region of Solnholfen in Germany, amazing fossils of great detail revealed the tiny *Compsognothaurus* and the first known bird, *Archaeopteryx*, while in the south of France, in Aix-en-Provence, some of the largest fossil dinosaur eggs, measuring 30 cm (12 in.) long- about five times larger than a hen's egg! - were found and believed to have been laid by the herbivorous *Hypselosaurus*.

Compsognothaurus, a carvivorous dinosaur whose name means 'pretty jaw', was only the size of a modern chicken.

In Canada in 1884 Joseph Tyrell uncovered the fossil remains of *Albertosaurus* in the Red Deer River area of Alberta. Tyrell was soon followed to the region by Barnham Brown of the American Museum of Natural History in 1910, known affectionately as 'Mr Bones'. Brown would find the first *Tyrannosaurus rex* fossils and would describe and name *Ankylosaurus* and *Corythosaurus*.

In 1912, the Sternberg family, led by their father Charles H. (1850-1943), made many spectacular discoveries in the Red Deer River region, and developed the technique of 'jacketing' fossil bones in a protective cast. Sons Charles M. (1885-1981) was famous for his skills in 'reading' the ground for dinosaur remains, while George F. (1883-1959) found an impression of dinosaur skin which belonged to *Anatosaurus* and then discovered the hadrosaur (meaning 'duck billed') *Edmontosaurus* in 1909. Levi (1894-1976) developed the jacketing method further and devised a latex casting technique that was used to duplicate fossils.

T.Rex
– one of the most famous of all dinosaurs.

So important was the Red Deer River region in Alberta, Canada that the area was designated the Dinosaur Provincial Park and is a United Nations World Heritage Site –a status enjoyed by important historical monuments like the Pyramids of ancient Egypt.

At the other end of the Americas, in South America, a great number of finds were made in the 20th century, in particular in Argentina by Jose Bonaparte and Fernando Novas, who in 1985 found fossils of *Carnatosaurus*. While Bonaparte and Novas were 'professional palaeontologists', discoveries were also being made by amateurs: the first *Herrerasaurus* bones were found by an Argentinean farmer called Victorino Herrera in the 1960s. These fragments were the only ones known until 1985 when scientists working in the Valley of the Moon, a desert region in the foothills of the Andes found a near complete specimen. Some of the biggest of all the dinosaurs- including the carnivorous and appropriately named *Giganotosaurus*- and the huge, herbivorous *Argentinosaurus*, were found in Argentina, while other important fossil finds have been made in recent years in Colombia, Chile, Brazil, Uruguay and Peru.

Carnatosaurus, the 'meat–eating bull', was found in Argentina in 1985.

Africa

The first major discoveries of dinosaur fossils in Africa were made as recently as 1908. These came from Tendaguru, in present day Tanzania in east Africa and were excavated by the German palaeontologists Edwin Hennig and Werner Janensch from the Berlin Museum of Natural History. Between 1908 and 1912, the pair excavated more than 250 tonnes (245 tons) of fossil bones and rock which were then carried by native bearers for over 65 km (40 miles) to the nearest port for shipment to Germany. Hennig and Janensch found some remarkable dinosaurs including the giant, giraffe-like *Brachiosaurus*, a smaller dinosaur they called *Dicraeosaurus* and the stegosaur-like armoured dinosaur, *Kentrosaurus*.

Later finds on the vast continent include those from Morocco and Egypt in the north (*Cetiosaurus* and the huge sail-backed *Spinosaurus*), from Niger in central Africa (*Camarasaurus*, a 20 tonne 19 tons plant-eater) and from Zimbabwe, in southern Africa (*Barosaurus*, and the 6 m long (20 ft) *Vulcanodon*).

Asia and Australia

Discoveries of dinosaurs date back to the early part of the 20th century, but the most significant discoveries in these regions have been made far more recently. Some of the most exciting finds have come from Australia- of dinosaurs found nowhere else in the world. One of the major sites is 'Dinosaur Cove' in the Otway-Strzelecki mountain range on the coast near Melbourne, Victoria, where the remains of *Leaellynasaurus* were found. In Queensland the remains of the large herbivorous *Muttaburrasaurus* (named after Muttaburra, the site of the remains) were found, while near Winton, the tracks of around 130 dinosaurs passing by are preserved in more than 3000 trace fossil footprints!

In India, the remains of a huge plant eating dinosaur *Titanosaurus* was uncovered near Umrer in central India. *Titanosaurus* lived some 70 million years ago, was a staggering 12 m (40 ft) long and is estimated to have weighed somewhere around 10 tonnes (nearly 10 tons)! Other major finds include *Dravidosaurus*, found near Tirunchirapalli in southern India. This is a dinosaur of the stegosaur group but which lived much later than other stegosaurs, in the Late Cretaceous Period, about 70 million years ago.

In Asia, most of the dinosaur fossils that have been found so far were discovered in the Gobi Dessert, in Mongolia, Central Asia and in present-day China. The first expeditions to the Gobi Desert took place in 1922 and were led by Roy Chapman Andrews (1884-1960) , Henry Fairfield Osborn, and Walter Granger of the American Museum of Natural History. The initial aim of this expedition was to find evidence regarding the origin of man, but the most significant finds the team made were in fact of dinosaurs. Between 1892 and 1925, four expeditions to the region collected a number of specimens- all of which were brand new to science: *Pinacosaurus*, *Saurornithoides*, *Oviraptor* and *Velociraptor*. Most significant was the discovery not only of *Protoceratops*, but of its' nests and eggs- the first of any dinosaur eggs to be discovered.

Brachiosaurus, or 'arm lizard' grew up to 16 m (50 ft) high. Its thigh bones alone were over 1.8 m (6 ft) long.

Velociraptor, the 'fast thief' of the Cretaceous period, had some 80 extremely sharp teeth, and a sickle-shaped claw on each foot for slashing.

Dinosaur fossils had been found for centuries in China, but were identified as belonging to the magic creatures of Chinese folklore – dragons! Systematic and scientific study of dinosaur fossils began in the 1930s and was led by Professor Yang Zhong-jian – (known to his colleagues in the west as C.C. Young) who in 1941 found the remains of *Lufangosaurus* in China's southern province of Yunnan.

Following the establishment of the People's Republic of China in 1949, and the country's political and cultural isolation, all dinosaur research in China was concentrated on the Institute of Vertebrate Palaeontology in Beijing which has co-ordinated much of the work since then. In the 1950s, Chinese scientists discovered *Tsintaosaurus* and *Mamenchisaurus*. These were followed in subsequent decades by the important discoveries of *Shantungosaurus*, *Psittacosaurus*, *Tuojiangosaurus* and *Avimimus*. Today China is an area of 'dinosaur fever'! Its important finds, including 'feathered dinosaurs' like *Sinosauropteryx* have astounded scientists across the world and are causing many to alter long-held ideas. A few of the existing dinosaur finds in China have also captured the world's imagination – but have turned out to be clever fakes!

With its horny 'beak', and small frill at the back of its head, Psittacosaurus, or 'parrot reptile' was a light, long-tailed herbivore.

THE SEARCH CONTINUES

While the vast majority of dinosaurs are known from only a few fossil parts, occasionally, remains are sometimes found of a dinosaur body that has 'dried out' very rapidly, so that quite a number of its parts were preserved as mummified fossils. One of the best known, part-mummified dinosaur fossils is 'Sue', the biggest and most complete preserved specimen of female Tyrannosaurus ever found. Sue was found in 1990 in South Dakota, USA and named after her finder, fossil-hunter Susan Hendrickson of the Black Hills Institute of Geological Research. Not only was Sue a very important specimen in scientific terms, she was extremely valuable: in 1997 Sue was sold for more than $8.3 million to the Field Museum in Chicago!

Almost all the continents- excluding Antarctica- have yielded- and continue to yield- dinosaur remains, and even Antarctica is likely to have some. The obvious problem here is that the rocks which most likely contain them are covered by thick ice sheets. Even this icy continent though has not always been inhospitable: the remains of an early Triassic period mammal-like reptile called *Lystrosauris* were found here, and scientists are hopeful that one day, dinosaur remains will also be discovered.

Naming dinosaurs

Chances are, there are many more dinosaurs waiting to be 'unearthed' but, for any dinosaur, enough fossils need to be found for a panel of scientists to be sure that it is a distinct type so they can estimate its size- and give it a scientific name.

Each dinosaur has a scientific name which is usually made up from Latin or Greek words. Each of the dinosaurs' names in this book is written in *italics*. This is in order to distinguish individual dinosaurs from their 'groups'. Some of the dinosaur 'groups' are themselves named after the first-discovered, or, major one of its kind – such as the tyrannosaurs and stegosaurs.

Still at work – the search for dinosaur remains continues.

For example, *Velociraptor* (which means 'speedy predator') and *Deionychus* (which means 'terrible claw') are both members of the group of dinosaurs known as dromaeosaurs. They are called dromaeousaurs (which means 'running reptiles') after the major, or first, specimen of this type of dinosaur to be found, *Dromaeosaurus*. All the dinosaurs in the dromaeosaur group share similar characteristics: they were medium-sized, meat-eating dinosaurs, with a large curved claw on each foot.

Euoplocephalus (which means 'well armoured head') belongs to the group of dinosaurs called Ankylosaurs (meaning 'fused reptiles'). These dinosaurs all had a protective armour of outer body plates and a large lump of bone at the end of their tails which they used as a hammer or to swing like a club!

Dromaeosaurus was a small fast-moving dinosaur whose remains were first discovered in 1914 in Canada. It gave its name to a group (the dromosaurs) of which Velociraptor is also a member.

Built like a tank, Euoplocephalus
*means 'well-armoured head'. It is a
member of the ankylosauria group
– armoured, quadrupedal herbivores.*

As you can see, many dinosaur names end in *-saurus*,
which some people say means 'reptile', while others say
it means 'lizard'- even though dinosaurs were not lizards!
Some of the Latin and Greek names can be real tongue
twisters, but most refer to a unique feature: the dinosaur
Opsisthocoelicaudia (pronounced 'owe-pis-thowe-see-lee-
cord-ee-ah'!) means 'posterior tail cavity' and refers to
the unique formation of this dinosaurs joints between the
vertebrae in its tail.

Some of the more modern dinosaur finds are also
named after the place where the remains were found
or the people who found them. *Minmi* takes its name
from Minmi Crossing in Queensland, Australia, while
Riojasaurus was found in Rioja, Argentina.

The duckbilled *Lambeosaurus* was named in honour of
the great Canadian fossil expert Lawrence Lambe (1853-
1919). *Baryonyx* which means 'heavy claw', a name
it got from the massive claw on its thumb, is properly
known as *Baryonyx walkeri*, in honour of Bill Walker,
an amateur fossil hunter and quarry man who in 1982
found a 'massive claw' in a clay pit in Surrey, England.
Leaellynasaura, found in Australia, was named in honour
of Lea Ellyn, the daughter of one of the dinosaurs'
discoverers.

Who knows, maybe one day, you too will find- and
name- a dinosaur!

CHAPTER 1

When dinosaurs ruled the earth

The changing earth

Geologists and palaeontologists divide the past into several different periods called *eras* which are then further subdivided into *periods*, each of which lasted for millions of years. Some periods are subdivided further into smaller 'units' called *epochs*. The 'milestones' of the main geological eras or epochs are the *orogenetic* (mountain-forming) periods. In these periods, the distribution of the land and seas were changed. This in turn affected the environment which supported life: life either adapted to its environment, or it became extinct. Consequently, new and more advanced forms of life originated at the same time that those which were incapable of transforming and evolving died out.

According to many scientists, the history of the Earth begins only at the time when the solid crust of the Earth was formed: this occurred in the Archaean or Archeozoic Era around 2100 million years ago. This era is divided into two periods: the first period is called the Anhydric (waterless) period, and the second, later period is called the Primeval Oceanic period during which air temperatures lowered and made the water vapour condense and form the first primeval oceans in the hollows of the solidifying crust of the earth. This was a period of great volcanic activity when immense lava flows solidified both on the surface of the earth and below it and were transformed into rocks which weathered and crumbled and were carried away by the first rivers to be deposited at the bottom of the oceans to form the first sediments.

Life begins

Of this very early period in the Earth's history- the Precambrian Era- we know very little. But what is apparent though, is that the history of the Earth, and life on it, has happened over millions of years. The trail that leads to dinosaurs begins really in the Palaeozoic Era, the first era in which a variety of complex living things were produced. In the first 200 millions years or so of the Palaeozoic Era – through the Cambrian, Ordovician and Silurian periods – almost all life on Earth remained beneath the seas. By the Cambrian period, seaweed and many of the groups of invertebrates (back boneless) animals had appeared. There were soft-bodied jellyfish and worms, but there were also *trilobites* and *brachiopods* which produced lime to make hard shells to protect their bodies.

In the seas of the Ordovician period, corals, molluscs and the ancient relatives of octopus and squid colonised the waters, while the ancestors of the modern starfish were beginning to give rise to small, fishlike animals- the first animals to 'make' bones. The ability to grow internal bones was a gigantic step forward: the skeleton protects the inner organs of an animal in the same way as the outer shell of a crab. But unlike a crab, an animal with an internal skeleton does not have to shed its protective armour when its inner body grows too big for its 'case'- its bones grow in size with it! Having an internal skeleton also allows for a greater degree of mobility. The advent of internal skeletons would help animals move out of the sea and onto land.

TABLE OF GEOLOGICAL TIMES		
ERA	PERIOD	How many million years ago (**approx.**)
ARCHAEAN	1st: Anhydric (waterless period) 2nd: Primeval Oceanic period (origins of life)	at least 2500
PROTEROZOIC (Eozoic)	1st: Huronian} 2nd: Algonkian}	1200
Development of Invertebrates		
PALAEOZOIC *Age of Invertebrates Fishes & Amphibia*	Lower Cambrian Ordovician Silurian Devonian Upper Carboniferous Permian	600 500 440 395 345 280
MESOZOIC *Age of Reptiles*	Triassic Jurassic Cretaceous	225 193 136
TERTIARY (Cenozoic/Kainozoic) *Age of Mammals*	Paleogene Paleocene } Eocene } Oligocene } Neogene Miocene } Pliocene }	65
QUATERNARY (Anthropozoic) *Age of Man*	Pleistocene } Holocene (present age) }	1.8

Plant life

The move to land by vertebrates occurred in the Devonian period - about 395-345 million years ago. But before anything animal could colonise the land, there had to be plants, since all animals depend on plants for food at first- or second-hand: herbivorous (plant-eating animals) feed on plants and carnivorous animals (meat eating animals) feed on herbivores. The soft seaweed – which was rootless – could not have survived either the dry air or the effects of gravity, but, by 400 million years ago, a relative of the seaweed had evolved a stiffened stem along with fine, hair like roots and an internal 'tube' system that allowed it to suck up water and nutrients.

Because these early plants were still evolving, they clung to the edges of land alongside rivers, lakes and seas, and it would be here that the aquatic animals would also first come ashore. The first creatures were the ancestors of millipedes, centipedes, wood lice and scorpions and other arthropod (jointed-leg) creatures.

The Carboniferous period saw very favourable living conditions and the well-watered basins at the feet of mountains were the perfect environment for luxurious plant growth. These plants formed forests covering much of what is now Eastern Europe and North America: the hot, wet forests of the Carboniferous period, lying just above sea level may have resembled the dense lush forest that can be seen in the tropical regions of the earth today. The plants, though, were very different. Under treelike plants such as the giant club mosses *Lipidodenron* and *Calamitina* which grew to heights of over 100 feet, grew a rich undergrowth of mosses and ferns. Some of these ferns wound themselves around the trunks of taller plants, others grew treelike themselves and up to 45 feet high. The tallest trees of the Carboniferous forest were the *Cordaites:* richly branched with long, ribbon like leaves and a smooth trunk, these could reach heights of 145 feet. The remains of these plants became the basis of the present day deposits of coal.

The first winged insects flew through the Carboniferous forests and fossil remains show that a few of these insects- such as dragonflies and cockroaches- would have looked very similar to present day species- only much larger. Scorpions grew to more than 60 cm (24 in) long, while the *Arthopleura*, a flat bodied millipede was a mighty 2 m (6 ft 6 in.) long! The primitive dragonfly *Meganeura* with its wingspan of around 60 cm (24 in.) was over three times that of the dragonfly *Tetracanthagyna plagiata* from Borneo – the largest dragonfly species still living today. Because insects are generally small and delicate, fossil remains are rare because their bodies most likely rotted away before they could be trapped in sediment (or amber) and fossilised. With little fossil evidence, scientists are still trying to work out how insects actually evolved.

LOBE-FINNED AMPHIBIANS

Most of the waterside dwelling insects would have provided food for the first vertebrates who ventured ashore. These vertebrates were rhipidistians, a group of now extinct, lobe-finned amphibians which evolved some 360 million years ago from fish. Because they had evolved from fish, the rhipidistrians still had fish-like features; but with long, fleshy, muscular lobed fins which looked a little bit like legs with which they pulled themselves out of the water and onto the land. Unlike modern fishes, rhipidistrians had lungs- but they were still fishes and were not designed to spend long periods out of the water.

By the late Devonian period, the lobed fins of some rhipidistrians had evolved into legs with five-toed feet and were now at home on land as well as in the water. Ichthyostega, an early amphibian from the Devonian period, had some fish-like features – a tail fin, and small scales – combined with a distinctly amphibian body. It also had fewer skull bones- making its head lighter to carry – and legs that were now suited to walking. For the first time on Earth, there were creatures with a skeleton whose basic design foreshadowed that of the dinosaurs.

REPTILES

The amphibians only managed to gain a toehold on the moist edges of land:
the first truly land-based vertebrates to venture further into the dry inland
areas were reptiles. They were uniquely suited to this 'adventure' thanks to
their body design and their breeding habits. Where amphibians have moist,
soft skins which soon dry up if over exposed to warm dry air, reptiles have
a tough, waterproof outer covering of thick, dry scales which traps moisture
inside their body.

Their bones, too, underwent changes, especially in the hips and feet which
allowed them to run – unlike the restricted wriggling motion of, for example,
a salamander. Bursts of activity- such as a sprint run after some tasty morsel
of prey – were fuelled by more effective respiratory and circulatory systems
than amphibians had. But it was possibly the reptiles, breeding habits which
freed them the most from the dependence on water.

Reptile fossil.

Most male amphibians scatter their sperm haphazardly over eggs laid in water by the females, but male reptiles fertilise the female's eggs while they are still inside her body. Amphibians' eggs, encased in their jelly-like blobs, would dry up if they were laid on land, but reptile eggs, whether 'leathery' or hard-shelled, carry protective linings which keep the contents moist even when they are deposited in hot desert sands. In the Permian period (which ended the Palaeozoic Era) the swampy forests were replaced by drier desert-like conditions, and the reptiles, unlike many amphibians, were ideally suited to the new landscape and climate and began to colonise new regions.

By the Permian period, several early reptile groups had evolved. First there were the small, low cotylosaurs – named because of their cup shaped vertebrae. Cotylosaurs called captorhinomorphs had sharp teeth and hunted insects and amphibians in the forests and swamps. Second, there were the much larger, 'man sized' reptiles called diadectomorphs, or 'broad-toothed forms', which had blunter teeth better designed to grind up plant material. So, by Permian times, there were herbivores (plant eaters) and carnivores (meat eaters) among the vertebrates.

Scientists believe that from the primitive cotylosaur reptiles, other kinds of species, including mammals evolved. One reptile 'offshoot' was a group known as pelycosaurs. These were the size of a rhinoceros and roamed largely across what are now the south-western states of the USA. Pelycosaurs had a 'skin web' or 'sail' which grew between spiny growths from its backbone. It is believed that these cold-blooded creatures used the 'sail' as a body temperature control system: by angling the sail to the sun, the pelycosaur could speed up – or slow down – the rate at which its body heated or cooled down. This ability to control body temperature is something that crocodiles also do today.

SYNAPSIDS

As the Permian period continued, mammal-like reptiles were to evolve from these pelycosaurs. These included the slow moving, but immensely powerful plant-eating dicynodonts or 'two dog teeth' whose forelimbs were splayed out sideways, but whose back legs were erect, like those of mammals. The dicynodonts were synapsids, which means 'with arch' and comes from the name given to the large hole low in the skull behind each eye. The muscles that operated the jaw passed through these holes and gave the synapsids very large gapes and an immensely powerful bite. The synapsids formed a separate group from the 'true' reptiles who gave rise to the dinosaurs.

The age of dinosaurs

The 'age of the dinosaur' corresponds to the time period that geologists call the Mesozoic Era, from about 248-65 million years ago. The Mesozoic – which literally means 'middle life'– is divided into three shorter time spans: the Triassic, Jurassic and Cretaceous periods. Throughout these periods, different dinosaurs lived and died, and each species may have lived for only 2 or 3 million years.

In the Triassic period – about 248-208 million years ago – dinosaurs began to evolve. The Jurassic period – about 208-144 million years ago – was the time of the largest (and smallest!) of the dinosaurs, while during the Cretaceous period- about 144-65 million years ago- the dinosaurs were at their most varied.

Pangaea: the super-continent

There are good reasons for the early evolution and spread of dinosaurs: when the Lower Permian period ended and the magnificent carboniferous forests disappeared from the surface of the Earth, the Upper Permian period began and striking changes took place in the plants and creatures. Most of the land was warm, which suited the reptiles, but also, the continents, as we now know them, were gathered together in one great land mass forming a single 'super continent' called Pangaea. Consequently, the animals that were evolving in one place during the Triassic period were able to travel across the land mass: a curious pig-like dicynodont called *Lystrosaurus* was to be found in Australia, Antarctica, China, India and in South Africa. Almost everywhere on this super continent, the climate was tropical or sub tropical with many areas of desert.

Throughout the Mesozoic Era the super continent Pangaea that straddled the equator and that was evident in the Triassic period was also to undergo slow, almost invisible changes due to the process called continental drift. This is the name given to Alfred Wegener's theory of 1915 whereby the great sheets of the Earth's crust – known as tectonic plates – very slowly (only a few centimetres each year) moved apart to form the continents as we know them today.

Laurasia and Gondwana

By the Jurassic period, Pangaea were gradually splitting into two huge land masses or continents: in the north was Laurasia, which was made up of a number of large land masses and smaller islands, while in the south was the continent of Gondwana. The 'modern' southern continents – South America, India, Antarctica, Africa and Australia – had begun to pull away from Europe and North America with the formation of a narrow sea way to the east called Tethys and the very small beginnings of the Atlantic Ocean to the west. By the middle of the Jurassic period, another sea, the Turgai Sea, would begin to separate Europe from Asia. Despite the movement of the continents, there appears to have been some 'contact' remaining between these areas because palaeontologists have found that various Jurassic period dinosaurs such as diplodocids, brachiosaurids, and iguanadontids, are very similar in both North America and Africa during this time.

The largest and the smallest of the all the dinosaurs lived during the Jurassic period in the warm wet forests thick with ferns and horsetails by river banks or in the drier inland areas which supported gingkoes, conifers and cycads- palm-like plants with large leafy crowns from which sprout pine-like cones. Many of the creatures that had lived during the Triassic period had all but died out and were replaced by others: dinosaurs now replaced the mammal-like reptiles such as the dicynodonts, while the big, aquatic reptiles like ichthyosaurs and plesiosaurs roamed the seas. By the end of the Jurassic period, the air was filled with flying animals and early birds which had evolved from reptiles.

Formation of modern continents

By the early Cretaceous period, Laurasia and Gondwana were themselves splitting further into the continents that exist today and were drifting into their now familiar positions on the globe. Africa and South America had drifted apart and India was moving across the Indian Ocean. In the north, while not physically separated to the same degree, the continents here were 'subdivided' by inland seas which covered parts of Laurasia. Consequently, western North America and eastern Asia were still 'in contact' with each other across the Bering Straits, and Europe and eastern North America were also connected. The distribution of dinosaur remains reflects these 'contacts', with some species found only in Asia and western North America, and others found only in Europe and eastern North America.

With the movement of the continents came climate changes and overall, the Earth's climate became cooler. The more temperate climate favoured the spread of flowering plants, the seeds of which grow inside a protective 'case', more familiarly known as a fruit. The new plants which appeared in this period include the very familiar 'modern' plants and trees such as oaks, aspens, and magnolias. Alongside these new plant species, in the northern continents, biped and quadruped – two- and four-legged – dinosaurs evolved, and many fed on the plant life. In turn these herbivores were themselves the prey of carnivorous dinosaurs. Mammals were also around, but they remained small and furtive. In the air, the giant skin-winged gliding animals, the largest ever airborne creatures, flew through the air alongside a widening variety of birds – some of which were not too different from those alive today. But by the end of the Cretaceous period, the dinosaurs, along with many other ancient life forms had disappeared from the earth. About 65 million years ago, the last dinosaurs lay dead. What killed them on land, in the sea and in the air, remains one of the great unsolved mysteries of prehistoric life on earth.

CHAPTER 2

Dinosaur anatomy

Dinosaurs are related to a very large group of diapsid (or, 'two arched') reptiles which include the now extinct dinosaurs and flying reptiles or pterosaurs, as well as some living animals such as snakes, crocodiles and lizards. The diapsid reptile group also included a not-so-well known group called the *thecodontians*.

Palaeontologists believe that the thecodontians paved the way for the dinosaurs because in the structure of their hips and hind legs, thecodontians were able to change the angle that their back legs made between their bodies and the ground when they walked. The femur, or upper leg bone, of thecodontians was curved and their hip joints were socketed in a way that allowed them to either hold their legs out at the sides of their bodies – like a lizard does – or hold their legs partly underneath their bodies which allowed them to lift their bodies clear of the ground when they walked. This was a much more efficient way of walking and it also allowed the thecodontians to have much larger body weights that were carried on legs rather than having a huge belly resting on the ground. This alteration in the range of leg positions would make it possible for dinosaurs to achieve immense body sizes.

The increased weight now carried on the thecodontians' legs would in turn affect the structure of the ankle bones. Small animals like lizards with their legs at the sides of their bodies do not require really strong or stable ankle bones: instead they need ankles with a great deal of flexibility. Theocodontians, and later, the dinosaurs, with their much larger size and more varied gaits, required much greater strength and stability. So, instead of rows of small bones which 'slide' past each other (as in lizards) the theocodontians developed the much stronger 'ball and socket' type of ankle joint.

The new 'leg position' of the dinosaurs was in many ways the key to their success: their upright posture meant they did not have to expend huge amounts of energy just keeping their bodies off the ground. Instead, they were able to develop much more active lifestyles.

During the Mesozoic Era around 248 to 65 million years ago, dinosaurs formed the single but most diverse group of reptiles that completely dominated life on land. The very first dinosaurs were probably biped carnivores (two-legged meat-eaters) who were not much larger than a medium-sized dog. Soon however, dinosaurs were to evolve into a huge variety of shapes and sizes, from as small as a farmyard hen to as large as a whale! No individual dinosaur species lived for more than a few million years, but there were always new ones evolving to take the place of the ones that had died out.

Bird-hipped and lizard-hipped dinosaurs

The dinosaurs that eventually evolved from the theocodontians at the end of the Triassic Era
are divided into two groups: saurischians, or 'lizard-hipped', and, ornithischian or 'bird-hipped'
dinosaurs. All dinosaurs had four limbs: unlike some other reptiles, such as snakes. Dinosaurs did
not lose their limbs as they evolved through the Mesozoic Era.

SAURISCHIAN DINOSAURS: KEY FEATURES

The saurischian (lizard-hipped) dinosaurs included the sauropodomorph ('lizard-foot form')
dinosaurs, which were usually quadrupeds (walking on all four legs) herbivores (plant-eaters)
of often enormous size, and all the therapods ('beast-feet'), which were bipedal (two-legged)
carnivorous (meat-eating) dinosaurs of varying sizes.

The saurischian dinosaurs are characterised by having a pelvis in which the
three bones the ilium, ischium and pubis as in most other reptiles, radiate
outwards from one another in different directions from the hip joint of
the socket. In most of the saurischian dinosaurs, the pubic bones pointed
forwards – like in lizards – but in some other saurischians, the pubic bones
pointed backwards. Unlike other reptiles though, the saurischians had
an opening in the hip socket called the acetabulum. Above this was an
outwardly projecting lip or ridge against which the femur was pressed: this
ridge allowed the joint to rotate but stopped the ball-shaped head of the

*An example of
lizard-hips*

femur from slipping out of the hip socket. The saurischian dinosaurs had knee joints and ankle joints
that were simple hinges – rather than the more complex ball-and-socket joints of the theocodontians.

ORNITHISCHIAN DINOSAURS: KEY FEATURES

The ornithischian dinosaurs share the same leg structure as the saurischian dinosaurs but their
pelvis was different. The ornithischian dinosaurs had a downwards and backwards pointing pubis
bone which lay parallel to the ischium, as it does in living birds- hence the name ornithischian.
But, in spite of their appellation, it was the therapod saurischian dinosaurs (and not the
ornithischian) which would give rise to birds!

As well as the different hip structure, the ornithischian dinosaurs were also distinguished by bony
rods on either side of their spine along their backs, and, by a strange U-shaped, horn-covered bone
called the predatory at the front tip of their lower jaws. In most ornithischian, the predatory
bone formed the lower half of a toothless, horn-covered beak which was designed for grasping and
cropping leafy vegetation. Further back, inside the jaw were cheek teeth designed for cutting up
and chewing leaves and stalks.

The ornithischian dinosaurs were all herbivores but they can be further subdivided into three main groups: thyreophorans, which were armoured and plated quadrupeds; marginocephalians, which had heads with bony frills or horns and, ornithopods, the bipedal herbivores.

Warm or cold-blooded?

Although palaeontologists know a great deal about the anatomy, the life cycle, breeding habits and diets of dinosaurs, whether they were cold or warm-blooded has not been established. Reptiles are *exothermic* (cold-blooded) creatures which means that they rely on the temperature outside their bodies, such as the heat from the sun if they live in their natural habitats, or from heating bulbs if they are kept in vivaria. Lizards spend a great deal of their time basking in the heat of the sun in order to raise their body temperature to a level where it can work properly. To avoid overheating, lizards cool off in the shade. But if it is too cold, for instance, at night or in winter, reptiles become inactive. *Endothermic* (warm-blooded) animals, such as mammals, produce their body heat from the food they eat, and have hair or fur to keep them warm and sweat glands to help them cool down.

What is puzzling to scientists is that although dinosaurs were reptiles, much of their behaviour is more like that of warm-blooded mammals. Being warm-blooded would have allowed dinosaurs to stay warm and active during the day and night and in colder weather conditions. This would have allowed them to hunt for prey for greater lengths of time: if dinosaurs were endothermic, they would have needed to eat at least 10 times more food than if they were exothermic, in order to 'burn off' calories to keep then warm and give them the energy that allowed them to run at great speeds.

Two further arguments for dinosaurs being endothermic (warm-blooded) have been offered, firstly, by the evidence that many lived in herds and 'raised' families of young. This type of very complex lifestyle is common to many birds and mammals, but in reptiles, is very rare (although Nile crocodiles do display a great deal of parental care in that they respond to their offspring's calls and break open the nests to release their young, then carry them protectively in their jaws to special crocodile 'nurseries' where they grow and develop while being carefully watched over by the adults).

Secondly, there is dinosaur posture. Most dinosaurs stood upright on straight legs: this posture is common to endothermic creatures, but not to other, cold blooded reptiles.

Brachiosaurus

Furthermore, dinosaurs had bones which were more like mammals than reptiles: mammal bones contain far more blood vessels than reptile bones. The huge sauropodomorph dinosaurs like *Brachiosaurus*, with its very long neck, needed a strong heart and to have a very high blood pressure in order its blood could be pumped to their brains – its head was probably about 13 m (43 ft) from the ground! But lower down in its body, at the level of its lungs, such a high blood pressure would have been fatal.

Endothermic animals have a 'twin pressure' system in so far as they have a fully divided heart- it is divided into a 'lung circulation' and a 'body-and-head' circuit which makes for an efficient circulatory system because there is no 'mixing' of oxygenated and deoxygenated blood in the heart. In reptiles which have only a semi-divided heart there is mixing of deoxygenated and oxygenated blood in the heart which is regulated by a pressure sensitive valve. In order that massive bleeding because of high pressure bursting the thin blood vessels in *Brachiosaurus*' lungs did not occur, *Brachiosaurus* must have had a divided heart which kept the blood pressure in the lung circuit lower than in the body-and-head circuit. Therefore, since dinosaurs had divided hearts, they may well also have been endothermic (warm-blooded).

Sexual dimorphism

In dinosaurs – and in many other animals – any difference between the sexes, either in size or in specific features, is known as sexual dimorphism. This can present problems to palaeontologists attempting to study fossilised remains: are the differences between male and females of the same species to be expected? Since it is the female of the species that bears the young, differences in pelvic anatomy have helped to distinguished male and female dinosaurs.

Sometimes, though, it is difficult to tell whether differences are really just variations in the normal range for the species (think how many different shapes and sizes there are of dogs- or even, human beings)- or, could it be that the differences found in two sets of fossilised remains mean that in fact, the two are completely different species!

These problems are made more difficult because no complete fossilised dinosaur with all its bones and all its soft parts like skin, eyes, muscles and organs, has ever been found. Most dinosaurs are reconstructed from the fossils of their hard parts- and chief among these are their teeth, bones, horns and claws. But the vast majority of dinosaurs are, in fact, known only from a very few fossil parts.

Because there are no living dinosaurs to study, scientists have to make 'educated guesses' based on comparisons with living forms. Consequently, many think that like many living reptiles, female dinosaurs were larger than the males- an idea that is further supported by evidence of 'Sue', the biggest and most complete preserved *Tyrannosaurus rex* found in South Dakota, USA in 1990.

With this in mind, perhaps the 'king' of the dinosaurs should be renamed 'Tyrannosaurus regina'!

Lambeosaurine

A further marker of sex in some dinosaurs, in particular the hadrosaurs (duckbilled dinosaurs), were the head crests of ambeosaurines. As a result of investigations by Dr Peter Dodson of the University of Pennsylvania, we now know that some examples of *Lambeosaurus* that had been earlier identified as a different species were in fact simply male, females and juveniles of a small number of species: some had short, rounded main crests with small, spike-like spurs pointing upwards and backwards, others had a large, angular main crest, with a large spur pointing upwards and backwards.

Crests, horns, spikes and frills

Dr Dodson's work showed that the crests on some hadrosaurs were related to growth stages in life and were probably used as 'indicators' of sex. It is most likely that the crests, frills, horns and spikes which adorned the heads of many other dinosaurs served the same purposes. Such devices would have helped dinosaurs to distinguish one another- for courtship and mating, as well as in territorial disputes- and perhaps the dinosaur with the largest and most 'attractive' head adornment marked it out as the 'leader of the pack'!

Parasaurolophus

The internal anatomy of the crests of some hadrosaurs has given rise to a number of theories about other possible functions. One theory suggests the elongated tubular crest of *Parasaurolophus* was a snorkel that allowed the dinosaur to breathe while it was feeding underwater. A variation suggested that the crests were self contained air storage compartments- like the air tanks of scuba divers. This is unlikely given the amount of air that could be contained in the crest- especially in relation to the size of dinosaur! A third theory suggests that the cranial crests were the sight of salt glands. Since many living reptiles have these glands in their nasal or ocular cavities to regulate the salt levels in their bodies- the perpetual tears in turtles' eyes when on land are produced by these salt glands- and it seemed reasonable to suggest that large, herbivorous dinosaurs such as hadrosaurs might well have them too. The problems however, with this idea, is that if the crests were used to house salt glands, why were there so many different shapes and sizes of crests, and what 'system' for regulating salt was available to those hadrosaurs which didn't have crests- and to those which had solid crests?

Another theory suggested that the crests on lambeosaurines functioned as 'foliage detectors'-a sort of antenna device to stop their heads getting knocked about by branches as they ran through thickly wooded areas. By far the most widely accepted theory, though, is that the crests were used for making sounds. Air blown through the head crest passages could have made the entire crest vibrate. The huge variety of shapes and sizes of crests must have made it possible for a range of sounds to be emitted, from very low pitched and deeply resonating rumbles to more high pitched 'trumpeting' blasts. Such sounds may have been part of the mating rituals as well as being used to intimidate rivals and frighten away predators. It is possible that like other herd animals, such calls and noises were made to call the herd together to form a massed defence.

HORNS AND FRILLS

Like head crests, dinosaurs' horns got bigger as the animals matured and grew in size. The horns and frills of the cratopsians (which means 'horn-face') dinosaurs were the defensive armour required by herbivores to keep them safe from attack by predatory carnivorous dinosaurs especially as ceratopsians had no teeth in the front of their hooked, beak-like mouths!

The 'ancestor' of all the ceratopsians- the horn-face dinosaurs- was *Psitticosaurus* ('parrot reptile') which lived in China and Mongolia in the early Cretaceous period. What distinguished *Psitticosaurus* and gave it its name- was its deep skull which ended in a parrot-like beak. But the first truly 'horned face' dinosaur was named *Protoceratops*. Its crest formed a large shield covering the neck and shoulders and may have helped to guard the neck and the vital nerves and blood supplies running through the neck to the brain.

As the ceratopsians evolved, each 'line' had its own frill and horn design. One of these lines included *Chasmausaurus* which had a long, swept back bony frill, a small nasal horn and two larger horns that jutted from its brows. *Pentaceratops* ('five-horned face') was a much bigger beast with larger horns and an additional pair of horn-like bony projections on the cheeks. Later still would come *Torosaurus* with huge brow horns and a frill that extended beyond the shoulders.

Psitticosaurus

A second 'line' comprised the short-frilled ceratopsians, of which the most famous is *Triceratops* (three-horned face) who was also the last, and the largest of all the ceratopsians. While its nasal horn was short, a pair of horns nearly 1 metre long (3 ft) projected from its brows.

Meanwhile, the pachycephalosaurs – or 'thick-headed reptiles' – which were hornless beasts, may have defended themselves by charging their enemies head first as they were equipped with a very thick domed bone on the tops of their heads. It's also likely that at mating times, males fought each other in head-butting contests.

Necks

Because *Triceratops* had an extension at the rear of its skull made of solid bone which could have weighed as much as 50 kg (110 lb), ceratopsian dinosaurs had short, stout necks which needed to be very strong to support the huge weight of their skulls and horns. Meanwhile, the herbivorous dinosaurs *Barosaurus* required a much longer and much more flexible neck to enable them to crop leaves from low-lying vegetation while standing still as well as enabling them to reach up to tender shoots and leaves in the tall trees. The long flexible neck of *Barosaurus* was composed of 15 vertebrae which had deep hollows inside them. These hollows made the vertebrae lighter in weight while keeping the bones strong. The tough ligaments which supported the neck ran along a series of notches in the top of each vertebra.

Beaks and Teeth

Some of the most common fossil remains of dinosaurs are their teeth. These are most common because, like us, it seems that dinosaurs lost teeth- either in fights or perhaps even through dental problems. But like reptiles, dinosaurs grew new teeth to replace old, broken or worn ones. Consequently, individual teeth were replaced at different times. They are also among the most common finds because teeth are made of the hardest bodily substance and are therefore more likely to 'turn up' as finds. Consequently, many dinosaurs have been named after their 'dental deposits'.

Dinosaur teeth varied greatly in shape: sharp dagger and knife-like teeth were suited to ripping flesh. There were also peg-shaped, comb- and rake-like teeth; rows of rasp or file-like teeth, and, teeth designed for flattening and crushing. The shape, number and arrangement or 'layout' of a dinosaur's teeth have enabled scientists to work out which were herbivores and which were carnivores.

Hadrosaurs (duckbilled dinosaurs) had more than 1000 teeth- all at the back of their mouths, while *Tyrannosaurus Rex* had saw-like edges on the backs and fronts of their fang-like teeth- which left very distinctive puncture marks in the fossilised remains of their prey!

A typical herbivorous dinosaur had a toothless beak and 'cheek teeth' which were used for grinding up leaves and which were all one type. *Hypsilophon* means 'high ridged tooth' and was so-named because it had grooved, high-ridged cheek teeth which made it an effective chewer of tough vegetation. Because its jaws hinged at the level of the teeth, as its upper jaw moved out, the lower jaw moved in and consequently the upper and lower teeth constantly sharpened each other.

Spinosaurus teeth

Heterodontosaurus which means 'different-tooth reptile' had three distinct types of teeth: sharp upper incisors which bit against a tough, horny toothless beak in the lower jaw; ridged, high crown cheek teeth to chew plant food to a pulp, and long curved canine teeth on the upper and lower jaws to the front of the cheek teeth, which were used as weapons.

Heterodontosaurus.

Dinosaur teeth came in a huge range of sizes- some of the largest teeth belonged to *Daspletosaurus*, a Tyrannosaurus-like carnivore whose teeth measured 18 cm (7in.) long.

Claws

Like reptiles today, dinosaurs had claws or similar hard structures at the ends of their digits (fingers and toes) which were probably made of keratin, the same hard substance that formed their horns and from which our own fingernails and toenails are mad.

Because different dinosaurs varied greatly in size, so too did the size and shape of their claws. Many dinosaurs had five-clawed digits on their feet, but others, like *Tyrannosaurus* had only three clawed toes on each foot. The huge carnivores like *Diplodocus* had claws on elephant-like feet that resembled hooves, while many of the carnivorous

Coelophysis claws.

dinosaurs that ran on their two back legs, had claws on their fingers which were long and sharp, ideally suited to slashing and ripping flesh.

Some of the largest claws belonged to *Deinocheirus* a gigantic ostrich-like dinosaur which lived during the late Cretaceous period in Mongolia. Only parts of its fossilised hands and arms have been found but its massive finger claws were more than 25 cm (over 8 inches) long. The fossil found in southern England by Bill Walker in 1982 which gave *Baryonyx* ('heavy claw') its name is truly justified: the long thumb claw was a massive 35 cm (13 in.) long

Tails

All dinosaurs had tails although some may have lost theirs in accidents or in attacks! Like the dinosaurs themselves, tails varied in both size and in function: *Diplodocus* had 73 caudal vertebrae (bones relating to the tail and lower back) while *Camarasaurus* had 53. *Seismosaurus* ('earthshaking reptile') found in New Mexico was one of the longest dinosaurs of all measuring around 34 m (110 ft) and weighing around 30 tonnes (33 tons). Long tails such as these were needed to counterbalance the weight of the neck. It is possible also that some dinosaurs like

Saltasaurus, with its muscular tail composed of ball-and-socket jointed vertebrae, would have used the strength in their tails to help 'prop' them up if they reared their bodies up onto their back legs.

While the long, flexible tails ending in a fine taper of thin bones was the hallmark of the giant quadruped sauropod dinosaurs, dinosaurs which ran on two legs had tails that locked stiffly together to help them balance when they ran or jumped. It also seemed that theses stiff tails acted as rudders, helping the dinosaurs to steer their course at speed.

Ankylosaurus

It is possible that *Diplodocus* may also have used its tail as a whip to defend itself against attackers. Meanwhile, other dinosaurs' tails were more obviously designed as part of their 'armoury'. The smaller, yet heavier ankylosaurids ('fused lizards') which were also slow-moving and could not rely on speed as their defence, used their tails as weapons. At the tips of their tails four bony lumps – two large and two small – were fused together and to the tail tip vertebrae to form a club which was further stiffened by tendons. The powerful muscles in the tail allowed the ankylosaurids to swing their club-ended tails from side to side to deliver mighty blows to their attackers. In other dinosaurs, the danger was not so much under the skin (or scales!) of the tail, but on it: sticking out from the end of *Stegosaurus*' tail were at least two pairs of, long, sharp bony spikes covered in horn. Standing 'broadside' to an attacker, by swinging its spiked tail, *Stegosaurus* would have been able to deliver a deeply penetrating wound to the flanks of a predator – or to a rival for a female's affection!

Skin and Armour Plating

A representation of how dinosaur skin might have looked.

Like reptiles (lizards, snakes, turtles and crocodiles) dinosaurs also had scaly skin. Because skin is soft tissue, in most cases when a dinosaur died, this would have rotted away, or been eaten by another dinosaur, very quickly. In a very rare find, a 65-million-year-old fossil of *Edmontosaurus* shows that the dinosaur's dead body dried and shrivelled up instead of rotting away so that the skin impression is preserved and is wrapped around the skeleton. This find showed that *Edmontosaurus* was covered in thousands of small scales like little pebbles with larger lumps called 'tubercules' spaced among them. In other instances, dinosaur skin has been preserved in clay or silt as 'imprints' showing the pattern of scales or nodules on the skin.

As in crocodiles, dinosaur scales were deeply embedded in a thick, tough, and leathery hide rather than lying on top of its skin and overlapping, as in snakes. The scaly skin would have offered some protection against the claws and teeth of other dinosaurs, and would have also proved effective against smaller pests, such as mosquitoes!

Dinosaur skin was probably similar in appearance and texture as crocodile skin.

Some dinosaurs had more protective armour, *Saltosaurus* had two types: while closely packed pea-sized lumps toughened its skin, on its flanks it had 50 or so hand-sized bony 'scutes' (lit. 'shields') or plates. But undoubtedly the most 'armour plated' skins belonged to the ankylosaurs and nodosaurs which were protected by bony plates and spikes: *Stegosaurus* ('roof-reptile') could be as big as a bus and had huge oesteoderms or bony plates along its back, while *Gastonia* (named after its finder, Robert Gaston) was as big as a family car and had huge spines sticking out sideways from its shoulders and tail while two rows of long spines ran down its back. In between the larger spines were smaller spines and a bony shield protected its hips.

While a great deal of knowledge has been gained about the structure of dinosaur skins and scales, we still cannot tell what colour dinosaurs were, since their remains are fossilised and therefore 'stone coloured'. Some scientists suggest that they may have been similar in colour to crocodiles, which would have given them useful camouflage. Without evidence to suggest otherwise, it may be that dinosaurs were as brightly and beautifully coloured as many living lizards and snakes. It is also quite possible that dinosaurs 'acquired' colours as they matured or perhaps during 'mating seasons'. Microscopic examinations of dinosaur skin and scales have shown that there were patterns of ridges on the surface: it seems that some dinosaur scales reflected light like mirrors or sequins. This means that they would have 'taken on' some of the colour of their immediate surroundings as the reflected light was bounced off their scales.

Brains and the senses

In general, there is a link between the size of an animal's brain compared to the size of its body and to the level of its intelligence. The human brain accounts for 1/50th of the weight of the human body, but *Brachiosaurus'* brain was a tiny 1/100,000th of the weight of its whole body. Nevertheless, this tiny walnut-sized brain located about 13 m (43 ft) in the air (over twice as high as a giraffe) was quite sufficient to 'work' this giant plant eater! The smartest dinosaur- if we use the brain size/body weight and intelligence correlation – may well have been the small carnivore *Troodon* whose brain was about 1/100th of the weight of its body. This means that we humans are only twice as smart as *Troodon*!

Troodon!

Like other soft tissues, the brains of dinosaurs have not been preserved: what we have instead are fossilised skulls which have preserved the brain cavity which indicate its approximate size and shape, and in some cases lumps of rock that have formed casts inside the skull cavities, taking on the size and shape of the brain.

It was once thought that the tiny brain of *Stegosaurus* was far too small to control such a large animal and that it had a 'second' larger 'brain' at the base of its' tail. This 'second' brain is now thought to be a nerve junction – a point where a bundle of nerves joined. These nerves 'controlled' the hind legs and tail movement and stored glycogen, food energy for powering the muscles.

It is apparent from fossilised skulls and skull casts, that some dinosaurs had large bulges called optic lobes in their brains, suggesting that this sense was well developed. While we don't know if dinosaurs could see in colour, the size and position of their eyes would have affected the image their brains received: small-eyed dinosaurs probably only had good 'daytime' vision, while larger-eyed dinosaurs like *Troodon* could probably see quite well in darker circumstances. Frontally placed eyes are more common in carnivorous animals, and allow them to see in detail and judge distances. Eyes placed on the sides of the face or head are more common in herbivorous animals which gave them 'all round vision'– vital as they needed to keep an eye open for hungry carnivores!

In either case, well developed senses such as sight, smell and hearing were vital to the dinosaurs' existence. These senses were needed for hunting (tracking prey by scent and sound) and for defence, as many dinosaurs lived in family groups or herds and protected their young by being alert for predators.

CHAPTER 3

Dinosaur Lifestyles

From the beginning of the Mesozoic Era around 200 million years ago, to its end about 65 million years ago, dinosaurs ruled the earth. In the space of around 140 million years, some of the most awesome, and terrifying, animals evolved. There were carnivorous predators, some standing more than 20 ft (6 m) tall and herbivorous giants measuring up to 85 ft (26 m) long. No matter how great or large, by the end of the Cretaceous Period, the dinosaurs had perished with the sole exception of modern crocodiles, which are the only surviving members of these archosaurs- the 'ruling reptiles'.

The Egg That Changed the World

Reptile, and hence the dinosaurs' success on land, is due to their ability to conquer their new environment. Life on land would have been impossible if reptiles did not evolve to lay eggs with shells. Life on land for tiny vertebrates is almost impossible: their body weight is too great for them to bear on their limbs and they would loose moisture from their bodies very rapidly. Amphibians developed a solution to this by having two 'stages' to their life: the egg is laid in water and matures into larva which then develops and grows into 'miniature adults' fully formed and able to leave their watery birthplace for life on land.

THE AMNIOTIC EGG

Reptiles evolved a different and ingenious solution which freed them completely from laying eggs in the water: they took the 'water' with them onto land in the form of amniotic eggs. Amniotic eggs have a semi-permeable shell that protects the embryo from drying out on land. Inside the egg, an internal membrane called the amnion surrounds the embryo. A second membrane surrounds the yolk from which the embryo gets its nutrition. A sac called the allantois stores waste material, while oxygen passes through the porous shell from the outside atmosphere to the embryo via a membrane called the chorion.

Female dinosaurs laid elongated sausage-shaped eggs with tough leathery shells which not only protected the developing embryos from drying out, but also offered protection from potential predators. Safe inside their own 'watery world' of the amniotic egg, the 'baby' dinosaur only emerged when they had grown to a size that made them able to survive on land. As with today's' reptiles, the incubation period – the time between the eggs being laid and the babies hatching out – is also likely to have varied by weeks, or even months, depending on the temperature off the eggs in the nest which most likely were warmed by the heat of the sun.

Nests and nurseries

The first discoveries of fossilised dinosaur nests and hatchlings were made by Roy Chapman Andrews (1884-1960) who made a number of expeditions to the Gobi Desert in Outer Mongolia between 1919 and 1930.

In some instances, such as with the small herbivore *Orodromeus*, as soon as the young dinosaurs hatched from their eggs, they were left to fend for themselves. In recent years scientists have found many dinosaur nesting sites which have shown that in some cases, the hatchlings (the newly hatched dinosaurs) stayed in their nests and were looked after by adults until they were old enough to leave.

A representation of a carnatosaur's nests

The female *Maiasaura* - whose name means 'good mother reptile'- appears to have cared for her young who were in constant danger from predatory carnivores, in particular tyrannosaurids. Fossilised nests discovered by John Horner in Montana in the late 1970s contained trampled eggshells, as well as the remains of hatchlings which are identifiable by their much shorter, juvenile heads. Some of the hatchlings had leg bones and joints that were not fully developed which suggests that they were not quite able to move about and gather their own food. Like baby birds, they needed to be fed by their parents. However their teeth were worn which suggests that they had been eating 'solid' food for some time in their nests.

Oviraptor - whose name means 'egg thief'- was also a devoted mother. When the dinosaur was first described in 1924 by its finder George Olsen, it was believed that the *Oviraptor* had died while raiding a nest of *Protoceratops'* eggs. In remarkable finds at Ukhaa Tolgod in Mongolia by Mark Norrell and Michael Novacek in the 1990s, more *Oviraptor* remains were found in nests and, in one lay the remains of eggs, one of which contained tiny bones of an *Oviraptor* embryo. Although the egg was a mere 7 cm (3 in) across, had it hatched, the baby would have grown to be around 2m (6 ft 6 in) long! Far from stealing eggs, in this case the mother Oviraptor had died protecting her own.

It also appears that some dinosaurs like *Maiasura* and *Protoceratops* bred in large colonies and occupied the same nesting sites every year, as scientists have found the remains of old nests on top of newer ones. The female *Protceratops* made nests that were shallow, bowl-shaped pits about 1 m

(3 ft) in diameter which had been scraped into dry, sandy earth with the bowl's contents arranged to form low protective walls. Into this pit, the female laid a clutch of around 20 eggs, arranged neatly in a circle or spiral shape. It is likely that the eggs were then covered with earth to keep them warm. *Maiasura's* nests were similarly constructed in the earth, but they added a comfortable lining of twigs and leaves onto which they laid around 25 eggs. From fossil remains, it appears that a young *Maiasura* was about 30 cm (12 in) long when it hatched, but they remained in the nest to be reared by one, or perhaps both, parents until they had grown to around 1.5 m (5 ft).

In 1998 scientists in Auca Mahuevo in western Argentina, found the first sauropod fossil eggs. Thousands of crushed, round eggs about the size of ostrich eggs were scattered across a huge nesting ground. The fossilised egg remains contained tiny bones and skin, but the most significant discovery was of pencil-shaped teeth which identified the remains as sauropods, possibly *Titanosaurus*, the only sauropods to inhabit South America during the late Cretaceous period.

Size and maturity

Calculating the weight of dinosaurs when they were alive offers a number of problems. Using reptiles such as crocodiles as comparisons, scientists estimate dinosaur weights using scaled down models of skeletons which are 'fleshed out' with muscles, inner organs, and skin. The model is then immersed in water and its volume calculated and then the model is mathematically 'scaled up' to full size to estimate its possible 'live weight'. The big problem scientists have is that most dinosaurs are known from only a few bones: they have to 'reconstruct' dinosaurs using combinations of bones from similar dinosaurs. And even when there are lots of bones as in the case of *Apatosaurus* which is known from around 12 skeletons giving scientists practically every bone in its body an accurate size (about 21 m/62 ft) is possible, but 'fleshed out' body weights still vary from 20 tonnes to more than 50 tonnes!

No one really knows how fast dinosaurs grew, how long they took to reach their full size, or even how long they lived. Scientists can only estimate growth rates and ages by making comparisons with modern reptiles. Some living reptiles reach an optimum size at maturity, others continue to grow in size during their lifetime, although

Apatosaurus

the rate of growth does slow down with increasing age. Scientists have offered some estimates: a fully grown *Tyrannosaurus* may have reached maturity aged around 20 years and lived until it was 50 years old. The giant sauropods like *Diplodocus* may have lived for up to 100 years. In each case, potential growth and life expectancy would have been dependent on a number of contributing factors not least of which was diet.

Diet

Growth, health and age for dinosaurs would most likely have been increased with a plentiful food supply. Just as scientists use the shape of dinosaurs' pelvic bones and the arrangement of muscles that would have been attached to them to work out how they would have walked, they also use jaws and teeth to work out how they ate their food. In the case of carnivorous dinosaurs, their teeth and jaws were 'designed' for stabbing and biting off chunks of flesh which were swallowed quickly and then digested in the stomach.

PROLIFIC PREDATOR OR SCAVENGER OF SCRAPS?

Tyrannosaurus had more than 50 dagger-like teeth, some more than 15 cm (8 in.) long set into a head that was an incredible 1.2 m (4 ft) long. Its jaw was hinged at the back of its head which allowed it to open its mouth extremely wide, while powerful neck and jaw muscles allowed it to swing its head while it ripped and tore at its victim's flesh. *Tyrannosaurus* certainly needed a jaw of this design: because its arms were so small, food could not have been passed 'from hand to mouth'! *Tyrannosaurus* may have been an active hunter, perhaps lying in wait to ambush passing prey and catching it after a short chase. But it may, as John Horner of the Museum of Rockies in Montana USA has proposed, that *Tyrannosaurus* was a scavenger that survived on carrion. When a dinosaur died, either of natural causes or as the result of injury, its carcass would have given off a very powerful odour that would have attracted the giant meat-eaters for miles around.

Coelophysis the Cannibal!

Coelophysis was one of the earliest and most primitive dinosaurs. A fleet-footed carnivore it probably dined on a varied diet of large and small insects, as well as smaller dinosaurs. In 1947 at a mass burial at Ghost Ranch in New Mexico, palaeontologists found the remains of juvenile *Coelophysis* inside the ribcages of adults. At first it was thought that the young skeletons were 'unborn infants' but this was impossible because it appears that all dinosaurs laid eggs and also these supposed 'embryos' were much too large and well

Coelophysis

formed to be from embryos within eggs. The shocking discovery was that these juvenile *Coelophysis* were in fact the 'last meals' of the adult of the same species!

GRAZERS AND GASTROLITHS

Herbivores faced a different problem because plant food is far less nutritious than meat: far greater quantities of vegetable matter were needed to compensate for its lower nutritional value, and the digestion of vegetable matter is a far longer process. Herbivorous dinosaurs would not only need to be constantly eating, but they would have had to 'pound' away at the tough fibrous material in order to release its goodness. Like modern cows, it is likely that many herbivorous dinosaurs had to 'chew the cud'.

Some herbivores were equipped with a sharp beak for snipping away twigs and leaves. Others had teeth – often in huge numbers – which were shaped for chopping, raking or crushing and chewing plant matter. Meanwhile *Barosaurus* didn't even chew its food – it swallowed tough leaves and twigs whole! In part of its stomach were gastroliths or 'gastric mill stones'. These were stones that had also been swallowed by the dinosaur and which acted like mill stones, grinding up the food in the stomach for digestion. As these gastroliths tumbled away inside the dinosaur's stomach, they became rounded, smooth and highly polished. Some fossil remains show gastroliths as small as peas and others the size of soccer balls!

Like modern cows, herbivorous dinosaurs probably 'chewed the cud'

It is important to remember, though, that during the Mesozoic Era many types of plants changed or evolved just like the dinosaurs themselves. Like dinosaur fossils, plant fossils have given scientists an insight into the changes in life on Earth during the Mesozoic Era.

In the Triassic period, early in the Mesozoic Era the main plants for herbivorous dinosaurs were conifer trees, gingkoes, cycads and the smaller seed-ferns, ferns, horsetails and club mosses. During this time only the prosauropds were big enough (or had long enough necks) to reach the tall cycad fronds and ginkgo leaves. During the warm, damp Jurassic Period, new plant life evolved and covered land that had previously been barren: tall conifers such as redwood trees and 'monkey puzzle' trees were widespread and their great heights required herbivorous dinosaurs to be incredibly large and very long-necked. It was not until the middle of the Cretaceous period that flowering plants appeared and which by the end of the period included magnolias, maples and walnuts. But because they did not appear on earth until 30-20 million years ago – long after the dinosaurs were extinct – no dinosaur ever ate grasses!

The prosauropods were they only dinosaurs tall enough to reach the tops of trees.

COPROLITES: DINO-DROPPINGS

Coprolites are fossilised droppings or dung and palaeontologists have discovered thousands at many fossil sites around the world. Believed to have been 'deposited' by a *Tyrannosaurus*, one of the largest dinosaur coprolites to be found measured 44 cm (17 ½ in) long! Like other fossils, the once soft (and no doubt smelly) coprolites have become solid rock and when they are cracked open they sometimes reveal what the dinosaurs had recently eaten.

Huge piles of coprolites were found in Montana, USA, left apparently by a large herd of herbivorous hadrosaurs, the duckbilled *Maiasura*. When examined, the coprolites were found to contain the remains of buds, cones, and the needle-like leaves of conifer trees on which they fed.

The coprolites of carnivorous dinosaurs often contain fragments of bone from their prey which can be analysed under a microscope to determine the approximate age of the prey when it was devoured. It seems from coprolite evidence that many carnivorous dinosaurs were opportunists, preying on the very young and the very old! As they were the most vulnerable to attack, the very young and the old would have been 'easy pickings' for a hungry carnivore in his (or her) prime!

Patterns of footprints would tend to support the theory that some dinosaurs lived in herds.

Herd living

The patterns of nests and the quantities of coprolites found in one place have suggested that some dinosaurs lived in herds or colonies. The herding behaviour of some dinosaurs is also supported by footprint track ways such as those found in Bandera County, Texas, which showed that more than 20 sauropods had been moving together across an open area in the same direction.

Living in a herd would seem logical for large sauropods: fully grown adults reached immense sizes which made them pretty much immune from attack by even the largest carnosaurs. Their young, however, would have been easy prey, so, herding together as they moved off to a new feeding ground would have offered some degree of protection. Some footprint tracks show larger footprints on the outer edges of the group, while smaller footprints belonging to juveniles are contained inside. Near Winton, in Queensland, Australia, more than 3300 footprints show that 130 dinosaurs once walked across the earth in a herd.

Furthermore, the discovery of numbers of dinosaur remains of the same type suggests that they may have died in the same place if they had lived there as a group. At the Red Deer River area in Alberta, Canada, the fossils of over 1000 *Pachyrrhinosaurus* suggest that a herd was caught in a flood. Many ceratopsians, the horned dinosaurs, appear to have been herding animals: remains have been found that suggest the herd panicked and drowned during a river crossing and their bodies and bones were subsequently trampled and scavenged by theropods.

Migration and hibernation

Using fossil evidence of skeletons, tracks, plants and knowledge of the positions of the continental plates at different times in the Earths' history, scientists have gained evidence to suggest that unlike living land reptiles, some dinosaurs appear to have migrated. In certain regions, cool winters would have meant that some plants would have died, forcing dinosaurs to move on to warmer parts to find food. In North America huge herds of *Centrosaurus* are known to have migrated north to feed on the plants which grew in the short sub-Arctic summer.

The same is true in very hot periods: fossilised evidence of plants shows that some stopped growing in 'summer' which would have meant the dinosaurs which fed on them would have had to migrate to cooler climes.

Those dinosaurs that did not migrate may have instead gone into hibernation during sustained periods of cold weather, protected perhaps in a cave or a burrow. Many living reptiles today hibernate in colder winter months, or at least shift into extended periods of inactivity to conserve energy when outside temperatures drop. The small herbivorous *Leaellynosaura,* whose remains were found at Dinosaur Cove on the coast near Melbourne, Australia, is believed to have hibernated, as the site was much closer to the South Pole when the dinosaurs lived there some 120-100 million years ago. While there were no polar ice caps at this time, the Australian dinosaurs would have had to cope with longer, cooler and much darker winters when fewer plants would have grown.

Extinction

The extinction of animal and plant life along with evolutionary lines is a 'natural phenomena', part of the history of life on Earth whereby the balance of the emergence and evolution of new life forms and species is maintained. Based on fossil evidence, scientists can demonstrate that extinctions occurred quite frequently and quite regularly: some dinosaurs lived in the Jurassic period (203-135 million years ago) but were extinct in the Cretaceous period (135-65 million years ago), but they did take several million years to die out.

There are also episodes when in a relatively short space of time 'mass extinctions' occurred. One such period was the during the K-T boundary (the border between the Cretaceous and Tertiary periods) around 65 million years ago, when the dinosaurs became extinct along with their 'cousins', the reptiles of the sea and air- although many animal groups including fish, crocodiles, turtles, lizards, birds and mammals (which appeared during the Triassic period and lived alongside dinosaurs) survived. There are no dinosaur fossils since this time 65 million years ago, but there are many theories for their extinction.

One theory suggests that a massive meteorite some 10 km (6 miles) across crashed to earth: indeed under – seabed mud off the Yucatan coast of Mexico is the huge 200 km (120 miles) wide Chixulub Crater which could mark the place of impact of a meteorite crashing to earth 65 million years ago. The impact would have no doubt triggered earthquakes and volcanic activities, belching poisonous fumes, as well as throwing up vast quantities of dust which would have obliterated the sun and darkened the skies. A single year of darkness would have caused the death of many plants – and the herbivores which fed on them and thus the carnivores at the top of the food chain. Supporting this cataclysmic theory is evidence provided by the American father and son team of geologists Luis (1911-88) and Walter Alvarez (born 1940), who in 1980 announced their discovery of world-wide deposits of rocks which contained abnormally high concentrations of rare metals like iridium, osmium and rhodium present in the same proportions in meteorites.

Because modern methods of dating rock samples is accurate only to within a few hundreds of thousands of years, it remains uncertain whether the extinction of the land living dinosaurs and the extinctions of marine and flying reptiles took place exactly at the same time. We know that, for example, ichthyosaurs became extinct before the end of the Cretaceous period and it seems that plesiosaurs, pterosaurs and dinosaurs themselves were less common towards the end of that period. This suggests to some that more gradual changes in the environment were taking place world-wide. During the Cretaceous period sea levels dropped, and as a result, the average air temperature also dropped and the climate became more variable world-wide. These gradual climate changes could have been the cause of the gradual decline of dinosaurs, especially if they were exothermic animals which relied on the heat outside their bodies to keep them warm. Climate change would have also encouraged the evolution of new plant species which may have been poisonous: herbivores that ate these plants would have died, and the carnivores would have also died later as their own food became less available. The carnivorous *Tyrannosaurus* was one of the last dinosaurs to become extinct.

Whichever theory is adopted – the cataclysmic mass extinction or the gradual decline and demise – to explain the extinction of the dinosaurs, one great puzzle remains: why did some very similar reptiles, like crocodiles, lizards and turtles, survive?

CHAPTER 4

Early dinosaurs

Early Theropod Dinosaurs
(see pages 55 – 61)

The first known dinosaurs appeared about 230-225 million years ago, in the latter part of the Middle Triassic Period. Fossils from Argentina and Brazil in South America- part of what was once the continent of Gondwana- show that many of these primitive dinosaurs were small-to-medium size saurischian (lizard-hipped) therapods (beast-feet): carnivorous predators which hunted small animals such as lizards, insects, and mammals- which were around at the same time as the dinosaurs. They were armed with sharp teeth and clawed, four toed-feet- the first toe short and high- and they ran on their muscular hind legs.

Coelophysis

Early Ornithopod Dinosaurs
(see pages 62 – 66)

Ornithopods or 'bird feet' were a sub-order of bipedal and bipedal/quadrupedal herbivorous ornithischian (bird-hipped) dinosaurs. They had feet which were rather like a birds', leaf shaped cheek teeth, a backwards pointing pubic bone and bony tendons that stiffened their tales to counterbalance their bodies while feeding or running. Some scientists believe that the earliest ornithopod is *Pisanosaurus* (Pisano's lizard) from the late Triassic period in Argentina, several million years before any other 'bird-hipped' dinosaurs appeared, although evidence is still very fragmentary. It is generally accepted that the earliest known ornithopods date back to the early Jurassic period, some 200 million years ago. In appearance they were small and lizard-like, but they ran upright on their slender back legs. Superficially, they looked like the smaller carnivorous theropod dinosaurs such as *Coelophysis*, but ornithopod were exclusively herbivores. All ornithischian dinosaurs, including the Late Cretaceous giant *Edmontosaurus* were descended from long legged bipedal ancestors such as *Lesothosaurus*.

Lagosuchus

Eoraptor
Pronounced: EE-oh-RAP-tor

Eoraptor is believed to have lived some 228 million years ago in Argentina. In 1992, a near complete skeleton was discovered and named by Paul Sereno, an American palaeontologist from the University of Chicago who is famous for his fieldwork in South America, Asia and Africa and for his research into early dinosaurs. It is thought that *Eoraptor* is very close to the common ancestor of all the dinosaurs. *Eoraptor* was a small primitive therapod, about the size of a large dog. Though small in size, *Eoraptor* was a fierce predator with long hind legs and a crocodile-like skull with sharp, curved teeth able to rip the flesh of lizards and small mammals. Although it resembled later theropods, *Eoraptor's* remains indicate that it was smaller and more lightly built. It also retained some more primitive features, in particular, fewer vertebrae supporting the hips, and, compared to *Herrerasaurus*, another primitive therapod found in South America (see page 56), *Eoraptor* had shorter grasping hands, and significantly, four fingers. The number of fingers indicates the primitive nature of *Eoraptor*: the trend in the more advanced dinosaurs was to have fewer fingers (and toes).

Name means: Early plunderer

Time: Late Triassic (250-203 MYA)

Location: Argentina, South America

Size: 1m (3 ft 3 in.) long

Weight: 11 kg (24 lb)

Diet: Carnivore

Herrerasaurus

Pronounced: eh-ray-rah-SORE-us

Herrerasaurus lived at the same time and in the same place as Eoraptor (see page 55): around 228 million years ago in Argentina, South America. The first *Herrerasaurus* bones were discovered in the 1960s by a goat herd, Victorino Herrera who gave the dinosaur its name. These first fossilised fragments were the only bones known to scientists until 1988. It had sharp teeth, short arms (less than half the length of its hind legs) and three-fingered hands with curved claws – the fourth and fifth fingers were mere 'stubs' and were clawless. Like most theropods (and birds) *Herrerasaurus* had a small hallux (first toe) that pointed backwards instead of forwards. But *Herrerasaurus* also had seemingly primitive leg and feet bones which at first led scientists to think *Herrerasaurus* was more primitive than any dinosaurs in the two mains groups of Saurischians and Ornithischians.

Name means: Herrera's Lizard

Time: Late Triassic (250-203 MYA)

Location: Argentina, South America

Size: 3-5 m (10-17 ft) long

Weight: 90-100 kg (200-220lb)

Diet: Carnivore

In the 1980s, further excavations were made in the Valley of the Moon in the foothills of the Andes Mountains, which revealed near complete skeletons, including one with a skull. The skull, which was long and narrow with small nostril holes showed that *Herrerasaurus* had a sliding lower jaw joint: the front half of the jaw was able to move against the rear half and provide a grasping bite, in the same way that some living lizards bite and overcome their prey. Because this flexible mandible was common to some other theropods, in 1992 Paul Sereno, working with Fernando Novas, proved that *Herrerasaurus* was in fact an early theropod and one of the most primitive dinosaurs.

An early bipedal, predatory dinosaur, *Herrerasaurus* was about the size of a small car and weighed about the same as a small pony. Even with relatively few species of predatory dinosaurs around in the late Triassic period, the upright stance and long hind legs meant that *Herrerasaurus* and its 'relatives' like Eoraptor were fast and effective killers. Its diet may have included the small bipedal herbivorous dinosaur *Pisanosaurus*, but reptiles such as the tusked, pig-like rhynchosaurs would probably have formed its main diet.

Coelophysis

Pronounced: SEEL-oh-FIE-sis

One of the earliest, and most well-known dinosaurs was *Coelophysis*, which had some features that were birdlike, and others which were reptilian. It was built like a large, slender bird with a narrow 'stork-like' head on an s-shaped neck, a slim body, a long bony yet flexible tail (which made up about half the length of its body) and almost bird-like legs. Like a bird, it also had hollow, thin-walled bones and fused bones of the pelvis (hips) and sacral vertebrae (spine) as well as fused tarsal (ankle bones) and metatarsals (upper feet). A ferocious hunter *Coelophysis* was lightly built for speed. Their bird-like feet had three walking toes with sharp claws, while the primitive clawed hands had four fingers, though only three were strong enough to grasp prey. Its long narrow jaw was equipped with sharp, serrated teeth.

Name means: Hollow Form

Time: Late Triassic (250-203 MYA)

Location: Arizona and New Mexico, North America

Size: 3 m (10ft)

Weight: 27 kg (60 lb)

Diet: Carnivore

The first remains of *Coelophysis* were found by amateur fossil hunter David Baldwin in Abiquiu, New Mexico in 1881 and identified by Edward D. Cope. The early finds consisted of various vertebrae, leg, pelvis and rib bones and remained all that was known of this early dinosaur until 1947 when the American Museum of Natural History organised an expedition to the area around Ghost Ranch in New Mexico. Excavating a section of hillside, scientists found a 'graveyard' of dinosaurs: dozens of skeletons, some of which were complete, ranging from the very young to the old and varying in length from 1-3 m (3 ft – 10 ft) were found lying across one another, all killed at the same time, perhaps in a flash flood. Finding so many specimens together suggested that *Coelophysis* lived in a herd, roaming the upland forests of Arizona and New Mexico, hunting in packs along the banks of streams and lakes, searching and killing lizards and the small, shrew-like animals that evolved in the late Triassic period.

Significant among the remains at Ghost Ranch were the tiny bones of hatchling *Coelophysis* which were discovered inside the rib cages of adults: since dinosaurs did not give birth to live offspring but laid eggs, and the bones were too large and too well formed to be from embryos within eggs, it appears that *Coelophysis* was not only a carnivore, but also, at least on occasion, a cannibal!

Dilophosaurus

Pronounced: die-LOAF-of-SORE-us

Name means: Two-ridge lizard

Time: Early Jurassic (208-144 MYA)

Location: Arizona, USA; Yunnan, China

Size: 6 m (20 ft)

Weight: 500 kg (1100 lb)

Diet: Carnivore

Dilophosaurus is the earliest of the larger theropods that is well known from remains found first in 1942 in Arizona by Navajo Indian Jesse Williams. At first though, palaeontologist Samuel Welles believed the remains belonged to a *Megalosaurus*, and it was not until 1977 that Welles named 'the terror of the Jurassic Age' *Dilophosaurus*. In the late 1980s, scientists made further discoveries in Yunnan Province, China.

Its name means 'two ridge lizard' which it was given because of the unique, tall crest made up of a pair of parallel bony ridges that stood like two halves of dinner plates on its head. Wafer thin in places, these crests were strengthened by vertical struts of bone. At the back of the head, the tips of each crest narrowed into a spike. The function of these crests remains a mystery: some scientists believe that they were for 'sexual display' and that only males sported them. This theory is supported in part by the fact that not all specimens had these crests: in fact none were ever found on the first few fossil remains (which led Welles to suspect they were *Megalosaurus*) and none of the crests have ever been found attached to the skull, but instead, lying nearby.

Dilophosaurus was a lightly built carnosaur (flesh lizard): some of the largest ever terrestrial carnivores such as *Tyrannosaurus* belonged to the carnosaur group. *Dilophosaurus* had a very large head – a typical feature of carnosaurs. But it was also light-boned, and with a long, slender but powerful and flexible neck; a tail that was as long as its whole body, and short arms, that were typical of the small lightweight theropods called coelurosaurs, the 'hollow-tailed lizards'.

The jaws of *Dilophosaurus* give clues to its lifestyle: the lower jaw was strong and full of long, sharp, thin teeth. Like *Coelophysis* (see page 58), *Dilophosaurus* also had a kink in its upper jaw called the subnarial gap: this gap separated a cluster of teeth at the front of the upper jaw from the rest of the teeth – a type of arrangement that can be seen today in the jaws of a modern crocodile. While it had a large head and very strong jaws, *Dilophosaurus* would not have killed its prey by biting them: the thin teeth and apparently delicate head crests would have been too vulnerable in a fight. It is more likely that *Dilophosaurus* ripped at its prey – perhaps the remains of corpses killed by larger and stronger carnosaurs – with its sharply clawed fingers (the first three of its four fingers bore these claws) and its feet as its hind limbs were long and powerful and ended in three, forward-facing sharp-clawed toes.

Lesothosaurus

Pronounced: le-SOO-too-SORE-us

Name means: Lesotho Lizard

Time: Early Jurassic (203-135 MYA)

Location: Lesotho Mafeteng, Southern Africa; Venezuela, South America

Size: 1m (3ft 3 in)

Weight: 11 kg (24 lb)

Diet: Herbivore

Lesothosaurus was no larger than a dog and ran from its enemies on its back legs across the hot arid plains of southern Africa and South America, but rested on all fours when grazing low-growing plants. Like a small ornithopod, *Lesothosaurus* had strong but short arms, and hands with five fingers (the fifth shorter than the rest), but very long legs designed for sprinting – the shins in particular were elongated and were 25% longer than its thighs – and its three toed feet were the same length as their shins. Bony tendons stiffened its tail and counter-balanced the body at the hips. An herbivore and without sharp teeth or claws to defend itself, *Lesothosaurus* depended on its speed and agility for its survival.

Lesothosaurus' skull was small, short and rather flat faced – a little like a modern iguana. There are very large eye cavities and fairly large openings in front of the eye which may have been for a salt gland. The lower jaw was tipped by a horn-covered predentary bone- a useful device for 'chipping' off foliage. The teeth were pointed and shaped like arrow heads with grooved edges: the upper teeth fitting alternately between the lower teeth. This meant that when it was chewing, instead of using a rotating movement which ground up leaves, *Lesothosaurus* used a more primitive and less efficient up-and-down, chopping action which sliced leaves before they were swallowed.

It is possible that *Lesothosaurus* lived in herds: a pair of skeletons were found together in southern Africa. Their bodies were curled up and surrounded by worn, discarded teeth, although the skulls of both animals contained full sets. This led some palaeontologists to surmise that these small dinosaurs may have aestivated (or, slept) through the hottest and driest parts of the year in underground burrows or chambers. The worn teeth scattered around them may possibly have been shed while they slept and grew new ones.

In 1964 a fragment of jaw and a few teeth were found in southern Africa and were named *Fabrosaurus australis* ('Fabre's southern reptile') and eventually it gave it name to the family of fabrosaurs. In 1978, remains of a small animal were found in Lesotho which appeared to be very similar to *Fabrosaurus*. But because there was so little fossil evidence in the earlier find to make more accurate comparisons, the new skeleton was renamed *Lesothosaurus*. If the two sets of fossil bones do, in fact, turn out to be from the same dinosaur, then *Lesothosaurus* will be renamed *Fabrosaurus*! This is because in cases of 'duplicate identification', the name first given to an animal (or plant) takes priority over any names given later.

Lagosuchus

Pronounced: lah-go-su-chus

Name means: 'Rabbit Crocodile'

Time: Middle Triassic (250-203 MYA)

Location: Argentina, South America

Size: 30 cm (1 ft)

Weight: 90g. (3¹/₄ oz)

Diet: Insectivore, possibly also carnivore

The earliest dinosaurs appeared on earth in the middle Triassic period, around 220-235 million years ago, so their ancestors, scientists assume, were around for some time before this. Many believe that the thecodonts, or 'socket-toothed' group of reptiles (so called because their teeth grew from roots fixed into pit-like sockets in the jaw bones) may have been the dinosaurs' ancestors as they both shared the same 'dental' structure. The thecodonts are grouped into five suborders: Proterosuchia; Rauisucha; Phytosauria; Aetosauria, and Ornithosuchia. It is this last subgroup, the Ornithosuchia, which became extinct by the end of the Triassic period, that many palaeontologists regard as the ideal intermediaries between 4-legged, lizard-like thecodontians and the 2-legged dinosaurs.

Lagosuchus was one of the most 'dinosaur-like' of the thecodontians, and many regard it as the ancestor of the dinosaur as all shared a common feature: a diapsid skull. The subclasses of reptiles are recognised by the patterns of skull openings behind the eye socket: the synapsids (the reptilian ancestors of mammals) have a single hole – the temporal fenestra – low down on the side of the skull; the euryapsids (the extinct marine reptiles like the *plesiosaurs*) also have one temporal fenestra, but in a higher position on the skull. Anapsids (the earliest reptiles, but also the chelonians, today represented by turtles, tortoises and terrapins) have no temporal fenestra, while diapsids – dinosaurs and *pterosaurs* (as well as crocodiles, snakes lizards and birds) – the flying reptiles of the Late Triassic Period- had two temporal openings on each side of the skull behind the eye socket (see pages 216).

Lagosuchus was a reptile about 30 cm (12 in) long with extremely, long, slender limbs. It was able to run quite swiftly on its hind legs as these limbs were much longer than its forelimbs: the shin bones were almost twice the length of the thigh bones, which is a feature of 'runing animals' and is particularly evident in the later bipedal dinosaurs.

Staurikosaurus

Pronounced: stor-IK-oh-SORE-us

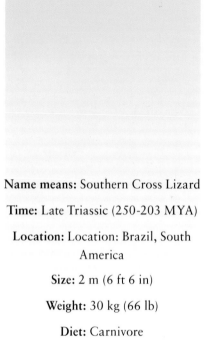

Name means: Southern Cross Lizard

Time: Late Triassic (250-203 MYA)

Location: Location: Brazil, South America

Size: 2 m (6 ft 6 in)

Weight: 30 kg (66 lb)

Diet: Carnivore

Named after the Southern Cross constellation, *Staurikosaurus* was a small, early theropod found in Brazil. So far, scientists have only incomplete skeletal remains with which to work on, but its seems that *Staurikosaurus* shared many of the physical features found in its larger relative, *Herrerasaurus* (see page 56) and that were common to theropods – the group all other known carnivorous dinosaurs belong to. Therapods had three weight-bearing toes on the foot, as the first toe, the hallux, did not reach the ground. This was some way up the foot and pointed backwards. The middle toe was the longest and bore most of the body's weight.

The primitive theropod *Staurikosaurus* perhaps had five-toed feet, but again only three toes would have carried its weight. Like *Herrerasaurus*, *Staurikosaurus* had a slim, curved neck, a large head with tooth-lined jaws and a long, stiff tail which acted as a counter-balance to the front of the body. Bipedal, it had long, strong yet slender, bird-like hind legs and it is also likely that it had four fingers on each hand. *Staurikosaurus* was more lightly built than *Herrerasaurus*, measuring about 2 m (6 ft 6 in) long and weighed only around 30 kg (66 lb). Able to run swiftly on its rear legs, *Staurikosaurus* could have easily out run the smaller moving, four legged prey on which it fed.

CHAPTER 4
Saurischian Dinosaurs 1
Theropods

The saurischian, or 'lizard-hipped' dinosaurs were one of the two great groups of dinosaurs and comprised both herbivores and carnivores. The saurischians inherited the primitive forward pointing pubis bone from their early ancestors. This pelvis – and the way their back legs were articulated from it- meant that they were able to walk on their hind legs, allowing them to become swift, and efficient killers.

The saurischian dinosaurs are subdivided into two distinct groups: theropods ('beast feet') and sauropodomorphs ('reptile-like feet'). The theropods tend to be bipedal carnivores of a variety of shapes and sizes, but are grouped together because of their associated skeletal structure and their predatory lifestyle. Other key saurischian features include a long second finger, and cavities in their bones which housed air sacs connected to their lungs and elongated necks.

Carnotaurus

Carnosaurs

(see pages 72 – 81)

The carnosaurs are one major group of theropod dinosaurs and were typically large- 6 m (20 ft) or more in length – heavily built, and stood on stout, strong pillar-like hind legs. Their forearms were short and relatively weak and they had large heads supported by a sturdy neck. The carnosaurs are well represented (although in many instances in very incomplete forms) in fossil finds from rocks from North America, China and Africa dating from the late Jurassic Period (203-144 MYA)- the oldest known carnosaur is *Piatnitzkysaurus* from the Jurassic period, but most carnosaur species existed in the last 10 million years of the Cretaceous period (144-65 MYA).

Albertosaurus

Tyrannosaurids

(see pages 82 – 86)

Some of the largest terrestrial carnivores that ever lived belonged to this family of 'tyrant lizards'. The fiercest predators in western North America and Asia in their time, the family tyrannosauridae as a whole was a small group. There are four well established species of tyrannosaurids: the famous *Tyrannosaurus Rex*; *Daspletosaurus torosus* and *Albertosaurus libratus* which come from Canada, and, *Tarbosaurus bataar* which comes from the Nemeght Basin in Mongolia. Though small, it was a highly specialised group and one that has given rise to the popular notions of what flesh-eating dinosaurs looked like – and how they behaved! They were also a remarkably short-lived group: the tyrannosaurids first appeared on earth around 80 million years ago and were among the last dinosaurs to become extinct at the end of the Cretaceous period, around 65 million years ago.

Gallimimus

Ornithomimids

(see pages 87 – 90)

The so-called 'bird mimics' were a rather specialised offshoot of the coelurosaurs, the 'hollow tailed lizards' which were the lightweight predators among the theropods. The ornithomimosaurs were about the same height and proportions as a modern ostrich, but they did have the dinosaur features of clawed hands and a long, bony tail. All were long-necked and long-legged sprinters- perhaps capable of speeds of up to 70 km/h (43 mph). They probably travelled in herds over the opens plains of North America, Europe and East Asia in the mid-Cretaceous period, but appear to have died out before the end of that time. Unlike most other dinosaurs, but like the oviraptosaurs, ornithomimosaurs did not have teeth. Instead, they had a horny, bird-like bill but their wide mouth allowed them to snap up sizeable prey, such as small mammals and lizards, as well as insects and fruits. Other distinguishing features were exceptionally large eyes and very big brains, features which suggest they were well co-ordinated predators.

Oviraptosaurs

(see pages 91 – 94)

This small family of toothless, bipedal, bird-like theropods lived during the Late Cretaceous period in eastern Asia and were named the 'egg thieves' on account of their suspected diet. The first fossil of these extraordinary creatures remains which appear to have been the dinosaurs that are the most closely related to birds, were discovered during the American Museum of Natural History-Mongolian expedition in the early 1920s, which set out to find the remains of early humans and instead discovered dinosaurs! The remains consisted of a partial skull preserved in the sandstone of Shabarakh Usu in southern Mongolia and is notable for the curious prong on the tip of its snout. They differed further from their relatives, the ornithomimids or 'ostrich dinosaurs' (pages 87 – 90) in that oviraptosaurs had larger heads with short, stumpy beaks, and, hands with 'thumbs' shorter than the fingers with strongly curved claws.

Oviraptor

Troodontids

(see pages 95 – 97)

Towards the end of the Cretaceous period, a rare group of dinosaurs appeared. Their body design was similar to the ornithomimosaurs and at first scientists believed the remains belonged to a large lizard, such as a monitor lizard. The first discovery of troodontid remains consisted of a single tooth found by Ferdinand Hayden in the Judith River beds of Montana, USA and described by Joseph Leidy in 1856. The tooth, flattened and serrated along its edge named *Troodon* or 'wounding tooth'. In the early 1900s more remains were found in Wyoming and in Alberta, Canada,

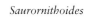

Saurornithoides

but again scientists attributed them to belonging to a *pachycephalosaur* or 'boneheaded dinosaur (see page 179). By the 1980s a much fuller picture was finally beginning to emerge when the teeth were matched with other bones which showed that *Troodon* was a bird-like theropod with a much bigger brain proportionally for its body size than any other dinosaur. Consequently, the new family name of Troodontidae was applied to this and its possibly related genera *Saurornithoides*, and *Bambiraptor*. These were 'small game' hunters, perhaps preying on hatchlings and juvenile dinosaurs, and belonged to the maniraptoran ('seizing hand') dinosaurs – the theropod group to which birds also belong. Like *Caudipteryx* (see page 93) it is also likely that down or feathers covered the North American theropods *Troodon* and *Bambiraptor*.

Dromaeosaurids

(See pages 98 – 101)

The dromaeosaurids are very restricted in their time of appearance in the fossil records: the earliest known, *Phaedrolosaurus*, appears as fossil remains in rocks from 130 to 120 MYA. The later species like *Deinonychus* is known from rocks only a mere 10 million years younger, and was followed very closely by *Velociraptor* and *Dromaeosaurus* .

Velociraptor

Although they were no larger than any of the other carnivores in the period, the members of this family of dinosaurs, the so called 'running lizards', were among some of the most fearsome predators of the Cretaceous period in North America and Asia. Armed with a particularly large and lethal, sickle-shaped claw on the second toe of each foot, rotatable through 180 degrees, structurally however, the dromaeosaurids seem to have been an 'intermediary' group of dinosaurs, with the light and speedy body of the coelurosaurs (the 'hollow tailed lizards') (see pages 102 – 103) and the large head of a carnosaur (see pages 72 –81). They also had very sharp, pointed teeth and grasping, clawed hands. With large brains, it is possible that they hunted in packs.

Coelurosaurs

(see pages 102 –103)
The Coelurosaurs, or 'hollow tailed reptiles' an odd mix
of small, generally lightweight theropods, were fast
running predators with small heads lined with small
sharp teeth, long flexible necks and long arms armed
with sharply clawed grasping hands. They appear to
have been very abundant throughout the 140 million year reign

Ornitholestes

in which dinosaurs 'ruled the earth', but because they were lightly built and
small, their chances of being preserved as fossils are greatly diminished; small
animals tend to decay more quickly, their bones scattered or completely
destroyed. We have already encountered *Coelophysis* ('hollow form') on
page 58. Here are two of the best known and, possibly related species:
Compsognathus whose remains have been found in France and Germany, and
Ornitholestes from Wyoming, USA.

Baryonyx and Suchomimus

(See pages 104 –105)
As we can see there is a huge variety of theropods and most have been put
into family groups. There are some, however, that are unique and don't fit
into any of the established family groupings. This family of Baryonychidae
(large, long theropods) was created in 1986 to cover just one single member,
Baryonyx , 'heavy claw', a skeleton of which was discovered by amateur fossil
hunter William Walker in 1983 in a clay pit in Sussex, southern England.
This unique specimen of a hitherto unknown dinosaur was also the best
preserved example of any dinosaur dating from around 130 million
years ago. Unlike other dinosaurs, *Baryonyx* had a peculiar skull
and forelimbs.

Also included in this section- because it may be related to
Baryonyx - is *Suchomimus*. Some palaeontologists believe that
this tetanuran (stiff-tailed) theropod was a larger example of
Baryonyx. In other instances, scientists group both dinosaurs
into the special group of tetanuran (stiff-tailed) theropods, the
spinosaurs (see *Spinosaurus* page 74). While neither *Baryonyx*
or *Suchomimus* have the tall skin 'sail' on their backs, they do
share *Spinosaurus'* long, low skull and kinked snout.

Baryonyx

Allosaurus

Pronounced: al-oh-SORE-us

Name means: Other Lizard

Time: Late Jurassic (203-144 MYA)

Location: Colorado; Montana; New Mexico; South Dakota; Utah; Wyoming, USA; Mtwara, Tanzania; Victoria, Australia

Size: 11 m (36 ft)

Weight: 1.5-2 tonnes (1 $\frac{1}{2}$- 2 tons)

Diet: Carnivore

The allosaurs – which include *Allosaurus* and *Yangchuanosaurus* (which was found in Szechwan Province in China in the 1970s) – were among the largest carnosaurs around during late Jurassic times. *Allosaurus* was named in 1877 after it was first discovered in Colorado, USA, by Benjamin Mudge who was working for O.C Marsh. It was by far one of the largest and the most fearsome of predators. It was a close relative of its contemporary *Megalosaurus* (see page 81) but was bigger and had two bony bumps above its eyes and a narrow bony ridge running between the eyes down to the tip of its snout. Its head was huge but not heavy as its skull consisted mainly of bony struts, or load-bearing bars that made a framework of openings or 'fenestrae' that surrounded the eyes, nostrils and muscles. The strongest bones were in the jaw: *Allosaurus* was able to open its jaws far apart and then expand the width of the 'gape' by sliding its skull back over its lower jaw. This meant its narrow, knife-like teeth sliced through flesh as *Allosaurus* bit into its victims.

Pillar-like legs supported the squat body which was counter-balanced over the hips by the massive tail. The high-ankled, scale-covered foot looked a bit like that of a huge, giant, flightless bird: three large toes bore the body weight, while the *hallux*, the first toe, was placed higher up, off the ground, on the inside of the leg and facing backwards. The toes also bore curved, narrow claws made up of a bony core and covered in horn. The neck, although short, was strongly curved so that *Allosaurus*' head was held almost over its shoulders rather than forwards. The forelimbs were quite short compared to the hind limbs.

Spinosaurus

Pronounced: SPINE-oh-SORE-us

Name means: Thorn Lizard

Time: Middle Cretaceous (144-65 MYA)

Location: Marsa Matruh, Egypt; Taouz, Morocco; Tunisia; Niger, Africa

Size: 15 m (49 ft)

Weight: 4 tonnes (3.8 tons)

Diet: Carnivore

Spinosaurs were a group of large theropods that may have evolved from the megalosaurs (see page 81) in the Cretaceous period. Spinosaurs had a particular feature: an elongation of the back vertebrae which produced a pronounced ridge down the centre of the back bone. *Spinosaurus* was the most spectacular: it was as big as the largest carnosaurs, but its ridge was a large 'sail' down its back which alone was taller than an average man! The 'sail' was formed by a row of broad, club-like 'spines' about 2 m (6 ft 6 in) tall which projected from the back bone and would have been covered with skin. What the sail's function was is unknown: perhaps it was a a 'solar panel' which regulated the dinosaur's body temperature, or, perhaps, a highly visible sign used to attract females and warn off competing suitors.

The forearms of *Spinosaurs* were larger than those of other theropods which suggests that it may have spent some time on all fours – an unusual posture among the bipedal carnosaurs. A fossilised maxilla (upper jaw bone) found in Morocco and examined by the French paleontologist, Eric Buffetaut, is thought to be from *Spinosaurus* and suggests that it had a long, narrow snout and crocodile-like teeth designed more for eating fish than other dinosaurs. It may have stood on a river or lake bank and grabbed fish with its jaws (a bit like a heron) or it may have waded into shallow water and grabbed them with its claws, although to date, no claws of *Spinosaurus* have been found. The finest fossilised remains of *Spinosaurus* were found in an oasis in Egypt in 1912. These were examined by the German palaeontologist Ernst Stromer von Reichenbach in 1915, who also named the dinosaur. However, an Allied bombing raid over Germany during World War Two destroyed the best fossil finds, leaving scientists with only very fragmentary evidence.

Carnotaurus

Pronounced: kar-noh-TORE-us

Name means: Carnivorous Bull

Time: Late Cretaceous (144-65 MYA)

Location: Chubut, Argentina

Size: 12 m (40 ft)

Weight: 1 tonne (1 ton)

Diet: Carnivore

The discovery of this big, powerful dinosaur was only made in 1985 by Argentinean palaeontologists Jose Bonaparte and Fernando Novas from digs in the Chubut region of Argentina, South America. The near complete finds, lacking only half of the tail and parts of the feet but including detailed fossilised skin impressions, revealed a dinosaur like nothing seen before: *Carnotaurus* had a deeper (taller from top to bottom), shorter (from front to back) and more 'snub-snouted' or 'bull-like' head than other theropods. It had very short 'dwarfed' arms which could not reach its mouth, and therefore would have been almost useless, forward-facing eyes, and thousands of non-overlapping disc shaped scales covering its body, with rows of extra large semi-conical scales along its back and sides. Underneath its skin, bony wings projected from the top of some of its vertebrae. But even more extraordinary was the existence of two pointed horns above its eyes.

Carnotaurus proved to belong to a group of theropods which the scientists called Abelisauridae and which take their name from *Abelisaurus* ('Abel's lizard') named after Roberto Abel who discovered it in 1985. Because there were similarities with *Ceratosaurus*, which had a small horn on its snout, scientists believed the newly discovered abelisaurids were a previously unknown group of ceratosaurs ('horned lizards'). Soon more discoveries were made: *Indosaurus* and *Indosuchus* were found in India; *Majungatholus* was found on the island of Madagascar, off the south-east coast of Africa, and *Xenotarsosaurus* ('strange ankle lizard') was found in Argentina. The distribution across the world of the abelisaurids suggested to scientists that they had spread across the southern super continent of Gondwana after it had separated from Laurasia.

Eustreptospondylus

Pronounced: yoo-STREP-toh-SPON-die-lus

Name means: Well Curved
Vertebrae

Time: Late Jurassic (203-144 MYA)

Location: Wolvercote, Oxfordshire,
England

Size: 7m (23 ft)

Weight: 220 kg (485 lb)

Diet: Carnivore

Many of the later theropods are known as tetanurans which means 'stiff tails'. In early theropods, the muscles of the thighs were linked to the middle of the tail, which allowed it to wave from side to side as the dinosaur walked. Later theropods like *Eustreptospondylus* had evolved much shorter tail-to-thigh muscles which meant that their tails were much less mobile, and in time, some tetanurans would lose their tails completely.

The first known tetanurans included *Eustreptospondylus* which lived in southern England around 170 million years ago. A fairly complete skeleton, missing only a few parts of the skull was found near Wolvercote in Oxfordshire in the 1850s, but was named *Megalosaurus* (see page 81) because of other finds in the region. At this time very few dinosaurs had been discovered and identified and many scientists believed that in the Jurassic period in western Europe, only one large predatory dinosaur was living, to which they gave the conceptual name *Megalosaurus* (Great lizard). In 1964 British palaeontologist Dr. Alice Walker was able to show that the Wolvercote fossil specimen was a completely different animal and it was given the new genus name of *Eustreptospondylus* with the species name *oxoniensis* (from Oxford).

Eustreptospondylus was a large carnivorous dinosaur with short arms and three-fingered hands, thick legs and a stiff tail. Despite its size – up to 7m (23 ft) – *Eustreptospondylus* was lightly built and had weight

saving 'fenestration'(the window-like holes) in its skull. The jaws were
armed with a number of small, blade-like teeth, which in common with other
tetanurans, grew only in the jaw areas forward of their eyes. A carnivore,
Eustreptospondylus may have preyed on herbivorous sauropods like
Cetiosaurus (see page118) that also roamed the region at the time.

The fossil of *Eustreptospondylus oxoniensis* is so far, the only example of this
dinosaur to be found. Now mounted in the University Museum of Oxford, it
remains the best-preserved specimen of any European carnosaur discovered to
date.

Giganotosaurus

Pronounced: GIG-ah-noh-toh-SORE-us

Name means: Giant Southern Lizard

Time: Late Cretaceous (144-65 MYA)

Location: Southern South America

Size: 15-16 m (50-52 ft)

Weight: 7-8 tonnes (7- 7 $\frac{1}{2}$ tons)

Diet: Carnivorous

South America was home to some of the earliest dinosaurs, such as *Eoraptor* (see page 55), as well as the latest, like *Saltasaurus* (see page 132). Remains of the giant herbivorous sauropod *Argentinosaurus* and the huge carnivorous therapod *Gigantosaurus* have also been found there.

Giganotosaurus, from late Cretaceous Argentina, was the largest carnivore ever to walk the earth. More massive than *Tyrannosaurus* (see page 82) *Giganotosaurus* was a tetanuran theropod (stiff-tailed, beast-foot) dinosaur that was a close relative of *Allosaurus* (see page 72) and shared the deep skull with distinctive bones and weight-saving 'fenestration'– although its head was twice as large as that of *Allosaurus*! It jaws were immense with narrow, blade-like saw-edged teeth 20 cm (8 inches) long. On its head were bony ridges running down its snout. Short, but strong arms ended in sharp claws on the three-fingered hands, powerful enough to rip flesh-from living sauropods or from carcasses of the dead. Each enormous foot was capable of supporting up to 4 tonnes (3.5 tons) of body weight (about the same as around 75 adults!) and had three immensely strong clawed toes. *Giganotosaurus* lived around 90 MYA, and like all of the allosaurids, seems to have died out before the end of the Cretaceous period to be superseded by abelisaurids (see *Carnotaurus*, page 76) and tyrannosaurids (see page 82).

Megalosaurus

Pronounced: MEG-ah-loh-SORE-us

The first dinosaur bone on record which, was discovered in England in 1676, most likely belonged to *Megalosaurus*. *Megalosaurus* (or 'great lizard') is neither the biggest, or the heaviest dinosaur, but it can claim to be the first to be found and the first dinosaur to be given an official scientific name (even though the term 'dinosaur' was yet to be invented by Richard Owen in 1841). In 1819 William Buckland (1784-1856) clergyman (later Dean of Westminster Abbey) and geologist discovered part of the lower jaw, several vertebrae and parts of the pelvis and hind limbs in a quarry at Stonesfield in Oxfordshire which he described and named *Megalosaurus* (*Megalosaurus buklandi* as it was later to be known in his honour).

Name means: Great Lizard

Time: Middle Jurassic (203-144 MYA)

Location: Stonesfield, Oxfordshire, England; Western Europe: France, Portugal

Size: 9 m (30 ft)

Weight: 1 tonne (1 ton)

Diet: Carnivore

Although no complete skeleton has yet been found, from the fragments available (in England, France and Portugal), scientists have surmised that *Megalosaurus* was probably longer and stronger than *Eustreptospondylus* (see page 78) but shared the same body of the typical carnosaur, with a large head, a jaw set with great curved teeth (Buckland's jaw fragment shows new teeth beginning to grow ready to replace old ones when they fell out- or were lost in the flesh of their victims!) a thick neck and long powerful legs. The three digits on each hand, and the three weight-bearing toes also bore long sharp claws, making them well equipped to attack, kill and feast off the large, long-necked plant eating dinosaurs of the day. Track marks left by *Megalosaurus* in the limestone rocks of southern England show how these heavy bipeds walked upright on their two hind legs, their toes pointing slightly inwards, and perhaps moving their long stiff tails from side to side with each step to counter-balance their body weight.

Tyrannosaurus Rex

Pronounced: tie-RAN-oh-SORE-us recks

Until the discovery of mighty *Giganotosaurus* in Argentina in the late 1980s, scientists believed that *Tyrannosaurus Rex* was the largest carnivorous animal ever to walk on earth. In spite of this, *Tyrannosaurus* was still a remarkable and very impressive creature. *Tyrannosaurus* is not only one of the most well known dinosaurs, it is also one about which scientists know a great deal as several discoveries have yielded fossilised bones, teeth, entire skeletons and other remains. Living at the very end of the 'Age of the Dinosaurs' about 68-65 million years ago, *Tyrannosaurus'* time on earth was very short lived – only about 15 million years.

Name means: King of the Tyrant Lizards

Time: Late Cretaceous (135-65 MYA)

Location: North America: Colorado, Montana, New Mexico, Texas, Wyoming, USA; Alberta, Saskatch- ewan, Canada; Asia: Mongolia, China.

Size: 13-15 m (46-50 ft) long, up to 6 m (20 ft) tall

Weight: 6-7 tonnes (6-6.5 tons)

Diet: Carnivore

When fully grown the 'King of the Tyrant Lizards' was as long as the width of a tennis court, as tall as a double-decker bus, and weighed about the same as a modern, adult African bull elephant. Its head alone was around 1.25 m (4 ft) long and its jaw was armed with more than 50 teeth that were serrated on both the front and back sides which left very distinctive marks in the flesh of its prey. The longest fangs measured an impressive 18 cm (7in). Its mighty jaw was powerful and big enough to swallow an adult whole – because the lower jaw was hinged at the rear of the head allowing for a huge gape when the mouth was open. The upper and lower jaws were curved, so that when *Tyrannosaurus* closed its mouth, all the great teeth met together.

Its massive head (nearly half the length of its backbone between its hips and legs, with a short deep snout), was carried on a strong, thick, but flexible neck supported by short, wide vertebrae and immensely powerful muscles.

Thick, strongly boned legs bore its enormous weight, and three large, clawed toes touched the ground, but two-fingered claws ended its ridiculously short (but nevertheless very powerful) forearms. The arms and hands were so small that it would have been impossible for *Tyrannosaurus* to pass food to their mouths with them. With large areas of its (relatively small) brain devoted to the senses of sight and smell, and with possible binocular vision, *Tyrannosaurus* it seems, was an active predator of the herds of hadrosaurs (duckbilled dinosaurs) that roamed the forests of North America.

Daspletosaurus
Pronounced: das-PLEET-oh-SORE-us

Name means: Frightful Lizard

Time: Late Cretaceous (135-65 MYA)

Location: Alberta, Canada

Size: 8.5-9 m (28-29.5 ft)

Weight: 3.5 tones (4 tons)

Diet: Carnivore

Daspletosaurus comes from the Red Deer River near Steveville, Alberta, Canada and was a large bipedal carnivore resembling *Tyrannosaurus* (see page 82). Most of the skeleton was found in 1921 by C.M. Sternberg. It was smaller than *Tyrannosaurus,* but with a body length of around 9 m (over 29 ft), it was still a fearsome carnivore, and it had larger teeth than any other tyrannosaur! Although they were fewer in number, each tooth was razor sharp, curved and saw-edged. The forearms, while quite small as in all the tryannosaurids, are larger than those of all the other known species. Its massive head and strong jaws suggest that it may have preyed on the quadrupedal armoured and horned ceratopsians, sinking its teeth into the unprotected flanks of its prey. Once *Daspletosaurus* had locked its curved jaws together, the victims were unlikely to have been able to escape, especially if they were pinned to the ground with one or both of its clawed feet, and would have died of blood loss.

As well as a short time on earth, the tyrannosaurids seem to have had a very limited distribution across it, with fossil remains largely confined to North America and Asia, although a number of fragmentary fossil finds have been referred to the family. They appear to have replaced the earlier carnosaurs (see page 72 –81) as the main predators, and while it is possible that they were in existence before 80 million years ago, fossil evidence is yet to be found to support this.

Albertosaurus

Pronounced: al-BERT-oh-SORE-us

Albertosaurus is another North American tyrannosaurid and this 'small' tyrannosaur shares all the features common to the family. Two partial skulls were discovered on the Red Deer River in Alberta, Canada in the early 1890s: at first the species was referred to by E.D. Cope in 1892 as *Laelaps,* an early name that had also been given to *Tyrannosaurus.* Later, the pioneering Canadian palaeontologist Lawrence Lambe (1863-1919) transferred it to the genus *Dryptosaurus* ('wounding reptile') but in 1905, the remains of these large theropods were reviewed by H.F. Osborn who subsequently renamed both *Tyrannosaurus* and *Albertosaurus.* Understanding of *Albertosaurus* was further enhanced in 1913 when C.H. Sternberg discovered a well-preserved skeleton at Berry Creek on the Red Deer River, although this was named *Gorgosaurus libratus* ('Free Dragon Lizard). While the majority of theropods had a three-fingered hand, *Gorgosaurus,* had only two, quite small fingers. The small forelimb and the two fingers are now characteristics that distinguish the tyrannosaurids as a whole. Even so, in 1917, *Gorgosaurus* was not 'related' to *Tyrannosaurus* because Osborn had reconstructed the latter with three fingers! It was not until 1970 that Dr Dale Russell was able to 'untangle' all the threads and confirm *Albertosaurus* in its own right.

Name means: Alberta Lizard

Time: Late Cretaceous (135-65 MYA)

Location: Alberta, Canada

Size: 8-9 m (26-29.5 ft)

Weight: 3 – 3$\frac{1}{2}$ tonnes (3 – 3$\frac{1}{2}$ tons)

Diet: Carnivore

Like *Tyrannosaurus*, *Albertosaurus* was a large, massively built theropod with a big head and a short body that was balanced at the hips by a long, strong tail. Like other tyrannosaurs, *Albertosaurus* had a large 'foot' on the pubis and a well developed second set of ribs on the underside of its body. A possible explanation for these is that they could have been adaptations for lying prone on the ground. The innards would have been supported by the extra ribs and not crushed by the great body weight. When *Albertosaurus* rose to its feet, its tiny but strong arms would have stopped it from sliding forwards. The body would then have been steadied by the forearms as the rear legs were straightened. By tilting its head and upper body backwards, *Albertosaurus* may have been able to raise itself upright onto its back feet.

Struthiomimus

Pronounced: STRUTH-ee-oh-MEEM-us

Struthiomimus, the 'ostrich mimic' is the best known of North Americas' fast running, bird-like dinosaurs. Its tail counter-balanced the front part of its body, but the stiffened aspect of the tail – long prongs of bone joined the vertebrae together and restricted movement – also meant that it acted as a stabiliser when it changed direction. Pretty well defenceless, apart from perhaps being able to deliver power kicks to drive away small predatory theropods, *Struthiomimus* had to rely on its speed and agility to escape. The feet bear a resemblance to those of modern running birds such as ostriches: the claws are narrow and flattened to provide traction with the ground and stop the foot slipping as it was pushed backwards during running.

The neck was long and slender and presumably, highly mobile as if *Struthiomimus* was always alert for danger, scanning the landscape with its huge eyes. The vertebrae of the back, however, appear to have been held stiffly in place by very strong ligaments. Belly ribs, or gastralia, are found in many reptiles, but not in mammals and no-one really knows what their function is: they may perhaps have helped support the abdomen in some way. The long and slender, toothless jaw was probably covered with tough horn and the thin, light bones suggest they may have been flexible, allowing movement in the skull and offering a greater degree of precision in manipulating food in the mouth, rather like modern parrots which can hold a nut in their jaw, move their upper and lower beak and tongue in unison and quite deftly take the shell off. The forelimbs were very slender and quite long, ending in three very long clawed fingers. These may have been used to hook and pull down leafy branches towards its mouth, or to scrape into the earth in order to uncover eggs on which to feast.

Name means: Ostrich Mimic

Time: Late Cretaceous (135-65 MYA)

Location: New Jersey, USA; Alberta, Canada

Size: 4 m (12 ft 6 in) long, 2 m (6 ft) tall

Weight: unknown

Diet: Carnivorous (insects, small mammals, eggs and lizards), possibly fruit and leaves

Dromiceiomimus

Pronounced: droh-MEE-see-oh-MEEM-us

Name means: Emu Mimic

Time: Late Cretaceous (135-65 MYA)

Location: Canada

Size: 3.5 m (11 ft) long, 2 m (6 ft 6in.) high

Weight: 150 kg (330 lb)

Diet: Carnivorous (insects, small mammals, eggs and lizards) possibly fruit and leaves

The first ornithomimosaur remains were of a partial foot found by George Cannon in 1889 in rocks near Denver, Colorado, USA. Later fragments found in Montana, including fragments of a pelvis, were described by Marsh in 1892 and he recognised that the remains were not ornithopods (bipedal, herbivorous ornithischian, or 'bird-hipped' dinosaurs) as first suspected, but theropods, or carnivorous 'beast-feet' dinosaurs. In the 1920s two specimens found on the Red Deer River in Alberta, Canada were originally described *Struthiomimus breviterius* and *Struthiomimus samueli* by William Parks. In 1972 Dr Dale Russell in Ottawa reassessed the various species proposed since the late 19th century and revealed that there were three genera of ornithomimosaurs in the late Cretaceous period of North America: *Ornithomimus; Struthiomimus,* and, *Dromiceiomimus*, or 'emu mimic' of which Parks' specimens were a part.

All ornithomimids had long slender legs: their tibias (shin bones) were on average about 20% longer than their femurs (thigh bones), but *Dromiceiomimus* had even longer shins than average, indicating that it was a very fast runner. Only its toes touched the ground: the foot bones were locked into a single, bird-like extension of the tibia. The ten neck vertebrae made a very flexible stem on which its head was mounted. The size of the brain cavity and eye sockets in its skull show that *Dromiceiomimus* had an exceptionally large brain – proportionally larger than a modern ostrich – and enormous eyes: *Dromiceiomimus* was in all likelihood a nocturnal hunter of small mammals and lizards in the forests of North America and Canada.

Gallimimus

Pronounced: gal-lee-MEEM-us

Name means: Chicken Mimic

Time: Late Cretaceous (135-65 MYA)

Location: Omnogov, Mongolia

Size: 6 m (20ft)

Weight: 400kg (880 lb)

Diet: Carnivorous (insects, small mammals, eggs and lizards), possibly fruits and leaves

Gallimimus, or 'chicken mimic', is an Asian ornithomimosaur and comes from the Late Cretaceous period in Mongolia, Asia. Over twice the length of a modern ostrich, *Gallimimus* was the largest of the lightly built, bird-like theropods. Remains found in the Gobi Desert include two near complete skeletons, a complete skeleton except for the skull, a skull and fragments of a skeleton, and fragments of different skeletons. From this range of material, scientists have deduced that *Gallimimus* differed from the North American ornithomimids not only in size – it was the largest ostrich-dinosaur discovered to date – but in the shape of its skull and proportions of its limbs. The slender hind limbs are shorter than *Struthiomimus* and its small, lightweight head was long and narrow, the snout ending in a broad, flat-tipped horny beak. Its jaws also appear to have been weaker than other ornithomimids. The hands of *Gallimimus* are also proportionally shorter than other species' and seem poorly designed for grasping, although its claws were more curved. This is probably because *Gallimimus* lived much deeper inland, in more arid and drought-prone regions than its North American cousin.

Oviraptor (O. philoceratops; O. ingenia and O. mongoliensis)

Pronounced: OHV-ih-RAP-tor

The circumstances of preservation of the original remains of the 'egg thief' provide the reason for its name, *Oviraptor philoceratops* ('egg thief, fond of ceratopsian eggs'): its skull and skeleton were found in 1923 by George Olsen at the *Protoceratops* site in Shabarakh Usu in southern Mongolia, lying on top of a clutch of *Protoceratops* eggs. It's possible that *Oviraptor* had died while in the process of raiding the nest, its skull crushed by an angry parent. It is possible that *Oviraptor* did feast on eggs, cracking them open with is horny beak and supplementing its diet by scavenging for berries, insects and on the carcasses of dead dinosaurs in the arid, semi-desert conditions. In the 1990s, further *Oviraptor* remains were found on top of egg-filled nests: this time however, the tiny bones in the embryos proved to be those of hatchling *Oviraptors*. Rather than stealing the eggs of other dinosaurs, this devoted mother had died protecting her own.

Oviraptor's toothless jaw skull was deep but lightweight, with many of the bones acting as struts surrounding windows for the eyes, nostrils and jaw muscles. The jaw ended in a horny beak but inside the mouth, jutting down from the roof, were two bony prongs which could have been used for egg crushing. As with other theropods, *Oviraptor* had a pubis bone which ended in a 'foot', and as with other swift running dinosaurs, its tibias (shin bones) were elongated and there were three weight-bearing toes on each foot with a backwards-facing hallux (first toe). The long tail core, used to counter-balance the body weight and perhaps use as a steering 'rudder' when running at speed, consisted of 40 caudal vertebrae.

Name means: Egg Thief (Philoceratops: 'fond of ceratopsian eggs')

Time: Late Cretaceous

Location: Shabarakh Usu, Southern Mongolia

Size: 2 m (6 ft 6 in.)

Weight: 33 kg (72 lb)

Diet: Eggs, molluscs

One of the most distinguishing features of *Oviraptor* was the head crest: two species, *O. philoceratops* and *O. mongoliensis* appear to have crests sheathed in horn, perhaps brightly or differently coloured. The bony crests resemble the 'casque' on the head of the modern cassowary, the large (2.5 m/5 ft high) flightless bird of Australia, New Guinea and adjacent islands. The cassowary uses its bony helmet to butt its way headfirst through forest undergrowth. Different oviraptosaurs appear to have had different shaped crests: *O. mongoliensis* had a tall, domed crest, much larger than that of *O. philoceratops*, while *O. ingenia* may have been crestless and had a brightly coloured skin on its head instead. In 1971, a Polish-Mongolian expedition, followed by a Soviet-Mongolian expedition both recovered further *Oviraptor* remains which revealed a wider range of skull and crest shapes and crest development than expected. It is possible that many of the differences may be due to the degree of maturity of the specimens.

Caudipteryx

Pronounced: caw-DIP-ter-icks

Of all the recent discoveries, none is more amazing than *Caudipteryx* from China. For centuries, dinosaur fossils found in China were identified as the dragons of traditional folklore and it was not until the 1920s and 1930s that fossil finds in China were first studied scientifically. Since the 1980s, fossil finds from the country (including some remarkable hoaxes) of dinosaurs, non-bird dinosaurs and birds, have been causing scientists across the world to rethink many long-held theories about dinosaurs, their inter-relationships and their descendants.

Caudipteryx was a long-legged, bird-like creature, about the size of a turkey. What is unusual is that it had both dinosaur and bird features. Its dinosaur features include sharp buck teeth in the front of its beak, the pubis bone which pointed forwards, while the caudal or tail vertebrae also hint that it was a close relative of *Oviraptor*. Long legs and bird-like toes (some scientists claim it had a reversed big toe like a bird although this is as yet unproved) indicate that it was capable of running quite fast. It also had short forearms (although shorter than than those of other advanced theropods) with long, three-fingered hands ending in claws to mark it as a non-bird, theropod dinosaur.

Name means: Tail Feather

Time: Early Cretaceous (135-65 MYA)

Location: China, Eastern Asia

Size: 75 cm (2 ft 6 in.) tall

Weight: 10kg (22lb)

Diet: Possibly carnivorous

But *Caudipteryx* also seems to have been covered in different types of feathers: short down feathers for insulation suggest it may have been warm-blooded, while longer feathers with 20 cm (8 in.) long quill shafts sprouted from the arms, fingers and tails. *Caudipteryx*, however was not able to fly: its 'wing' feathers were symmetrical in shape, not asymmetrical as in flying birds. The feathers may then have been camouflage, or formed a display for mating purposes.

Therizinosaurus

Pronounced: THER-ih-ZINE- oh-SORE-us

Name means: Scythe Lizard

Time: Late Cretaceous (135-65 MYA)

Location: Mongolia, China

Size: up to 12 m (39 ft) long

Weight: unkown

Diet: Possibly carnivore/insectivore, possible herbivore

In 1948, a large amount of dinosaur material was collected by a Soviet-Mongolian expedition to the Gobi Desert which included some extremely large, bony claws – one was 70 cm (28 in.) long and this does not include the horny part of the claw which would have made it even longer! The other two claws were shorter, but no less impressively curved like scythe blades, flat bladed and gently tapering to a very narrow point. The claws were so long that scientists suspected that 'scythe lizard' as it was named, would have to walk on its knuckles if it went down on 'all fours'. Later in 1957, 1959, and 1960 more huge claws were discovered in Kazakhstan, Transbaykalia and in Inner Mongolia along with a partial forelimb, incomplete hind limbs and a tooth. These remains demonstrated that *Therizinosaurus* was not a huge turtle (as many originally thought) but a large theropod and yet another remarkable Late Cretaceous period dinosaur from China. The wrist bones of the forelimb remains and the toe bones of the hind limb remains show that *Therizinosaurus* was a tetanuran (stiff tailed) theropod that was related to *Oviraptor* (see page 91).

From various finds scientists have suggested that *Therizinosaurus* had a small head supported on a long, flexible neck, and was largely bipedal. Despite their immense size, the claws do not appear particularly well suited to aggression, especially when compared to the claws of the dromaeosaurids (see page 98 –101). This has led some scientists to suggest that *Therizinosaurus* did not use them for slashing skin, but for raking the ground and tearing open termitaria (anthills). Others, however, find it difficult to believe that such a large dinosaur could sustain itself on just termites or ants, unless they themselves were very large!

Troodon

Pronounced: TROH-oh-don

Named for its small, triangular, saw-edge tooth which was flattened from side to side like the blade of a knife, *Troodon* or 'wounding tooth' had up to 25 teeth on each side of its upper jaw with exactly 25 teeth on each side of it lower one. It flourished in North America about 70 million years ago, right at the end of the Age of the Dinosaurs, the Mesozoic Age (250-65 MYA). The long, bird-like head had very large, partially forward-facing eyes. Scientists believe that the overlapping visual fields of the two eyes may have allowed *Troodon* to accurately judge distances and enabled it to pounce on fast-moving small prey. Its slim, elongated legs certainly allowed it to run very fast on its three weight-bearing clawed toes. However, the second toe appears to have been held above the ground and was also articulated so that it could 'swivel' around, and this, too, was armed with a long, deep switch blade-like claw, a little like that of *Deionychus* (see page 100). Nevertheless, this toe claw would not have been sufficient for *Troodon* to attack and kill large prey, although it could have seized them with its sharply curved claws on the ends of three-fingered hands.

Name means: Wounding Tooth

Time: Late Cretaceous (144-65 MYA)

Location: Location: Montana, Wyoming, USA; Alberta, Canada

Size: 2 m (6 ft 6 in.) long

Weight: 50kg (110 lb)

Diet: Carnivore

Saurornithoides

Pronounced: sore-OR-nith-OID-eez

Name means: Bird-like Lizard

Time: Late Cretaceous
(144-65 MYA)

Location: Mongolia, Asia

Size: 2 m (6 ft 6 in.) long

Weight: 15 – 20 kg (32 –50 lb)

Diet: Carnivore

In 1923 Henry Fairfield Osborn described the incomplete remains of a bird-like theropod dinosaur found in rocks at Shabarakh Usu in the Gobi Desert of Mongolia. This dinosaur was named *Saurornithoides mongoliensis* ('bird-like reptile from Mongolia') and at first was thought to be an early toothed bird because its skull had a long narrow, bird-like muzzle. The skull housed a large brain and large eyes, which may suggest nocturnal habits. It had 38 teeth in the upper jaw which were unusual in that only their back edges were serrated. An incomplete back foot showed that the toes were articulated in a typical theropod fashion, with a small, spur-like first toe and three longer 'walking toes'. Like *Troodon*, *Saurornithoides* had a second toe which was jointed in such a way that could it have been raised clear of the ground. While *Troodon* was native to North America, *Saurornithoides* has been found only in Mongolia. The two may be related, having spread across the northern hemisphere by way of the land bridge across the Bering Straits and then evolved differences to suit the different environment.

In 1974 more finds were discovered in Bugeen Tsav in Mongolia which were described by Rinchen Barsbold and named *Saurornithoides junior* ('younger bird like reptile') because it was found in slightly earlier rocks and was around one-third larger than Osborn's specimen and had a greater number of smaller teeth which were only serrated along their back edges. The well-preserved skull also showed strange swollen areas around the ears and on the floor of the brain case. These differences led Barsbold to propose that *Saurornithoides* should, in fact, be placed not with the Troodontids, but in a family of its own, the saurornthoidids.

Bambiraptor

Pronounced: BAM-bee-RAP-tor

Bambiraptor is one of the most recent dinosaur discoveries. The remains, discovered only in 1994 in Montana, USA, made one of the most complete fossil skeletons of the bird-like (but non-avian) North American dinosaurs. At only 1 m long, it appeared that this specimen of *Bambiraptor* was a juvenile, and not yet fully grown. While some of its bones contained air sacs that were linked to its lungs (as in a bird) and provided extra oxygen to the body when the animal was active, *Bambiraptor* also shared some of the features of *Troodon*, such as the elongated shins and huge eye sockets. Its much larger head also displayed a rather deeper snout with much bigger teeth, giving *Bambiraptor* a much less bird-like appearance. The skull size also indicates that *Bambiraptor* had the largest brain for the size of its body than any other dinosaur. The wrist bones were articulated to allow it to fold its hands (in the same way a bird folds its wings), while the wishbone and shoulders allowed it to swing its long arms out to grab at its prey. The stiffened tail would have acted to counter-balance the weight over the hips and probably swung from side to side as it ran. It is also thought that *Bambiraptor* may have been warm-blooded and covered with a downy feathering to help maintain its body heat.

Name means: Bambi raider

Time: Late Cretaceous (144-65 MYA)

Location: Montana, USA

Size: 1 m (3 ft 3 in) long

Weight: 15kg (32 lb)

Diet: Carnivore

Dromaeosaurus

Pronounced: droh-Mee-oh-SORE-us

Name means: Running Lizard

Time: Late Cretaceous (144-65 MYA)

Location: Montana, USA; Alberta, Canada

Size: 1.8 m (6 ft) long

Weight: 15kg (33 lb)

Diet: Carnivore

Dromaeosaurus, discovered in 1914 in Alberta, Canada, was the first of the sickle-clawed dinosaurs to be discovered and it gave its name to the entire family. But it was not until 1964, when *Deinonychus* was discovered that scientists were able to understand the species more fully. Until that time, *Dromaeosaurus* was considered either as a large coelurosaur, or as a small carnosaur. Although it is only known from its skull and fragments of its arms and legs, palaeontologists have been able to piece together a picture of *Dromaeosaurus* as a small but agile predator. The head had a deep, rounded snout, but for the rest of him, it is assumed that *Dromaeosaurus* was similar to, but smaller than, *Velociraptor* (see page 99) and *Deinonychus* at just under 2 m (7 ft) long.

The relationship of the dromaeosaurids to other carnivorous dinosaurs is still hotly debated: some claim their nearest relatives to be the saurornithoides or troodontids, (see page 95 – 97) as these also have the peculiar sickle-shaped toe claw, but not the same hip structure.

Velociraptor

Pronounced: vel-O-see-RAP-tor

Living some 75-70 million years ago in Central Asia, *Velociraptor* had all the fearsome features of the dromaeosaurids, including the 'terrible claw' on each second toe. The fossil remains of *Velociraptor* have been largely confined to finds in the Djadochta rock formation in Shabarakh Usu in Mongolia, and the first finds were discovered by teams led by the American naturalist and explorer, Roy Chapman Andrews, on expeditions between 1919 and 1930.

Although it was about the same size as *Deinonychus*, it can be distinguished from other dromaeosaurids by its very low, narrow head which may be accounted for by dietary differences. One of the most dramatic fossil finds in Mongolia was of two skeletons found in 1971: a *Velociraptor* locked in mortal combat with the horned dinosaur *Protoceratops* (see page 186). *Velociraptor* was found grasping the great head shield of *Protoceratops* with its clawed hands while at the same time it ripped into its belly and throat with its long sickle-clawed feet. But *Protoceratops* had also mortally wounded its attacker by caving in *Velociraptor's* chest, perhaps with its horny beak.

Name means: Quick Plunderer

Time: Late Cretaceous (144-65 MYA)

Location: East Asia: Mongolia and China

Size: 1.8 m (6 ft) long

Weight:15 kg (33 lb)

Diet: Carnivore

Although no evidence has yet been found related to this particular species, it is also possible that *Velociraptor* and other dromaeosaurids – especially those from China and Mongolia – may have had a body covering of feathers rather than scales. The recent discoveries of other small theropods, including the dromaeosaurids *Sinornithosaurus* ('Chinese bird lizard') and *Microraptor* ('tiny robber'), which were only found in the 1990s, also revealed fossil feathers.

Deinonychus

Pronounced: die-NON-i-kus

Name means: Terrible Claw

Time: Early Cretaceous (144-65 MYA)

Location: Montana, USA

Size: 3-4 m (10-13 ft) long, 1.8 m (6 ft) tall.

Weight: 68 kg (150 lb)

Diet: Carnivore

The discovery in 1964 in Montana, USA of near complete fossilised skeletons of *Deinonychus* showed a dinosaur built for the chase and the kill. This agile killer really undermined the long-held notion that dinosaurs were 'tiny-brained' slow-moving reptiles. *Deinonychus* had the lightweight body that was characteristic of the coelurosaurs and stood on average around 1.8 m (6 ft) tall and weighed around 68 kg (150 lb). All in all, *Deinonychus* was about as tall as a man and weighed about the same. The head, however was typical of the carnosaur: large and well equipped with numerous flesh-tearing, backward curving teeth with serrated edges. Its jaws opened wide and then would clamp onto its prey; by tugging its head backwards, it could slice through its victims' flesh. Its long tail stood out from its body because all the caudal vertebrae (tail bones), except for the ones closest to its body, were 'locked' together by overlapping bony chevron-shaped tendons. As it ran, the body was most likely held horizontally, with the tail counterbalancing the weight of the body in front of the hips.

The legs were slender with long shin bones designed for running, and each foot had four toes. The first toe was tiny and non-functioning as in most of the later theropods, while the third and fourth toes carried the weight. The second toe on each foot gave *Deinonychus* its most lethal weapons: both bore a huge, hinged, sickle-shaped claw up to 15 cm (6 in.) long. The arms were unusually long for a theropod, but still much shorter than the hind legs, and ended in long clawed three-fingered hands. These strong arms (the humerus (upper arm bone) is very broad and has roughened areas for attachment of powerful arm and chest muscles) suggest that *Deinonychus* used its arms to actively grasp its struggling prey. To overcome their prey, scientists suggest that the highly intelligent *Deinonychus* hunted in predatory packs, first harassing a potential victim – perhaps slowing it down by grasping their tails – exhausting them and then finishing them off with lethal blows from their feet claws to the victims unprotected flanks or underbelly.

Ornitholestes

Pronounced: Or-nith-oh-LEZ-teez

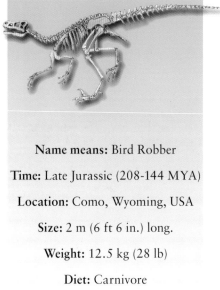

Name means: Bird Robber

Time: Late Jurassic (208-144 MYA)

Location: Como, Wyoming, USA

Size: 2 m (6 ft 6 in.) long.

Weight: 12.5 kg (28 lb)

Diet: Carnivore

This type of coelurosaur was discovered in 1900 at Bone Cabin Quarry near Como, Wyoming and the fossil remains consist of a partial skeleton including the jaws, skull and other small fragments. It was first described and named by its discoverer, H.F. Osborn in 1903 (and again in more detail in 1916) and apart from an incomplete hand of another individual, it remains the only example of *Ornitholestes*, the 'bird robber' so far discovered.

Like its 'relatives' *Coelophysis* (see page 58) and *Compsognathus* (see page 103), *Ornitholestes* had a body similarly balanced at the hips by a long tail held clear of the ground, and a slender, flexible s-shaped neck. It did, however, have a stronger, deeper skull than the two other theropods and some scientists believe that it also had a bony crest at the end of its shorter snout. The teeth were also numerous and quite large: the front ones were almost conical, while those further along the jaw were small and curved. This suggests that *Ornitholestes* had a more powerful bite than than either of the other species, and was perhaps more capable of tackling larger and more active prey. Although named 'bird robber', *Ornitholestes* more likely preyed on the eggs and hatchlings of other dinosaurs as well as small lizards and mammals. The forearms were long in proportion to those of *Coelophysis* and *Compsognathus* and the hands were also unusually proportioned: the second and third fingers were long and slender and almost equal in length, while the first finger or 'thumb' was much shorter. These features suggest that *Ornitholestes* had a much greater ability for reaching and grasping its prey.

Compsognathus

Pronounced: komp-soh-NAY-thus

One of the smallest known dinosaurs (the German example stood no taller than a chicken although the French specimen was as large as a turkey) we also know *Compsognathus* - as a swift footed, bipedal predator of insects and small animals of various types. This is because like *Coelophysis* (see page 58), the skeletal remains of *Compsognathus'* last meal of a small lizard named *Bavarisaurus* have been preserved in its ribcage. In order to have caught such a fast moving animal *Compsognathus* must have had very keen eyesight, been able to accelerate very quickly and kept up a high speed while all the time manoeuvring its body through undergrowth and around rocks. For such a small theropod, *Compsognathus'* skull was large and narrow, lightly constructed with huge openings for the orbits (eye sockets) and tapering to the snout. The teeth were sharp, curved and widely spaced along its upper and lower jaws. Typical of the fast running dinosaurs, *Compsognathus* had long hind legs with elongated tibias (shin bones) and feet, running on its second, third and fourth toes.(The tiny first toe pointed backwards.) Uniquely, the short forearms appear to have borne two-fingered and clawed hands, much like the huge Tyrannosaurids of the late Cretaceous period. It is because of this two-fingered hand that some scientists classify *Compsognathus* as the sole known member of it own family, the Compsognathidae.

Name means: Pretty Jaws

Time: Late Jurassic (208-144 MYA)

Location: Var, France; Bavaria, Germany

Size: 70 cm-1.4 m (2 ft 4 in. - 4 ft 6 in.) long.

Weight: 3 kg (6 ½ lb)

Diet: Carnivore, possibly insectivore

Baryonyx

Pronounced: bar-ee-ON-icks

Name means: Heavy Claw

Time: Mid-Cretaceous
(144-65 MYA)

Location: Sussex, southern England

Size: 10.5 m (34 ft) long,
3 m (10 ft) tall

Weight: 2 tonnes (2 tons)

Diet: Fish, carrion

Two unusual features distinguish this large theropod from others: firstly, it had an enormous, curved claw about 30 cm (12 in.) long, hence it name *Baryonyx*, which means 'heavy claw'. Unfortunately, the claw became unattached from the skeleton when fossil hunter William Walker's geological hammer hit it, so it it not known whether the claw was part of the hind or forelimbs, although most scientists know it as the 'thumb claw' and presume it belonged to the forelimbs as these bones were unusually thick and powerful for a theropod.

The second peculiar feature of *Baryonyx* was its skull which was long- about 1.1 m (3 ft 7 in) – and narrow. In appearance, *Baryonyx's* skull was more like that of a modern crocodile than a carnivorous dinosaur. The jaws (of which the upper one was kinked at the front) were lined with a vast number of small pointed teeth – twice as many as other theropods – and there was also evidence of a small bony crest on top of the head. The long stiff tail counter-balanced the body weight at the hips as the longer and straighter neck and head were held low and jutting forwards. This was an unusual feature as most other theropods had a more curved, flexible, s-shaped neck. The arms were very powerfully built and when all these features are combined, we have a picture of a huge animal, craning its neck out over water and grabbing at fish with its giant hooks of thumb-claws. That *Baryonyx* ate fish is known for certain: palaeontologists found the scales of the large (1 m/ 3 ft 3 in long) fish *Lepidotes* in its ribcage, while in its stomach cavity were some half-digested bones of a young *Iguanodon*.

Suchomimus

Pronounced: soo-CHO-meem-us

Suchomimus, 'crocodile mimic' was discovered only in 1997 in the Sahara Desert in North Africa. The fossilised remains show a creature 11 m (36 ft) long but scientists believe that this specimen was not fully grown when it met its death. *Suchomimus* had a long, narrow head which ended in a flattened, 'paddle' or 'spoon-' shaped tip. Inside the jaw were numerous small sharp teeth, ideal for catching slippery fish. Its naris (nostrils) were placed far back along the head like a crocodiles', so perhaps *Suchomimus* could also lay almost completely submerged in water as it waited for its prey. But *Suchomimus* was also well armed with powerful forelimbs and hooked thumb claws which suggest that it was equally adept at 'fishing' from the banks of rivers and lakes by hooking its prey out of the water. It is also possible that these claws were used to rip at the flesh of corpses of already dead animals on which *Suchomimus* may have also scavenged. While very similar to *Baryonyx* (in fact some scientist suggest that they are one and the same same species) *Suchomimus* did appear to have one distinguishing feature: it had a low ridge running from the top of its head down its back, with the highest ridges above its hips.

Name means: Crocodile Mimic

Time: Early Cretaceous (144-65 MYA)

Location: North Africa

Size: 11 m (36 ft) long

Weight: 5 tonnes (5 tons)

Diet: Fish, carrion

CHAPTER 5
Saurischian Dinosaurs II

Sauropodomorphs

The second suborder of the Saurischian ('lizard-hipped') dinosaurs were the sauropodomorphs ('lizard foot forms'). Their lifestyle was completely different to their contemporaries, the theropods. Although both were saurischians, the theropods were bipedal carnivores, while the sauropodomorphs were largely, quadruped herbivores. Sauropodomorphs inherited the large thumb claws from their bipedal ancestors and had small heads and teeth that were shaped for cropping and chewing plants. Their necks were long, which allowed them to browse for tender shoots in tall trees, and their bodies were often enormous because they needed the extra room to process enough nutrition out of tree leaves and ferns.

By late Triassic times (250-203 MYA), there were two types of sauropodomorphs grazing across the earth: prosauropods ('before the lizard feet'), which ranged from small bipedal forms to the enormous quadruped 'monsters', and, the sauropods ('lizard feet'), gigantic herbivores supported on four pillar-like legs. The prosauropods died out during the Jurassic period, but the sauropods lived on right through to the end of the 'Age of the Dinosaurs'.

Riojasaurus

Prosauropods
(See pages 112 – 116)

Although the prosauropods, as their name implies, lived 'before the sauropods', current theory rejects the once-held notion that the prosauropods were the direct ancestors of the sauropods. Instead, they are now regarded as a side branch of the sauropod family tree. The prosauropods lived in the late Triassic period and are themselves thought to have evolved from theropod-type ancestors, possibly *Staurikosaurus* (see page 66) from the mid-Triassic period, or *Herrerasaurus* (see page 56), from the late Triassic period, both of which were from South America. Scientists in 1990 drew up a list of prosauropod features which included: small 'saw-edged', leaf-shaped teeth; a jaw that was hinged below the level of the upper teeth; paired pubic bones which form a sort of 'apron'; a skull that was half as long as the thigh bone; large, pointed thumb claws and traces of a very small fifth toe on each foot.

SAUROPODS

Between 200 and 65 million years ago, the largest herbivores – in fact the largest creatures ever to have lived on land– were the giant, four-legged, long necked sauropods. In order to support their immense bodies, they evolved some adaptations to their skeletons: firstly, great hollows were carved out of their vertebrae, lightening the load of their enormous bones while maintaining the structural strength, and secondly, their massive hip girdles were fused to their backbone by four (and later by five) sacral vertebrae to form a solid support for the body and the massive tail.

The infra order of sauropods includes some nine families of these very large quadrupeds, some of which weighed 50 tonnes (49 tons) or more, although some of the various family relationships still remain unclear: Vulcanodontidae; Barapasauridae; Cetiosauridae; Brachiosauridae; Titanosauridae; Camarasauridae; Euhelopodidae; Dicraeosauridae, and, Diplodocidae. The sauropods survived as a group for some 50 million years, evolving in the late Triassic/early Jurassic period and reaching their peak in the late Jurassic period. Like all the dinosaurs, they were extinct by the end of the Cretaceous period, around 65 million years ago.

FAMILY VULCANODONTIDAE

(See page 117)
While there are number of distinct sauropod families, there are also a number of less well-known early sauropods, including *Vulcanodon* who lived 208–144 million years ago in early Jurassic Zimbabwe (see page 117). It probably existed alongside later sauropods such as cetisoaurs. The fossil remains are missing skulls, and until more evidence is found and they are re-assigned to another family, Vulcanodon are termed part of the family Vulcanodontidae.

Vulcanodon

Family Cetiosauridae

(See pages 118 – 20)
These early sauropods lived world-wide during the Jurassic period and into the Cretaceous. Their name means 'whale lizard' which relates to their enormous size, not to a marine lifestyle. Members of the cetiosaur family retained two primitive features: their vertebrae were only partially hollowed out, so their body would have quite considerable weight, and their hips were attached to their backbone by only four sacral vertebrae which was a weaker and less efficient arrangement than in later sauropods.

Shunosaurus

Family Camarasauridae

(See pages 121 – 123)

Living in late Jurassic western North America and western Europe, the members of this family of sauropods were somewhat smaller than their 'relatives', the brachiosaurs and diplodocids: their necks and tails were shorter, their skulls were higher and they had much blunter snouts. The Camarasaurids also had different teeth to other sauropods: these were long, forward-pointing and spoon-shaped. This suggests that these sauropods had a different diet to the other larger sauropods in the vicinity, so they were not competing for the same food. Less closely related sauropods in this family lived in Asia, in Mongolia, China and in Thailand, south-east Asia.

Opisthocoelicaudia

Family Brachiosauridae

(See pages 124 –125)

The members of this family were giants of sauropods: until recent finds this family could claim *Brachiosaurus* as the most massive dinosaur to have ever lived, and as the largest animal ever to have walked on Earth. Although overtaken in the size stakes, they remain a very impressive family. From the mid-Jurassic period to the early Cretaceous times, these great herbivores roamed across North America, eastern Africa and Europe. They all shared a similar body structure: small heads perched on top of extra long necks, deep bodies and shortish tails. These sauropods differed from others as their front legs were longer than their hind legs, so that their bodies sloped downwards from their shoulders, a little like a modern giraffe.

Brachiosaurus

Family Diplodocidae

(See pages 126 –130)

This family of sauropod dinosaurs, the diplodocids, included the most spectacular of all dinosaurs. These had enormously long necks- and even longer tails! They also had slender bodies and tiny heads. Despite their great lengths, the diplodocids were actually 'light weights' among the sauropods because their vertebrae had been reduced to a complex framework of bony struts which saved weight but were also very strong. The diplodocids ranged across the world during the late Jurassic period and into the Cretaceous period, although the most famous members, *Diplodocus*, *Apatosaurus* , *Barosaurus* and the mighty 'earth shaking' *Seismosaurus*, all hail from the western region of United States of America. The diplodocids take their name (which means 'double beams') from the twin extensions called chevrons in the caudal vertebrae (tail bones) in the middle of their tails.

Family Titanosuaridae
(See pages 131 –132)
This family of sauropods was the largest, was spread world-wide, especially in
the southern continents, and lived right to the end of the 'Age of the Dinosaurs'
at the close of the Cretaceous period (65 MYA). Some 20 different kinds of
titanosaurs are known from finds in Europe, Africa, Asia, India and North
America, but the most significant finds have been in South America.
Named after the mythical 'giants' of Greek legend, not all the members
of this family were, in fact 'titanic': most averaged 'only' around 12.2-
15.2 m (40-50 ft), quite small in comparison to the diplodocids and

Seismosaurus

brachiosaurids. So far, only fragmentary remains of titanosaurs have been found,
but it appears they had a similar structure to *Diplodocus* (see page 126) but had
a shorter neck and a high, steeply sloping head. Unlike the diplodocids, however,
titanosaurs had solid vertebrae- they were not 'hollowed out' to give them a
weight-saving advantage, which limited their size. A striking feature, and unique
for sauropods, is that on some titanosaurs there is evidence of a bony armour on
their backs.

Family Euhelopodidae
(See page 133)
This family hail from China and has about a dozen genera, but because they
share similar characteristics with the diplodocids, some palaeontologists
do refer some of the dinosaurs in this family to the Family Diplodocidae.
The 'Chinese sauropods' which include *Euhelopus*, *Omeisaurus* and
Mamenchisaurus, varied in length from 10 m to 26 m (33-85 ft) and they lived
in the late Jurassic period until the early Cretaceous. The striking feature of this
family is that they appear to have very, very, long necks!

Mamenchisaurus

Family Segnosauridae
(See page 134)
The infra-order Segnosauria was named as recently as 1980 for some very strange
dinosaurs that were found in south-eastern Mongolia: *Segnosaurus* ('slow
reptile'), *Erlikosaurus* ('king of the dead reptile') and *Enigmosaurus* ('enigma
reptile'). This family is an unusual group of saurischian dinosaurs, with
features reminiscent of theropods, prosauropods and ornithischians. They
were lightly built bipeds with curious skulls and unusual hips. These three
segnosaurs may form part of a group of dinosaurs that lie between the
saurischians and the ornithischians.

Segnosaurus

Plateosaurus

Pronounced: PLAT-ee-oh-SORE-us

Name means: Flat lizard

Time: Late Triassic (248-208 MYA)

Location: Doubs, France; Baden-Wurtemberg, Germany; Aargau, Switzerland

Size: 8 m (26 ft)

Weight: 1.5 tonnes (1¹/₂ tons)

Diet: Herbivore

This 'flat lizard' is one of the most well-known of the larger prosauropods: dozens of their skeletons have been found in the Triassic rocks of central Europe and this also suggest that they may have lived in herds and possibly migrated to avoid droughts. *Plateosaurus* was a large animal whose flexible tail constituted about half its overall length. It had a stronger, deeper head than most other prosauropods and its fairly short neck was also somewhat thinner than usual. Its many small, leaf shaped teeth and the 'low-slung' jaw which made for greater leverage suggest that *Plateosaurus* was primarily, if not wholly, herbivorous. Small cheek pouches held the leaves in the mouth as the jaws worked up and down, chopping up the leaves. It would have roamed across the arid plains and semi-desert landscape of central Europe on all fours, sometimes perhaps, rearing up on its hind legs to feast on various trees such as the cycads and conifers that were growing at this time. *Plateosaurus* had forelimbs with five digits of varying lengths: two short outer fingers; two longer middle fingers: and a huge curving thumb. This large, clawed thumb was partially opposable: it could be moved around, a little like human thumbs. This was useful since the thumb and its claw were so large they would have interfered with walking when on all fours. It seems that *Plateosaurus* overcame this problem by being able to turn and lift its thumb clear of the ground. The thumb would also have made a pretty useful weapon for warding off predatory theropods, and, along with the rest of the hand, it could also be used for grasping and pulling down tree branches as *Plateosaurus*

stretched and reared up to graze. An unusual feature of
Plateosaurus – the reason for which is as yet unknown –
was its very large nasal chamber: perhaps this functioned
as a resonating chamber, for 'calling' to the rest of the
herd or to frighten off predators.

Riojasaurus

Pronounced: ree-O-ah-SORE-us

Name means: La Rioja Lizard

Time: Late Triassic (248-108 MYA

Location: La Rioja, San Juan, southern Argentina

Size: 10 m (33 ft)

Weight: 1 tonne (1 ton)

Diet: Herbivore

Named after the Argentine province of La Rioja where it was found, *Riojasaurus* was one of the largest prosauropods, and one of the first truly large dinosaurs: it could grow as large as 10 m (33 ft) long and some scientists have calculated its weight as much as 4.5 tonnes (5 tons)! Its size alone would have offered it a good deal of protection from attack by carnivorous predators. As the prosauropods grew larger, the great weight of their intestines (plus that of the gastroliths (stomach stones) they swallowed to aid the digestion of plant material) in front of their forward sloping hip bones, made them 'front heavy' and consequently they were forced to live all the time on all fours in order to support their weight. Accordingly, the skeleton was modified: the limbs were thick, solid and strong and held vertically under the body, while the hips were fused at the backbone by three vertebrae making for a very solid attachment for the heavy hind legs. To keep weight to a minimum however, *Riojasaurus'* vertebrae were made lighter by deep hollows. With its elongated and flexible neck, *Riojasaurus* was one of the first land animals to be capable of feeding on vegetation growing high above ground level. Like other prosauropods, *Riojasaurus'* skull was also small for the size of its body and it also shared the leaf-shaped teeth of its European 'cousin' *Plateosaurus* (see page 112).

Anchisaurus

Pronounced: AN-ki-SORE-us

An early dinosaur, *Anchisaurus* was the first to be discovered in America, in 1818. At first it was thought the incomplete fossilised remains belonged to a human, but it was identified as a dinosaur in 1885. It was only in 1925, however, that the remains were formally identified as *Anchisaurus*. This 'near lizard' was typical of the small prosauropds in that it had a small head on a long, flexible neck, and a long, slim body. Its head was long and narrow and its skull was relatively flat. Its forearms were shorter than its hind legs by about one-third and each hand had five fingers- although the two outer fingers were quite short. On the first finger, or thumb, there was a large, curved claw which may have been used for both digging up roots and for fighting. Despite its shorter arms, *Anchisaurus* was 'designed' to walk on all fours, but it is possible that it may have been bipedal at least some of the time, or occasionally rearing up on its hind legs, using its tail to complete a weight-bearing 'tripod', in order to feed on tree leaves. From track marks left in the Connecticut Valley in eastern North America, it appears that *Anchisaurus* lived in herds, and shared its habitat with harmless ornithischian (bird-hipped dinosaurs) as well as some dangerous theropods. It must have been well adapted to the landscape and capable of defending itself with its claws (or perhaps it simply ran away on its hind legs when it faced danger) because living in the Jurassic period, *Anchisaurus* survived long after most other prosauropods evidently became extinct.

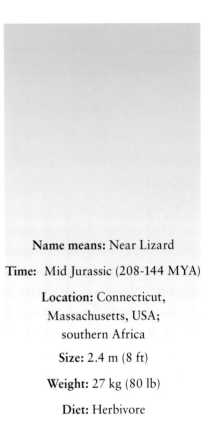

Name means: Near Lizard

Time: Mid Jurassic (208-144 MYA)

Location: Connecticut, Massachusetts, USA; southern Africa

Size: 2.4 m (8 ft)

Weight: 27 kg (80 lb)

Diet: Herbivore

Massospondylus

Pronounced: MAS-oh-SPON-die-lus

Name means: Massive Vertebrae

Time: Late Triassic (248-208 MYA)

Location: North America: Arizona, USA; Africa: Quthing, Lesotho; Matabeleland, Zimbabwe; Orange Free State, Transvaal and Cape Province, South Africa

Size: 5 m (16 ft 6 in.)

Weight: 150 kg (330 lb)

Diet: Herbivore

Massospondylus was the most common prosauropod in southern Africa. A few large but broken vertebrae were sent to England for examination by Sir Richard Owen who named it 'massive vertebrae' in 1854. New fossils were found later and now there are some 80 partial skeletons which have allowed scientists to reconstruct *Massospondylus*. The discovery of fossilised remains in North America also point to the widespread distribution of the species, distribution made possible by the fact that the land masses during the time in which it lived were joined together. *Massospondylus* was a medium-sized prosauropod with a particularly tiny head perched on the end of a very long and very flexible neck. Its five-fingered hands were massive and had a great 'spread' which they needed to support their weight when they walked, but they may also have been used for grasping food as each thumb had a large, curved claw. While *Massospondylus* probably spent most of its time on all fours, it could have reared up on its hind legs, using its tail as a support. While fossil remains show that in the stomach cavities of some specimens there were gastroliths (stomach stones swallowed to aid digestion by grinding up plant material to pulp) there have also been suggestions that *Massospondylus* was carnivorous. Scientist point to the unusually tall, strong front teeth which were ridged a bit like a steak knife, as well as the lack of wear which suggest that *Massospondylus'* teeth did not 'meet' as they would in a herbivore which needed them to grind up plants.

Vulcanodon

Pronounced: vul-KAN-oh-don

Vulcanodon belongs to the most primitive sauropod family, the Vulcanodontidae, which is composed of early Jurassic examples which measured up to 9 m (29 ft 6 in.) from Europe, Asia and Africa. Vulcanodon was found in early Jurassic (208-144 MYA) rocks in Zimbabwe, southern Africa and is one of the earliest sauropod dinosaurs to be discovered to date. Although the skeleton, first described in 1972 and then later in 1984 is incomplete, it is apparent that *Vulcanodon* was a very large, quadruped saurischian dinosaur. It had sauropod-like limbs but whether it was a large prosauropod or a 'true' sauropod is still hotly debated because *Vulcanodon* demonstrated some of the more 'primitive' prosauropod features, especially in its hips.

Name means: Volcano Tooth

Time: Early Jurassic
(208-144 MYA)

Location: Zimbabwe, southern
Africa

Size: 6.5 m (21 ft)

Weight: 4-5 tonnes (3$^{1}/_{2}$- 4$^{1}/_{2}$ tons)

Diet: Herbivore

Cetiosaurus

Pronounced: See-tee-oh-SORE-us

Name means: Whale Lizard

Time: Mid-Jurassic (208-144 MYA)

Location: England; Beni Mellal, Morocco, North Africa;

Size: up to 18.3 m (60 ft) long

Weight: 27 tonnes (26.6 tons)

Diet: Herbivore

In the 1830s when the first sauropod bones were discovered in Oxfordshire, England, they were identified by George Cuvier as whale bones. However, by the early 1840s, Richard Owen recognised that the remains were less likely to be whales (which are mammals) and more possibly a whale-like lizard or a whale-sized crocodile, perhaps, and he coined the name *Cetiosaurus* or 'whale lizard'. When more bones were discovered in 1848 and in 1869 (a near complete skeleton), scientist Thomas Henry Huxley recognised that *Cetiosaurus* was actually a land-living reptile.

Cetiosaurus was a massively built sauropod but with a shorter neck and tail, and much sturdier forelimbs than usual among sauropods The backbone was a solid mass since the vertebrae were hardly 'hollowed out' at all. A near complete skeleton unearthed in Morocco in 1979 revealed the true size of the animal: the thigh bone was a massive 1.8 m (6 ft) long (as tall as a man) and one of the shoulder blades measured over 1.5 (5 ft) in length. Its stiff neck stuck straight out and its weight was counter-balanced by its raised tail. For a long time it was thought that *Cetiosaurus* was a tree-top browser, but in fact it could not raise its head much above shoulder height, although it could lower it to drink and swing it in an arc about 3 m (10 ft) across to crop ferns and small, bushy trees. Judging by its enormous bones, *Cetiosaurus* must have consumed an incredible amount of food each day to maintain its weight and to power its limbs.

Shunosaurus

Pronounced: SHOON-oh-SORE-us

Name means: Shou Lizard

Time: Middle Jurassic period
(208-144 MYA)

Location: China

Size: 10 m (33 ft)

Weight: 10.1 tonnes (10 tons)

Diet: Herbivore

Shunosaurus or 'Shou Lizard' was a middle Jurassic period sauropod from China where there have been more than 20 discoveries of near-complete skeletons. This makes *Shunosaurus* one of the best-known sauropods, and only the second to be known in its entirety. These finds have revealed that this early sauropod already showed the basic characteristics of small head, long neck and tail, deep body and pillar-like legs, although these features were not yet fully developed. *Shunosaurus* had a relatively shorter neck and tail and fewer had fused to their hip bones to support their body and their spinal vertebrae were not yet 'hollowed out' to reduce the weight. *Shunosaurus* had only 12 neck vertebrae and 13 spinal vertebrae, four vertebrae fused to its hip bones and 44 tail bones. Later, larger sauropods like *Apatsaurus* (see page 128) would have nearly twice as many tail bones. The most surprising feature of *Shunosaurus* however, is the fact that it had a small, bony club at the end of its tail which were formed by enlarged vertebrae that had fused together. This means that *Shunosaurus* may have used its tail as a defensive weapon.

Opisthocoelicaudia

Pronounced: oh-PIS-thoh-SEEL-i-KOW-dee-a

The exact size and appearance of this
tongue-twister of a sauropod can only be
guessed at since the one skeleton unearthed
in the Gobi Desert of Mongolia, China, in 1965, is
missing the neck and head. The rest of the body was
fortunately well preserved and scientists have been
able to see that *Opisthocoelicaudia* was similar to the
other non-brachiosaurid sauropods in its general shape
and proportions and appeared to be a typical, though
relatively small and more streamlined camarasaur.
The heavy pillar-like legs supported a bulky body, the
shoulders were quite high and the tail was held straight
out. The curious feature of this creature – and what gives
it its name – is that at the front end of each caudal (tail)
vertebrae, there is a large hemispherical dome which fits
into a deep cup or socket at the rear of the preceding
vertebra. This arrangement makes the joints between each
vertebra extremely strong. Furthermore, it was noted that
the 'spines' of the tail vertebra were exceptionally
roughened and enlarged in order that
powerful muscles and ligaments
could be attached. Why exactly
Opisthocoelicaudia needed
such a powerful rigid tail is a
mystery: some palaeontologists
have suggested that the tail may
have been used as a body prop – a
sort of third leg – to steady the creature
as it raised itself up on its hind legs
to feed off the upper leaves of
trees.

Name means: Tail Vertebrae Cupped
Behind (aka: Posterior Tail Cavity)

Time: Late Cretaceous
(135-165 MYA)

Location: Mongolia, Asia

Size: 12 m (39 ft)

Weight: unknown

Diet: Herbivore

Camarasaurus

Pronounced: kam-are-ah-SORE-us

Name means: Chambered Lizard

Time: Late Jurassic (203-135 MYA)

Location: North America: Colorado, Utah, Wyoming, USA; Europe: Estremadura, Portugal

Size: 18 m (59 ft)

Weight: 20 tonnes (19$\frac{1}{2}$ tons)

Diet: Herbivore

Camarasaurus or 'chambered lizard' is possibly the most well-known North American sauropod with the most complete fossil skeletons. Furthermore, fossil remains have included juvenile specimens and the first fossilised embryo of a sauropod dinosaur ever found.

Camarasaurus was named in 1877 by Edward Drinker Cope and was called 'chambered lizard' on account of the roomy hollows in its backbone which helped to limit the mighty weight of this sauropod.

Camarasaurs had a high skull that was short from front to back with bony struts surrounding window like openings. The naris (nostril sockets) opened in front of very large eye sockets (orbits) and below each eye socket was a skull hole called the 'infra temporal fenestra' from which the muscles that worked the jaw bulged. The large size of the fenestrae suggests that *Camarasaurus* had highly developed senses of sight and smell. The jaw bones themselves were very sturdy and housed deeply rooted, spoon-shaped teeth that would have been able to deal with fibrous plant material such as horsetails and ferns. Its vertebrae included 12 short neck bones with long straight cervical (neck) ribs that overlapped those behind to stiffen the neck; 12 deeply hollowed dorsal (back) bones; five sacral bones fused to the hip bones, and 53 chevron-shaped caudal (tail) bones. The chevrons guarded the blood vessel that ran under the 'cores' of the vertebrae and the long, lower prong on each chevron provided a site for the attachment of muscles. The front legs were relatively long and ended in stubby toes with sharp thumb claws, while the shorter hind legs had three clawed toes. Because the remains of juveniles have been found with adult *Camarasaurus* in the same sequence of rock (the Morrison Formation in western USA) it is likely that *Camarasaurus* travelled in herds, perhaps on migrations to new feeding grounds.

Brachiosaurus

Pronounced: brak-ee-oh-SORE-us

Name means: Arm Lizard

Time: late Jurassic to mid-Cretaceous (approx. 153-113 MYA)

Location: North America: Colorado, Utah, Wyoming; Europe: Estremadura, Portugal; Africa: Wargla (Algeria), Mtwara (Tanzania)

Size: 25 m (82 ft)

Weight: up to 50 tonnes (49 tons)

Diet: Herbivore

The first *Brachiosaurus* bone to be discovered was found in 1900 by Elmer S. Riggs at the Grand River Valley, western Colorado, USA. One of largest, longest and heaviest of all dinosaurs, *Brachiosaurus* is also one of the most well known, as complete skeletons exist except for the neural arches of the vertebrae at the base of its long neck. Its relatively slim, yet pillar-like front legs were proportionally longer than the hind legs. The humerus (upper arm bone) averaged 2.1 m (7 ft) – which gives 'arm lizard' its name – and its shoulders were about 6.5 m (21 ft) from the ground. This gave *Brachiosaurus* a 'giraffe-like' stance and combined with its long neck, it is estimated that it could reach heights up to 16 m (50 ft), enabling it to feed on leafs and branches high above the ground. Plant material was bitten off with 26 chisel-like teeth on each jaw and located towards the front of the mouth. It appears that plant matter was swallowed whole and digested with aid of gastroliths (stomach stones) in its gizzard and gut. The weight of the relatively small, oddly shaped and high domed skull was reduced by replacing solid bone with a framework of light, bony struts which framed the orbits (eye sockets) and the nasal openings- which were placed above the eyes on the large bulge of the skull dome. This arrangement allowed *Brachiosaurus* to breathe while it ate- without getting leaves up its nose! Behind the eyes lay a tiny brain case: its brain was no more than one hundred-thousandth the weight of its whole body. A scaffolding-like framework of bones supported the body: 13 neck bones (each elongated to three times the length of the dorsal vertebrae); 11 or 12 dorsal (back) vertebrae and five vertebrae fused at the hips. To reduce weight, great hollows were 'scooped' from the sides of each vertebrae, to leave a structures that was 'anchor-shaped' in cross section and made of thin sheets and struts of

bone. Each vertebra was angled and articulated
to give optimum strength along the line of stress.
In contrast, the thick-walled limb bones were
immensely heavy and the feet all had five toes
with fleshy pads behind. The first toe on each
front foot bore a claw, while on the hind feet, the
first three toes were also clawed.

Diplodocus

Pronounced: di-PLOH-de-kus

Name means: Double Beam

Time: Late Jurassic (203-135 MYA)

Location: Colorado, Utah, Wyoming, USA

Size: 27 m (89 ft)

Weight: 12 tonnes (11³/₄ tons)

Diet: Herbivore

Resembling a suspension bridge, the longest complete skeleton ever found belonged to *Diplodocus*, a massive sauropod whose length on average was greater than a tennis court! Most of this length was accounted for by the long neck (around 7.3 m/24 ft long) and the extra long tail (about 14 m/46 ft long) as the body was on average only around 4 m (13 ft) long and the tiny head was a miniscule (proportionally in dinosaur terms!) 60 cm (24 in) long. In spite of these mighty measurements, *Diplodocus* weighed in, on average, at a mere 10-12 tonnes (9.5- 11.75 tons)- about 1/8 th the weight of *Brachiosaurus* (see page 124) and one third the weight of *Apatosaurus* (see page 128). This was because *Diplodocus* had a particularly lightweight framework of vertebrae which were hollowed out to form huge cavities. The boney areas and struts that remained were, however, strong enough to bear the body weight of this large creature. The name *Diplodocus* means 'double beam': this refers to the pair of anvil-shaped bones or skids that grew from the underside of each vertebrae in the middle section of the tail. These 'extensions' may have protected the delicate blood vessels and nerves that ran through the tail, when it was pressed on the ground. The tail itself was made up of at least 70 (and perhaps as many as 80) vertebrae, the first 19 of which were lightened with cavities. Towards the tip of the tail, the vertebrae diminished into simple rod-like bones that supported the whiplash tail tip. The pillar-like hind limbs rested on five-toed feet which were supported by fibrous 'heels' and only the first three toes were clawed. The hind legs were longer than the front legs, as was usual for most sauropods (brachiosaurs excepting) and the body sloped downwards from the hips. The forelegs had only one clawed toe on each foot. For some time it was thought that *Diplodocus* had three toes on the forefoot: this was because of the casts made from a well preserved, but incomplete, skeleton found in Wyoming during a dig financed by American steel magnate Andrew Carnegie in 1899. The bones of the feet of *Diplodocus* were missing, so the casts were constructed using feet modelled by the three-clawed toes of *Camarasaurus* (see page 122) that was also living in Wyoming at the same time. A total of eight casts were made- and sent to museums worldwide- before the 'error' was later discovered. The casts presented by Carnegie also showed *Diplodocus* with its tail dragging on the ground. Modern interpretations which are based on evidence provided by fossilised footprints and tracks, don't show 'drag marks' of a tail- so *Diplodocus* probably walked with its tail held well clear of the ground.

Apatosaurus (once known as Brontosaurus)

Pronounced: Ah-PAT-oh-SORE-us

Name means: Deceptive Lizard

Time: Late Jurassic (203-135 MYA)

Location: Colorado, Oklahoma, Utah, Wyoming, USA.

Size: up to 21.3 m (70 ft) long

Weight: 25 tonnes (24 tons)

Diet: Herbivore

Many people know *Apatosaurus* ('deceptive lizard') by its old name of *Brontosaurus* ('thunder lizard'– on account of the supposed noise its heavy footfalls would have made!). The name was changed when it was discovered that *Brontosaurus* fossils were in fact identical to the earlier named *Apatosaurus*. The body of this giant herbivore which roamed across the western states of America was well known to scientists for it had been discovered and then described first in 1877 by Edward Drinker Cope. But poor old *Apatosaurus'* head was a mystery! Many assumed it was a 'boxy' shaped skull like *Camarasaurus*, (see page 122) but when a skull was finally discovered in 1975, it was realised that this creature was a giant sauropod with the tiniest of long, low heads, only a mere 55 cm (22 in) long out of a total body length of over 20 m (65 ft)! While not as long overall as *Diplodocus* (see page 126), *Apatosaurus* was certainly weightier, as its cervical (neck) vertebrae and the limb bones were thicker and heavier. Both creatures did share the same body shape (the longer hind legs and shorter front legs) and had the same long, slender teeth at the front of their jaws. Both animals clearly could rise up on their hind legs to reach up into the tallest branches for tender leaves, but *Apatosaurus* had a longer tail than *Diplodocus*: no fewer than 82 interlocking vertebrae (as compared to *Diplodocus's* 70 or so caudal vertebrae) made up the tail which ended in a whiplash. Current thinking suggests that *Apatosaurus* did not drag its tail along the ground as it was once supposed, but held it clear of the ground. In doing so, it would have meant that other *Apatosaurs* in the herd wouldn't have stepped on it, and predatory theropods would have been less able to grab an *Apatosaur* by its tail.

Barosaurus

Pronounced: bar-oh-SORE-us

Name means: Heavy Lizard

Time: Late Jurassic (203-135 MYA)

Location: North America: South Dakota, Utah, USA; Africa: Mtwara, Tanzania

Size: 23-27 m (75-89 ft)

Weight: 20 tonnes (19½ tons)

Diet: Herbivore

The immensely long 'heavy lizard' has all the typical features of its family: a bulky body that stood highest at the hips, relatively short legs for its size, a long neck and tail, and, it is assumed a tiny head, although since Orthniel Marsh named *Barosaurus* in 1890 no skull has yet been discovered. Where *Diplodocus* (see page 126) had a very long tail, *Barosaurus* had a very long neck – it was one-third longer than *Diplodocus's* neck, and constituted one-third of its overall length. Although both dinosaurs had the same number (15) of cervical vertebrae (neck bones), each of *Barosaurus's* neck bones were 'stretched', and were up to 1 m (3 ft 3 in) long. Each of these cervical vertebrae bore long, strut-like ribs to support them but the vertebrae were also hollowed out to make them lighter in weight. Without this weight reduction, there was no way *Barosaurus* would have been able to project its head and neck the 9 m (30 ft) beyond its shoulders. This makes *Barosaurus* one of the tallest North American dinosaurs, whose head, if it reared up on its hind legs, would have towered a remarkable 15 m (49 ft) off the ground. Like its missing head, the structure of *Barosaurus's* tail tip is also a paleontological mystery: the known tail bones suggest that like *Diplodocus*, *Barosaurus* also had a whiplash tail that would have had to have been long enough to counter-balance its long neck.

Seismosaurus

Pronounced: SIZE-moh-SORE-us

From the sole specimen found to date in New Mexico in 1986 and described in 1991 by David Gillete, *Seismosaurus*, the 'earth shaking lizard' appears to be the longest dinosaur and one of the largest animals ever to have walked on Earth. Measuring around 36 m (120 ft) long and with weight estimates varying between a mere 30 tonnes (33 tons) up to an incredible 98.5 tonnes (100 tons), a few palaeontologists consider *Seismosaurus* to be an 'aged *Diplodocus*': while they share the same overall proportions and body structure, *Seismosaurus* seems to have had longer forelegs than *Diplodocus*. In spite of *Seismosaurus's* enormous size, it was very lightly built and had relatively short legs. As its extremely long neck would have required a very high blood pressure to maintain the flow of oxygen to the brain, it is possible that in fact *Seismosaurus* did not often raise its head up to its highest extent, but instead contented itself with browsing for food at relatively low levels. The late Jurassic rocks in which this monster was found have yielded even larger creatures including the aptly- though not officially-named '*Supersaurus*' from western Colorado who was found in 1972.

Name means: Earth Shaking Lizard

Time: Late Jurassic (203-135 MYA)

Location: New Mexico, USA

Size: 36 m (120 ft) long

Weight: 98.5 tonnes (100 tons)

Diet: Herbivore

Saltasaurus

Pronounced: sal-ta-SORE-us

Name means: Salta Lizard

Time: Late Cretaceous
(135-65 MYA)

Location: Salta Province, north-west
Argentina, South America

Size: 12 m (39 ft)

Weight: 20 tonnes (19 tons)

Diet: Herbivore

The incomplete remains of this medium-sized sauropod were found in Argentina's north-western Salta Province in 1970 and these consisted of a group of partial skeletons surrounded by thousands of bony plates. For some time it was believed that these bony lumps were the remains of armoured ornithischian dinosaurs but in 1980, analysis of a fossilised skin proved that *Saltasaurus* did indeed have armour. Furthermore, it had two types! Close-packed pea-sized lumps served to toughen the skin, while fist-sized bony plates were arranged along its back and flanks. These larger plates may also have terminated in a bony spike. That this South American sauropod had body armour suggests that the continent could have been separate from the great land mass that included North America and Eurasia in the mid-Cretaceous period, with present day Central America under water and forming a barrier between north and south. Sauropods in South America would then have developed in isolation and subject to different evolutionary forces. *Saltasaurus* had shortish, sturdy limbs and a flexible, whiplash tail. In its neck, a single bony spine rose from each cervical vertebra (neck bone) while its hip girdle featured an extra vertebra. The tail vertebrae were articulated with 'ball and socket' joints. These would have strengthened the tail, and perhaps allowed *Saltasaurus* to prop itself up when rearing on its hind legs to browse at higher branches: the bony neck tendons suggest that *Saltasaurus* was not particularly able to lift its small head much above shoulder height.

Mamenchisaurus

Pronounced: mah-men-chee-SORE-us

With the longest neck of any dinosaur by far, *Mamenchisaurus* also had more cervical vertebrae (neck bones) than any other sauropod. There were 19 cervical vertebrae, each more than twice the length of the dorsal (back) vertebrae, so that *Mamenchisaurs's* neck constituted more than half its overall length. These cervical vertebrae were, however, in parts very thin and lightweight and to support this great neck, each had two rod-like ribs or bony struts which overlapped the vertebrae. While these struts would have offered support, they would also have stiffened the neck, restricting movement between the head and the uppermost neck bones so that *Mamenchisaurus* would not have been able to hold its head much above shoulder height. The forelimbs were relatively long and like the hind limbs, very sturdy. Like *Diplodocus*, *Mamenchisaurus's* tail chevron bones bore front and back extensions and likewise, its tail may have ended in a whiplash. Because *Mamenchisaurus* is missing its skull, palaeontologists often reconstruct it 'wearing' the head (and teeth)of *Diplodocus*. It is possible however, that *Mamenchisaurus's* head was more like its Chinese 'relative' *Euhelopus* ('good marsh foot') which was shorter and deeper-snouted with larger teeth that grew from the sides of the jaws as well as at the front of the mouth.

Name means: Mamenxi (Mamen Brook) Lizard

Time: Late Jurassic (203-135 MYA)

Location: China: Sichuan, Gansu, and Xinjiang

Size: 22 m (72 ft)

Weight: 20 tonnes (19 tons)

Diet: Herbivore

Segnosaurus

Pronounced: SEG-noh-SORE-us

Name means: Slow Lizard

Time: Late Cretaceous (135-65 MYA)

Location: Mongolia, China

Size: 6 m (19 ft 6 in)

Weight: 1 tonne (1 ton)

Diet: Probable herbivore

The first segnosaur remains came to light in 1979 following the Soviet-Monglian expedition. *Segnosaurus* was the first of the three forms to be identified and was 'reconstructed' from a partial skeleton which included a lower jaw (but no skull), parts of the legs and backbone, and a complete pelvis. Several other fragments including a forelimb were later found in the area of late Cretaceous rocks known as the Bayn Shireh Horizon in south-eastern Mongolia. The first thing that struck palaeontologists was the pelvis which was unusual for a saurischian (lizard hipped) dinosaur: the arrangement of bones was more like those found in ornithischian (bird-hipped) dinosaurs. The second striking thing about *Segnosaurus* was its jaw: unusually for a supposed theropod, the front part of its jaw was toothless and the teeth at the rear of the mouth were small and pointed rather than being like serrated daggers. It appears that the front end of the jaw was likely to have been covered in a horny beak. The forelimbs were short and ended in three clawed fingers, while the hind limbs ended in a short, broad four-toed foot. In theropods, the feet are usually quite slender and 'bunched' together. At around 6-7 m (20-23 ft) long, the limbs (its thighs were longer than its shins) suggest that *Segnosaurus* was capable only of a brisk walk or slow run. This implies that *Segnosaurus* was unlikely to have been a predatory carnivore, but it was able to use its strong forearms and claws to dig at the earth, perhaps clawing at termite and ant hills. The limited amount of fossil evidence so far means that the exact appearance and the lifestyle of *Segnosaurus* remains a mystery. If and when more remains are discovered, scientists will be able to build up a much fuller picture of these extraordinary creatures.

CHAPTER 7

Ornithischian Dinosaurs

Members of the ornithischian (bird-hipped) order of dinosaurs were exclusively herbivores; the other great order, the Saurischian (lizard-hipped) dinosaurs, as we have seen, had members which were both herbivore and carnivore. The ornithischian dinosaurs can be recognised by several features: the bird-like pelvis (from which the group takes its name); a peculiar horn-covered predentary bone at the tip of the lower jaw; a trellis like arrangement of long, bony tendons along the backbone, and, in most but not all ornithischians, a strange bone called the palpebral in the eye cavity.

The ornithischian dinosaurs can be divided further into distinct types, or suborders: Suborder Ornithopoda; Suborder Thyreophora (which includes the infra orders Stegosauria and Ankylosauria); Suborder Marginocephalia (which includes the infra orders Ceratopsia and Pachycephalosauria).

Suborder Ornithopoda

Ornithopods, or 'bird feet', walked on two feet and may well have been the ancestral group from which all the other ornithischian (bird-hipped) dinosaurs evolved. As a suborder, they were a diverse group of animals in terms of their size, lifestyle and distribution, but structurally, they were all similar. They were also a highly successful group: they survived for nearly 150 million years and spanned the whole of the Jurassic (203-135 MYA) and the Cretaceous (135-65 MYA) periods.

The suborder of Ornithopoda comprised a number of families: Fabrosauridae (these earliest known ornithopods superficially looked like the small carnivorous theropod dinosaurs, the coelurosaurs, and one specimen called *Fabrosaurus*, may in fact be the same as *Lesothosaurus*, see page 62); Heterodontosauridae; Hypsilophodontidae; Iguanodontidae; and Hadrosauridae (which is further divided into two groups, the hadrosaurines and lambeosaurines).

Family Heterodontosauridae

(See pages 143 – 44)

Members of this family of ornithopods, the heterodontosaurs, were small and lizard-like in appearance, but ran upright on their long, slender rear legs. What distinguishes this family is their dental arrangement which is unique among dinosaurs, and indeed among most other reptiles. Heterodontosaurs were the first dinosaurs to have developed cheeks which kept their food inside their mouths.

Heterodontosaurus

They also had three kinds of teeth (hence their name of 'varied-toothed lizards') each performing a different function.

Family Hypsilophodontidae

(See page 145)

Among the most successful of the dinosaurs, the hypsilophodonts flourished as a group for about 100 million years from the late Jurassic to the end of the Cretaceous period 65 million years ago and were widespread across the world- except in Asia. They are an important family in the evolution of dinosaurs as palaeontologists believe that they gave rise to two other major groups of ornithopods: the iguanodonts (see page 147–9) and the 'duck-billed' hadrosaurs (see page 150–56). Although structurally they were similar to the

Hypsilophodon

fabrosaurs, even the primitive hypsilophodonts had developed the retaining cheeks that stopped their food from falling out of their mouths. Further, their upper and lower teeth occluded (met) in regular rows rather than interlocking alternately. But it was their hips that were significant and more advanced than fabrosaurs: part of the pubis bone projected forwards and provided an extra area to which the leg muscles could be attached which gave extra 'running power' to the hypsilophodonts.

Family Iguanodontidae
(See pages 147– 49)
This family of large, herbivorous ornithopods is named after its most famous member *Iguanodon*. The iguanodonts evolved in the mid-Jurassic Period (203-135 MYA) and spread worldwide: fossilised remains have even been found in what is now the Arctic Circle, although these lands would have been ice-free when the iguanodonts roamed the earth some 170 million years ago. Scientists suspect that the ancestors of the iguanodonts were the hypsilophodonts (see page 145) but unlike them, iguanodonts did not evolve as 'running' animals: their bodies were bigger, bulkier and their femurs (thigh bones) were longer than their tibias (shin bones), while both their fore and hind feet had heavy, hoof-like nails. These features suggest that iguanodonts were likely to be slow-moving, quadruped browsers of low growing plants.

Ouranosaurus

Family Hadrosauridae
(See pages 150 – 56)
The largest ornithopod family were the Hadrosauridae, the duck-billed dinosaurs, and they were also some of the biggest dinosaurs, although they were preyed upon by carnivorous theropods. Probably evolving in central Asia, by the late Cretaceous period, the Hadrosauridae rose to dominate as herbivores in most parts of the northern hemisphere and migrate eastwards into Europe and then across the land bridge that existed at the time, into North America. The southern land mass of Gondwanaland had by this time already broken up and the continents were drifting apart. While no hadrosaurids have been found in Africa, India or Australia, some did manage to reach South America, probably crossing from the north via the chain of volcanic islands that existed where Central America

Hadrosaurus

is now. As their name suggests, the hadrosaurids had a wide, expanded mouth packed with hundreds of teeth arranged in batteries on both the upper and lower jaws – with new teeth continuously replacing old or broken ones. This was a unique development in dinosaurs which no doubt contributed to their success. Superficially, hadrosaurids looked quite different: there were many variations in the crests and bumps on their heads and consequently hadrosaurids are divided into two distinct subfamilies. Some animals had flat heads crowned with solid, bony crests, others had no crest at all. These are the hadrosaurines (See pages 150 – 56). The second subfamily had high domed heads topped by quite magnificent hollow crests. This subfamily are the lambeosaurines and appear to have evolved and been largely confined to North America.

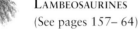

Lambeosaurines
(See pages 157– 64)

Hadrosaurids – duck-billed dinosaurs – with hollow head crests are known as lambeosaurs. Their head crests, which varied in size and shape between species- and individuals, appear to be linked to gender and maturity, although some theories proposed that they also functioned as 'snorkels' and 'air tanks' allowing the lambeosaurines to feed underwater, as sites for salt glands, as 'foliage detectors, or as signalling devices. The crests were hollow structures with a complex series of tubes inside and were connected to the noses and throats of the lambeosaurines, so it is possible the crests were used as resonating devices with each shape creating a different sound. The lambeosaurines seem to have been particularly widespread in the Cretaceous period across North America.

Corythosaurus

Suborder Thyreophora

Thyreophorans, whose name means 'shield bearers', were a diverse group of heavy- limbed, mainly quadrupedal and armoured ornithischian dinosaurs. They are distinguished by their rows of protective bony scutes (bony studs with a horny outer covering embedded into the skin), plates or spikes running along their backs. These dinosaurs are considered to be more primitive ornithischians than ornithopods or marginocephalians on account of their small cheek teeth and jaw formations. The most primitive thyreophorans were from the early Jurassic period and were relatively small animals (around 4m long) such as *Scelidosaurus* (see page 169), with the more developed species grouped into two infra-orders or 'families': Stegosauria and Ankylosauria.

Stegosaurus

Family Stegosauria

(See pages 165-68)

All of the familiar stegosaurs including the famous *Stegosaurus* belong to this infra-order. They evolved in Asia in the mid-Jurassic period, some 170 million years ago and reached their peak of diversity by the end of the Jurassic period. Stegosaurs were widespread throughout North America, western Europe, east Africa and eastern Asia. By the early Cretaceous period the stegosaurs had started to decline, although some species appeared to have survived in isolated pockets, such as in India, until the end of the Cretaceous period, and the end of the 'Age of the Dinosaurs' around 65 million years ago. Like their ornithopod relatives, stegosaurs were herbivores and probably lived in herds. Unlike the more agile ornithopods though, stegosaurs were exclusively quadrupedal and were unable to rise up on their hind legs. The stegosaurs were medium-to-large sized creatures, with toothless beaks, and most had long, thick pillar-like hind limbs: this meant that their back was arched and was highest over the hips. The most distinctive features, however, were the two rows of tall, bony plates and/or spikes which stood up along the back and ran from head to tail, and at least two pairs of tail spikes. A large area in the hip region- once mistaken for a 'second brain' helped to control the tail and hind legs. In addition to this armour, some stegosaurs were also equipped with shoulder spikes.

FAMILY ANKYLOSAURIA

Ankylosaurs ('fused' or 'joined together' lizards) were the tanks of the dinosaur era. They were 'low slung' dinosaurs with broad heads, rather short necks and heavy 'barrel-shaped' bodies carried on four sturdy limbs with a fairly long and muscular tail. Instead of tall plates of spines, these armoured ornithischians were equipped with bands of bony studs or plates, some of which were sheathed in horn. These covered the neck, flanks and backs and in some specimens, the belly. They are known chiefly from fossil finds in North America and Asia, but discoveries in Australia show that they also spread to the southern continents, replacing the stegosaurs by the early Cretaceous period. The ankylosaurs are divided into two sub families: Nodosauridae and Anklosauridae. The nodosaurs were the more primitive ankylosaurs and, lived from the middle Jurassic to the late Cretaceous times and occurred in Asia, Australia, Europe, and North

America. The ankylosaurs flourished from early to late Cretaceous time in Asia and North America. In a 'family' of its own but here placed 'alongside' the ankylosaurs, are the scelidosauridae. Some palaeontologists maintain that these early thyreophorans are primitive members of the ankylosauridae, while others maintain that they are the ancestors of the stegosaurs.

Family Scelidosauridae
(See page 169)

Scelidosaurus

The Scelidosaur family were primitive quadruped herbivores and ranged from heavily armoured dinosaurs to more lightly built creatures equipped for running, varying in size from 1 m–4.5 m long. They lived in the late Triassic–early Jurassic periods, possibly inhabiting wet, marshy areas.

Family Nodosauridae
(See pages 170 – 75)

Nodosaurus

The nodosaurs ('node' or lumpy lizards') were the earlier and more primitive of the two families of ankylosaurs. Their skulls had an unusual hourglass-shaped palate, and the skull overall was longer than it was wide. Solid bony plates covered the body from neck to tail, and while nodosaurs did not have a tail club, long spikes guarded the flanks. Nodosaurus remains are generally poorly preserved and consequently, their whole family tree and their relationships are subject to debate.

Family Ankylosauridae
(See pages 176-78)

Like the nodosaur, the ankylosaurs were heavily built, quadrupedal herbivores. They were also armoured but additionally had a 'club' of solid bone at the end of their tails. The ankylosaurs also differed from the nodosaurs in the shape of their skulls: where the nodosaurs had narrow skulls, ankylosaurs had broad skulls at least as broad as they were long with pointed 'corners' or 'horns' at the back and an intricate pattern of breathing passages. Ankylosaurs flourished from the early to the late Cretaceous period (135-65 MYA) and roamed Asia and North America. They ranged in size from 3-10 m (10-33 ft) long with massive boned hips which were fused to the back bone by at least eight sacral vertebrae to form an extremely strong anchor for the hindquarters.

Suborder Marginocephalia

The Marginocephalia ('margined heads') were a suborder of the ornithischian (bird-hipped) dinosaurs. Herbivorous, and, bipedal/quadrupedal, the marginocephalia had a narrow shelf or deep bony frill at the back of their skulls. They are also distinguished by the structure of their hip bones: they had no obturator process (a projection on the ischium) and no symphysis (the cartilaginous joining of the bones) between the pubic bones. The earliest marginocephalians were late Jurassic bipeds with a small skull ridge, but the later, late Cretaceous marginocephalians include the huge horned quadrupeds with large bony skull frills. The marginocephalians are divided into two infra orders or families: Pachycephalosauria and Ceratopsia.

Infra Order Pachycepahlosauria

(See pages 179 – 83)
The 'thick-headed lizards' ranged in size from very small to large bipedal herbivores which evolved thickened skulls: the skull roof was up to 25 cm (10 in) thick. Some, like the homalocephalidae (the 'even headed') were flat headed pachycephalosaurs from late Cretaceous East Asia, while others developed high, domed skulls. Some species also had bony frills, knobs and even spikes on the backs and sides of their heads, and sometimes on their snouts. Rows of bony tendons stiffened the middle sections of their tails and primitive ornithischian features include teeth in the front of the jaw and small, leaf-shaped cheek teeth. In many other respects pachycephalosaurs were like other ornithopods: bipedal herbivores with five fingered hands and three-toed feet (with a tiny hallux, or first toe).

Stegoceras

Infra Order Ceratopsia

The second infra order of the Marginocephalians is the infra order Ceratopsia. These 'horned faces' were bipedal and quadrupedal ornithischian dinosaurs and the infra order includes all the horned dinosaurs. It was one of the shortest-lived groups of dinosaurs as most lived during the late Cretaceous period in the last part of the 'Age of The Dinosaurs' which ended around 65 million years ago. They were, however, very numerous with many species arising although they were confined to the northern continents of North America and Asia. The infra order contains two primitive families – Psittacosaurids and

Psittacosaurus

Protoceratopids – and a larger, more advanced family, the Ceratopids, which some palaeontologists divide further into 'short-frilled' ceratopids and 'long-frilled' ceratopids, as the long-frilled forms appear to be more advanced and occurred right at the end of the 'Age of the Dinosaurs'.

Family Psittacosauridae
(See page 184)

The forms of ceratopians in this family represent an early evolutionary state. This rare group of 'parrot lizards' were bipedal herbivores with an 'old fashioned' ornithischian body- similar to hypsilophodonts (see Ornithopods, page 145) but with highly evolved skulls that suggests that they were the ancestors of the ceratopians. The snout was deeper than other ornithischians' and formed a narrow 'beak' with high nostril holes. The family of Psittacosauridae comprises only one known genus, *Psittacosaurus*, of which there are four known species living in the early Cretaceous period (135-65 MYA) in central, eastern and south -east Asia.

Protoceratops

Family Protoceratopidae
(See page 186)

The protoceratopids, or 'first horned faces' include some eight genera of quadrupedal and bipedal/quadrupedal herbivores which ranged in size from 1 m (3 ft 3 in) to 3 m (10 ft) long. They constitute the early, primitive horned dinosaurs (although only some of them had horns) but all had a bony frill at the back of the skull, and some had bumps above the brow and nose. Smaller than their later relative, they had teeth in their upper beak, which is considered a primitive feature. They arose in late Cretaceous times and occurred in central and east Asia and spread to western North America.

Family Ceratopidae
(See pages 187-94)

The most numerous, large herbivores of the late Cretaceous period, confined solely to western North America, were the 18 named genera of great horned dinosaurs of this family. Rhinoceros-like herbivores up to 9 m (29 ft 6 in) long, some (the Chasmosaurinae) bore deep, shelf-like bony skull frills and great horns on their brows, while others (the Centrosaurinae) had shorter neck frills with horns on their snouts. Exclusively quadrupedal, ceratopidae had pillar-like legs with heavy hoofed feet which supported stocky bodies covered in thick protective hide.

Triceratops

Heterodontosaurus

Pronounced: HET-er-oh-DONT-oh-SORE-us

In 1962, in Cape Province in South Africa, the rabbit-sized skull of *Heterodontosaurus* was discovered. Typical plant-eating dinosaurs had a toothless beak and cheek teeth which were all one type and designed for grinding up plants. *Heterodontosaurus* amazed palaeontologists because it had three distinct types of teeth, a dental pattern that was reminiscent of a mammal, even though this dinosaur had no connection with the mammalian line of evolution. At the front of the upper jaw were some small pointed teeth (like a mammal's incisors). There were no opposing teeth at the front of the lower jaw, but instead, the chin bone had a horny beak. This bone is called the predentary bone and is unique to ornithischian dinosaurs. Behind the upper teeth and the lower beak, there were two pairs of large, canine-type teeth or 'tusks', with the lower pair fitting into a socket in the upper jaw. Behind these canines were tall, chisel-like back teeth with cutting edges. The pointed front teeth were used to snip and nip off leaves and greenery from trees while the back teeth were used to cut up the leaves with a scissors like motion and grind them into small pieces. But what the two pairs of canine-type 'tusks' were used for is a mystery – except perhaps for fighting other males, since it seems from other skulls found, that the female *Heterodontosaurus* may have lacked these particular teeth. Living in the early Jurassic semi-desert regions of southern Africa, fossil remains show that *Heterodontosaurus* was about the size of a large turkey and had sturdy arms bearing five clawed fingers. Each foot had one short toe and three longer, forward facing clawed toes. The rear legs were more than one-third longer than the arms, and the tibia (shin bone) was one-third longer than the femur (thigh bone) making it capable of running at some speed.

Name means: Varied-Toothed Lizard

Time: Early Jurassic (203-135 MYA)

Location: Africa: Cape Province, South Africa; Quthing, Lesotho

Size: 1.2 m (4 ft)

Weight: 2.5 kg (5¹/₂ lb)

Diet: Herbivore

Hypsilophodon

Pronounced: hip-sih-LOH-foh-don

Hypsilophodon was an ornithischian (bird-hipped) dinosaur whose name means 'high ridged tooth'. It was first discovered in 1849 on the Isle of Wight, off England's' south coast, but experts at the time believed it was an *Iguanodon* (see page 147). Later finds examined by Thomas Huxley in 1870 revealed *Hypsilophodon's* distinctive teeth and a new dinosaur genus was named… except that Huxley conceived it as a tree-dwelling, plant-eating ornithopod! It was not until 1974 that palaeontologists agreed that there was no evidence to suggest it lived in a tree, but that it was in fact, perfectly adapted to life on the ground. Living in herds *Hypsilophodon's* small head had a horny beak and large eyes, and, in its mouth, its jaws were lined with 28 or 30 tall, grooved and self-sharpening cheek teeth and there were incisor like teeth on the front of the upper jaw. The upper and lower teeth met to form a flat surface for grinding up vegetable matter. *Hypsilophodon* has been described as a 'browsing sprinter': it had a very strong mobile jaws and cheek pouches for storing food and longer tibia (shin) bones than femur (thigh) bones. Unlike more advanced ornithopods (the four-fingered and three-toed hadrosaurs), the primitive *Hypsilophodon* had five-fingered hands and four, forward facing toes. The fifth toe was tiny and the fourth toe itself was too short to reach the ground. The legs appear to have swung backwards and forwards very quickly: in motion the head and neck was counter-balanced by the long, tapering tail which was stiffened by rows of bony tendons and unlikely to have touched the ground unless *Hypsilophodon* was resting or sleeping.

Name means: High Ridged Tooth

Time: Mid-Cretaceous (135-65 MYA)

Location: Europe: East Sussex, Isle of Wight, England; Teruel, Spain; North America: South Dakota, USA

Size: 2.3 m (7 ft 6 in.)

Weight: 68 kg (150 lb)

Diet: Herbivore

Iguanodon

Pronounced: ig-WHA-noh-don

Iguanodon was the second dinosaur to be discovered-although in 1809, the term dinosaur hadn't been invented! Part of its shin bone was found in southern England in 1809 and in 1819, some teeth and further bones were found. Scientists of the day thought the creature was some great mammal, but Gideon Mantell recognised the teeth as being more reptilian and that they resembled the teeth of the modern iguana of Central and South America. In 1825 Mantell described and named *Iguanodon* and using the rather sparse information he had, he attempted a reconstruction. Mantell's *Iguanodon* was a four legged beast with a heavy tail and small lizard-like head with a short horn on its head. This horn was in fact an *Iguanodon* thumb claw! It was in 1877 that the true nature of *Iguanodon* became clear when 31 skeletons were found in Bernissart, Belgium by coal miners. Originally believed to be primarily quadrupedal, *Iguanodon* is now thought to have been capable of bipedal walking as its legs were thick and sturdy and its forelimbs were considerably thinner and shorter. Since *Iguanodon* was first discovered scientists have found their fossilised footprints in the rocks of southern England: these show that when *Iguanodon* passed by, he/she was walking upright. Similar footprints, although no actual bones, have also been found as far away as South America and in Sptizbergen, to the north of the Arctic Circle, which demonstrates just how widespread the iguanodonts were.

Name means: Iguana Tooth

Time: Early Cretaceous (135-65 MYA)

Location: North America: South Dakota, USA. Europe: south-east England; Hainault, Belgium; Nordhein-Westfalen, Germany; Castellon, Cuenca and Teruel, Spain

Size: 9 m (29 ft 6 in.)

Weight: 4.5 tonnes (4 tons)

Diet: Herbivore

The rear legs of *Iguanodon* were pillar-like, with three stout toes ending in heavy, hoof-like nails. Each arm had a five fingered hand: the middle three fingers on each hand had hoof-like nails and were joined by a pad of skin, while the fifth finger could be curled to grasp food. Meanwhile, the thumb was armed with a sharp spike which stuck out sideways from the hand. The head of this great creature ended in a prominent snout and powerful, beak-like jaws. The cheek teeth needed to be especially strong because the bones in the upper jaw were hinged and could move apart when the lower jaw was raised up between them: the banks of cheek teeth moved past each other, grinding up the plant matter.

Ouranosaurus

Pronounced: OO-ran-oh-SORE-us

Ouranosaurus shared many characteristics with its famous relative *Iguanodon*, including longer hind limbs that were stronger than the forelimbs, hoof-like claws on the toes and the fingers, thumbs armed with smaller though equally vicious spikes, and leaf-shaped teeth with high-ridged crowns. But *Ouranosaurus* also had some very distinctive features of its own: a flat-topped skull with a low bump over its eyes, a hadrosaur-like (duck-billed) beak, and a bony, skin sail held aloft by blades jutting from its backbone. The very tall back spines were unique among ornithischians and the sail's purpose is as yet, unknown. If the males had taller sails than females, these might have been part of mating rituals, either to attract a mate or to scare off rivals for a female's affections. The sail may also have served as a temperature regulator, as it was made of skin and blood vessels must have flowed through it: *Ouronosaurus* (like the carnivorous Spinosaurus see page 74, which also had a back sail and came from the same arid region) may have angled its spine towards or away from the sun to either heat up or cool down its body. The structure of *Ouronosaurus'* hand suggests that it rested and perhaps ambled on all fours: the wrist bones were very strong and although the three middle fingers were hoofed and could not 'grasp' objects, they could be stretched out or bent back to form weight bearing 'feet' if it went down on all fours. To run, perhaps from dangerous predators like *Spinosaurus*, the adults would have reared up on their hind legs. It appears, however, from fossilised remains, that juveniles were bipedal until mature as their forelimbs were substantially shorter.

Name means: Brave Monitor Lizard

Time: Mid Cretaceous (135-65 MYA)

Location: Africa: Agadez, north-eastern Niger

Size: 7 m (23 ft)

Weight: 3.5 tonnes (3 tons)

Diet: Herbivore

Hadrosaurus

Pronounced: HAD-roh-SORE-us

Name means: Big/Sturdy Lizard

Time: Late Cretaceous (135-65 MYA)

Location: North America: New Jersey, Montana, New Mexico, South Dakota, USA

Size: up to 10 m (33 ft)

Weight: 7 tonnes (6½ tons)

Diet: Herbivore

Hadrosaurus, meaning 'big' or 'sturdy' lizard, has the distinction of being the first dinosaur ever to be discovered in North America. Its bones were found in New Jersey and they were reconstructed and named by Joseph Leidy in 1858. Leidy recognised that *Hadrosaurus* was structurally related to *Iguanodon* (see page 147) whose remains had been found earlier in 1825 in England. But unlike the quadruped described by Mantell, Leidy also recognised that although *Hadrosaurus* would have spent much of its time browsing on all fours, it could rear up to be bipedal as its forelimbs were much shorter than the hind legs. It probably used its tail, held outstretched to balance it as it walked. *Hadrosaurus* was typical of the duck-billed dinosaurs: its tough horny bill (used for snipping off vegetation) at the front of the jaw had no teeth, but at the back of the jaw, there were the ranks of hundreds of teeth for chewing vegetation, each tooth replaced by a new one as it wore out. *Hadrosaurus* had no head crest: it did, however, have a large bump on its snout which was made of bone and probably covered tough, thick skin.

Edmontosaurus

Pronounced: ed-MONT-toh-SORE-us

Many skulls of this large, flat headed hadrosaur have been found which display the many hundreds of teeth packing the jaws behind the beak to make an effective 'grinding machine'. It is estimated that at any one time *Edmontosaurus* had over 1,000 teeth, each with an outer edge coated with hard enamel which wore away more slowly than the rest of the tooth. The result: a tooth with a cutting edge of hard enamel, ideal for cutting through tough vegetation. The jaw structure of *Edmontosaurus* was like that of *Iguanodon*: the upper jaw could move over the lower jaw so that the teeth ground against each other when the jaw was closed. *Edmontosaurus* was a large dinosaur – one of the largest hadrosaurs – up to 13 m (42 ft) long with long, strong, pillar-like hind legs, and a long tail to balance the weight of the front of the body, the flexible neck and short front limbs. The fleshy pads between the digits (fingers) gave *Edmontosaurus* the hadrosaurid 'paddle-like' hands, while claws on the first two fingers were large and hoof-like. A trellis of bony tendons attached to the vertebral spines of the back tied the bones together so that the body didn't 'sag' on either side of the pelvic girdle. While it was crestless, many palaeontologists believe that *Edmontosaurus* was equipped with an inflatable sac on its nose that it could use to make noise, perhaps making distinctive bellowing calls to members of its family or group, in the same manner that elephant seals do today.

Name means: Edmonton Lizard

Time: Late Cretaceous (135-65 MYA)

Location: North America: Alberta, Canada; Montana, USA

Size: 10-13 m (33-43 ft)

Weight: 4-5 tonnes (3.9-4.5 tons)

Diet: Herbivore

Anatosaurus

Pronounced: AN-at-oh-SORE-us

Anatosaurus was a relatively common hadrosaur and it is one of the best known crestless forms. The popular name for the hadrosaurids, 'duck-billed dinosaurs', was coined after the discovery of the broad, flat skull of this creature in Alberta, Canada. The name *Anatosaurus* itself means ''duck lizard' and refers to the creature's horny beak or bill. Several, well preserved skeletons of *Anatosaurus* have been found and palaeontologists have been able to deduce that it was some 9-10 m long (30-33 ft) and stood around 4 m (13 ft) tall. It was also closely related to *Edmontosaurus* and to another North American hadrosaur, *Anatotitan* (so closely related that some scientists suggest that all three be referred to as *Anatosaurus*) although *Anatosaurus* appears to be distinguished by its skull shape and extremely long snout. A great deal of information was provided by the discovery of two 'mummified' specimens, complete with dried up tendons and the contents of their stomachs- including their last meals of pine needles, twigs, seeds and fruits intact! Also preserved were impressions of the skin showing it was covered in a thick, leathery hide and that it had 'webs' of skin between the three main fingers on each hand. At first, these 'webs' appeared to give substance to the notion that hadrosaurs were aquatic animals which used their hands and flattened tails as paddles for swimming. Closer examination showed that the skin could not stretch particularly wide and that these 'webs' were more likely to be the remains of shrivelled up fleshy pads used for walking on- a little like the fleshy walking pads on camels' feet. The 'pad theory' also ties in with the fact that *Anatosaurus* had hoof-like nails on two of the main fingers of each hand. *Anatosaurus* was then, a land-dweller which walked on all fours.

Name means: Duck Lizard

Time: Late Cretaceous (135-65 MYA)

Location: North America: Alberta, Canada

Size: 10 m (33 ft)

Weight: 4 tonnes (3.9 tons)

Diet: Herbivore

Maiasaura

Pronounced: MY-ah-Sore-ah

Name means: Good Earth-Mother Lizard

Time: Late Cretaceous (135-65 MYA)

Location: Montana, USA

Size: 9 m (30 ft)

Weight: 5 tonnes (4¹/₂ tons)

Diet: Herbivore

Maiasaura, whose name means 'Good Earth-Mother Lizard' is one of the most important recent dinosaur discoveries: in 1978 a skeleton of an adult was found in Montana by John Horner and Robert Makela, complete with her nest and young. It seems that scientists had found the remains of a dinosaur 'nursery' some 75 million years old.

The adult – the mother presumably – was about 9 m long (30 ft) and several youngsters were around 1 m (3 ft 3 in) long. Their presence suggests that the young *Maiasaura* remained with their parents for some time to be looked after. There was a also a group of hatchlings each about 50 cm (20 in) long together in their fossilised nest, while further nests revealed intact eggs and broken egg shells where the young had hatched. The nests themselves had been made of scooped up mud (now fossilised into solid rock) and was about 3 m (10 ft) in diameter and 1.5 m (5 ft) high with a crater like depression in the centre of the mound about 2 m (6 ft 6 in.) across and 75 cm (2 ft 6 in.) deep. The spacing between each nest was about 7 m (23 ft): given the size of the adults, the nests were placed quite close together. The fossilised sausage-shaped eggs found in the nests had been laid and arranged with great care in circles in the crater-depression, and layer upon layer, possibly with each layer carefully covered with sand to keep it safe and warm, and then finally covered with earth. With its broad, duck-billed beak and rows of self-sharpening teeth, *Maiasaura* was also a typical hadrosaurid. It had no hollow crest on its long, rather horse-like head, but instead it had a solid 'hump' above its eyes and triangular projections on its cheek bones.

Kritosaurus

Pronounced: KRITE-oh-SORE-us

Name means: Chosen Lizard

Time: Late Cretaceous
(135-65 MYA)

Location: North America: Alberta,
Canada; Montana, New Mexico,
USA

Size: 9 m (30 ft)

Weight: 5 tonnes (4$\frac{1}{2}$ tons)

Diet: Herbivore

In addition to the main distinguishing feature marking the difference between hadrosaurines (non-crested hadrosaurs) and lambeosaurines (crested hadrosaurs) which was on their heads, the hadrosaurines also had broad duck-like beaks and quite large nostrils. There was also a less 'obvious' difference though: the pelvis of crested hadrosaurs had a large plate-like extension on the front pelvic bone (pubis) and the rear pelvic bone (ischium) was wide and was shaped at the lower end like a hook. A medium-sized, and crestless hadrosaurid, *Kritosaurus* was in many respects, similar to *Hadrosaurus* (see page 150) but while it had no crest, there was the beginnings of one in the form of a large, bony 'hump' on the snout in front of the eyes. The function of the 'hump' is unknown: it is possible that only the males had one and that it was used in courtship and mating. Alternatively, the thickened bony hump may have served the same purpose as the thickened skulls of the pachycephalosaurs (see pages 179-83) - to absorb the impact during 'head butting contests' between males at the start of the mating season. It is also possible that *Kritosaurus* and *Hadrosaurus* were, in fact, two species of the same animal.

Lambeosaurus

Pronounced: LAMB-ee-oh-SORE us

Named in honour of Lawrence Lambe (1863-1918) the pioneering Canadian fossil hunter, *Lambeosaurus* was discovered in 1913 by Charles H. Sternberg. It was a large, sturdy hadrosaurid (duck-billed dinosaur) with a head crest often compared to a hatchet. In fact *Lambeosaurus'* head was quite unique in that it had two head structures: the tall hollow hatchet-shaped crest leaning over the snout and a tall, solid, and backward-pointing spike of bone behind it. The nostrils ran up from the snout and through the crest which may have supported a 'flap' of skin that ran down the head, back and tail. Some of the specimens found had larger crests than others: in some the crest was larger than the skull and it was first assumed that these were different species. It now appears that they may in fact be males, females and juveniles of the same species. *Lambeosaurus* was a large hadrosaurid, about 15 m (49 ft) long with massive bones: the Baja California, Mexico specimen however seems to have been a something of a giant at around 16.5 m (54 ft) long, making it one of the largest hadrosaurs known. Like other members of the family, *Lambeosaurus* had a deep narrow tail formed by tall vertebral spines and chevrons that made the tail stiff and immobile. It also moved around on all fours, browsing for plant food, using its flexible neck to reach around a wide area without it having to shift its whole body

Name means: Lambe's Lizard

Time: Late Cretaceous (135-65 MYA)

Location: North America: Montana, USA; Alberta, Canada; Baja California, Mexico

Size: 15 m (49 ft)

Weight: 4 tonnes (3 ¾ tons)

Diet: Herbivore

Corythosaurus

Pronounced: koh-rith-oh-SORE-us

Name means: Helmet Lizard

Time: Late Cretaceous
(135-65 MYA)

Location: North America: Montana,
USA; Alberta, Canada

Size: 10 m (33 ft)

Weight: 4 tonnes (3¹/₂ tons)

Diet: Herbivore

One of North America's best known hadrosaurids (duck-billed dinosaur) thanks to a complete skeleton found in 1912, 'helmet Lizard' is named for its huge hollow bony head crest which rose steeply from just in front of its eyes into a narrow fan shape- or as some describe it, half a dinner plate (about 30 cm (1 ft) high) that curved down to the back of the head. Not all *Corythosaurus*, however, had such well developed crests: according to extensive research by Dr Peter Dodson of the University of Pennsylvania, size and shape of the head crests are related to the sex and maturity of the *Corythosaurus*. Before this was established, there were seven species where now only one is recognised. While the actual function of the crest is still a mystery, Dodson's work has given us a major insight into the growth and development of hadrosaurids and the sexual dimorphism of the species. The domed crest was made up of expanded nasal bones: the hollows inside the crest were the actual nasal passages which ran up into the crest and then looped downwards into the duck-billed snout. The most likely function of the crest beyond distinguishing males and females, is that the tubular cavities inside the crest operated as a resonator allowing *Corythosaurus* to produce distinctive sounds and calls. Like other hadrosaurines, *Corythosaurus* was a land dweller, browsing in low growing vegetation and spending most of its time on all fours, although it could walk on its two hind legs alone. Living in the warm plains between the Rocky Mountains and the vast inland sea that in the late Cretaceous period divided North America into western and eastern halves, *Corythosaurus* lived in herds, browsing through the pine forests, fern prairies and coastal marshes. If threatened by hungry carnivorous theropods, *Corythosaurus* may even have sought refuge by wading into shallow water.

Saurolophus

Pronounced: Sore-oh-LOAF-us

Name means: Ridged Lizard

Time: Late Cretaceous
(135-65 MYA)

Location: North America: Alberta,
Canada; California, USA;
Asia: Mongolia

Size: 9-12 m (29 ft 6 in-40 ft)

Weight: 4-5.5 tonnes (3^1/$_2$ -5 tons)

Diet: Herbivore

Saurolophus was an advanced crested duck-billed dinosaur that is known from several skeletons ranging in size from 9-12 m long (29 ft 6 in.- 40 ft). The Asian species had a larger crest than its North American relative and a correspondingly larger body. The face of this large duck-bill swept up in a graceful curve from a broad, rather flattened and much shorter snout than other hadrosaurids, to the tip of a solid, bony horn-like crest that sloped backwards from the top of its head. The solid crest would imply that *Saurolophus* was a hadrosaurine (duck-billed dinosaurs with solid crests) rather than a lambeosaurine (a duck-billed dinosaur with a hollow crest). The crest was an extension of the nasal bones, and in *Saurolophus* the nasal passages would have run through it. *Saurolophus* then would be an 'intermediate' between the two subfamilies. Some palaeontologists think that there may have been a mass of nasal tissue which could have been inflated to produce a 'honking' noise through the nose, and so the bony crests would have acted as supports for the inflatable skin sac. As hadrosaurids were herd dwellers, communicating with each other, and signalling alarm, was vital to their survival.

Parasaurolophus

Pronounced: par-a-SORE-oh-loaf-us

Name means: Beside *Saurolophus*

Time: Late Cretaceous
(135-65 MYA)

Location: North America: Alberta,
Canada; New Mexico and Utah,
USA

Size: 10 m (33 ft) long

Weight: 4 tonnes (3¹/₂ tons)

Diet: Herbivore

Like *Saurolophus* (see page 160) this lambeosaurine had a shorter snout than other hadrosaurines, but is distinguished largely by the magnificent single backward-pointing, horn-like crest on top of its head. The crest was a hollow tube, unlike the 'solid' crest of *Saurolophus* - and could be as long as 1.8 m (6 ft). The shape and size of the crest seemed to be dependent on sex and maturity, with males apparently having the largest crests and there may also have been a brightly coloured frill of skin joining the crest to the neck. Inside the crest was a pair of nasal passages that ran from the nostrils right up to the tip of the crest and then curved back down to the snout. In the backbone of *Parasaurolophus* there was a unique notch, just behind the shoulders where the tip of the crest would abut the back of the neck when the animal held its neck and head in the s-shaped position. Some palaeontologists suggest that *Parasaurolophus* held its crest into its neck when it moved through dense forest growth, deflecting branches away from its head and body. *Parasaurolophus* also had a very deep tail which some researchers suggest was also brightly patterned and was used, along with the neck frill, as a signalling device, for social recognition and perhaps during courtship to attract a female.

Hypacrosaurus

Pronounced: HIGH-pak-roh-SORE-us

Hypacrosaurus was another hadrosaurid (duck-billed dinosaur) with a semi-circular head crest. The crest was similar to that of *Corythosaurus* (see page 158) but it was not as tall or narrow, and, it did not rise as steeply from its face. Instead *Hypacrosaurus'* crest sloped gently upwards. *Hypacrosaurus* remains were found in rock deposits that post-date those of *Corythosaurus* and some palaeontologists have suggested that the 'High Spine Lizard' in fact evolved from this species. Although they were both similar sized duck-bills, *Hypocrasaurus* differs in that it had dorsal vertebrae (back bones) that were extended upwards into tall spines which formed a prominent skin-covered ridge along its back, giving it its name. This 'skin sail' may have been a heat exchange mechanism used to regulate the body temperature. By angling the sail into or away from the sun, *Hypocrasaurus* could have 'warmed up' or 'cooled down' its body. A similar method appears to have been used by the carnivorous *Spinosaurus* (see page 74) which roamed what is now northern Africa.

Name means: High Spine Lizard

Time: Late Cretaceous (135-65 MYA)

Location: North America: Alberta, Canada; Montana, USA.

Size: 9 m (29 ft 6 in.) long

Weight: 4.5 tonnes (4 tons)

Diet: Herbivore

Tsintaosaurus

Pronounced: CHIN-say-oh-SORE-us

Name means: Tsintao Lizard

Time: Late Cretaceous
(135-65 MYA)

Location: Asia: China

Size: 10 m (33 ft)

Weight: 5 tonnes (4^{1}/$_{2}$ tons)

Diet: Herbivore

Tsintaosaurus was one of the most unusual crested hadrosaurs: its crest pointed forwards, rather like the horn of the mythical unicorn. The tall hollow tube of bone pointed straight up from between its eyes; the tip was expanded and notched, and, there was a connection between the base of the tube and the nostrils. These features have led some palaeontologists to suggest that *Tsintaosaurus* had a flap of skin attached to its horn, or perhaps stretched between the tip of the horn and its beak. The flap may have been inflatable like a balloon and used as a signalling device to call to other members of the herd or attract a female in the mating season. Other palaeontologists believe that the skull and skeletal remains of *Tsintaosaurus*, which were found in China, suggest that it was related to *Saurolophus* (see page 160) and that the 'horn' has been reconstructed facing the wrong way. This is quite possible, as both *Saurolophus* (as well as being found in North America) and *Tsintaosaurus* remains have been found in China. While the sea barrier which separated the southern continent of Gondwana (South America, Africa, India, Australia and Antarctica) from the northern continent of Laurasia in the mid-Cretaceous period, may have impeded the hadrosaurids from spreading from their northern area of origins southwards (except perhaps via an island chain running through what is now Central America), they were able to spread across the northern continents because the Turgai sea (which separated Europe and North America on one side from Asia on the other) was shallow, and although they were land dwellers, the hadrosaurids could certainly swim, especially across shallow water.

Stegosaurus

Pronounced: STEG-oh-SORE-us

The largest and most familiar of the stegosaurs, *Stegosaurus* had massive hind legs and heavy hooves which were over twice the length of their forelimbs. This was unusual in a four legged animal since it meant that the body sloped forwards from the highest point at the hips. Tall spines projected from the vertebrae of the hips and tail and probably acted as 'anchor points' for the immensely strong back muscles. *Stegosaurus* had a long, narrow head that was very small in relation to its size; it was about 40 cm (16 in.) long and housed a brain about the size of a walnut! To 'compensate' for the small brain, a large cavity in the hip vertebrae above the hind legs and where the spinal cord would have passed, held a mass of nerve tissues 'controlling' the rear legs and tails. All vertebrates (back-boned animals) have this so called 'second brain', but the size is related to the size of the animal's hips: in big-hipped animals such as dinosaurs, this 'brain' was often larger than the one in their skulls. *Stegosaurus* had a toothless beak at the front of its jaws and small cheek teeth. Consequently, in order to digest tough plant matter, *Stegosaurus* probably made use of gastroliths – small stones that it swallowed to help grind up the food in the gizzard and stomach. The most recognisable feature of *Stegosaurus* is undoubtedly its body armour: a double row of broad bony plates, covered in tough horn and shaped like huge arrowheads, some over 60 cm (2 ft) high, were embedded in the skin on its back. Since none of these plates have been found 'attached' to a skeleton, some palaeontologists maintain that the plates were arranged to lie flat in or on the skin like a tiled roof- to form a protective layer. The commonly held belief, however, is that the plates were arranged vertically to form a 'fence' down either side of the backbone from just behind the head to half

Name means: Roof Lizard

Time: Late Jurassic (203-135 MYA)

Location: North America: Colorado, Oklahoma, Utah, Wyoming, USA

Size: up to 9m (30 ft)

Weight: 2-3 tonnes (2-2$\frac{1}{2}$ tons)

Diet: Herbivore

way along the tail. This arrangement has suggested to some palaeontologists that the plates may have not been for defence but may have been covered in a blood-rich skin and were used as heat exchange mechanisms, warming up or cooling down the stegosaur by angling the plates into or away from the sun. The heavy tail itself was armoured with pairs of spikes, each about 1 m (3 ft 3 in.) long. The number of pairs of spikes and the size varied form species to species: *S. ungulatus* had four pairs while *S. stenops* had only two pairs. The spikes were probably used for defence, with the heavy tail being swung from side to side to ward off attacks from hungry carnivorous theropods.

Kentrosaurus

Pronounced: KEN-troh-SORE-us

Kentrosaurus is an East African contemporary of
Stegosaurus (see page 165) whose remains were found
in Tendaguru, Tanzania. Up to 5 m (16 ft) long,
Kentrosaurus had a long, narrow head which it held
low when walking and browsing for food, and its jaws
were equipped with small cheek teeth. It appears
likely that *Kentrosaurus* fed on low growing ferns
and shrubby vegetation that grew in the moist
soil alongside the prehistoric riverbanks in eastern
Africa. While it was smaller than its American relative,
Kentrosaurus was equally well-armoured, and its pattern
of 'plates' and 'spikes' was quite distinctive. A double
row of narrow, triangular, bony plates rose out from
either side of the backbone and were grouped in pairs
along the neck, shoulders and front part of the back. At
the middle of the back, these flat plates were replaced
by five pairs of sharp spikes, some as long as 60 cm
(2 ft), and these continued down the back and tail. In
addition, there was a pair of extra long spikes which
stuck out at hip level on each side and pointed diagonally
backwards. The arrangement of these spikes suggests that
Kentrosaurus may have been able to rush backwards at
predators- in the same way that modern porcupines do.
The flexible tail could have been swung from side to side
to lash at predators. *Kentrosaurus'* tail structure
was unusual in that in most stegosaurs, the caudal
neural spines (the high narrow tops of tail
vertebrae) slope backwards (toward the
tip of the tail): in *Kentrosaurus*, after
caudal vertebrae number 18,
the neural spines slope
forwards, towards the
base of the tail.

Name means: Spiky Lizard

Time: Late Jurassic (203-135 MYA)

Location: Tanzania, Africa

Size: 5 m (16 ft)

Weight: 1.5 tonnes (1¹/₂ tons)

Diet: Herbivore

Tuojiangosaurus

Pronounced: too-hwang-oh-SORE-us

Name means: Tuo River Lizard

Time: Late Jurassic (203-135 MYA)

Location: Sichuan, China

Size: 7 m (23 ft)

Weight: 1 tonne (1 ton)

Diet: Herbivore

The Chinese 'Tou River Lizard' is one of several armoured dinosaurs found in China and the first to be discovered in Asia. Known from an almost complete skeleton, *Tuojiangosaurus* was smaller than *Stegosaurus* (see page 165), averaging 6-7 m (18-23 ft), though structurally similar, with a small narrow head, low ridged teeth and and a heavy 'humped back' body. Up to 15 pairs of bony plates surmounted its back, neck and tail, becoming taller and more 'spine like' over the hips and down the tail. As in *Stegosaurus* there were two pairs of long, slim spikes stuck up from the end of the tail and a long spine jutted out from each shoulder. Unlike *Stegosaurus* though, *Tuojiangosaurus* appears not to have been able to rear up on its hind legs: the tail spines that projected upwards from the back vertebrae of *Stegosaurus* providing muscle attachment points are absent in *Tuojiangosaurus* – and in *Kentrosaurus* (see page 167) as well- which suggests these were exclusively quadrupedal animals. Holding its head low, *Tuojiangosaurus* browsed on ferns and cycads which grew in the rich river valley soil of southern China, cropping the vegetation with its horny beak and chewing it with its small ridged teeth.

Scelidosaurus

Pronounced: IDE-oh-SORE-us

Until the discovery of *Heterodontosaurus* (see page 143) in 1962, *Scelidosaurus* was the earliest known ornithischian dinosaur. Remains discovered in Dorset, southern England, in 1859 were first described by Richard Owen, and again by him in 1863 following the discovery of an almost complete skeleton. A third discovery was made as recently as 1985 by a group of amateur fossil hunters in Charmouth, Dorset which added greatly to the knowledge of this dinosaur. One of the most primitive ornithischian dinosaurs, *Scelidosaurus* was about the size of a small car and had a long heavy body with pillar-like hind legs longer than the forelegs (although *Scelidosaurus* was quadrupedal) and broad, four-toed feet designed for bearing the body weight. Its flanks were covered with parallel rows of bony studs while along the neck, spine and top of the stiffened tail was a row of bony spikes (the underside of the tail was covered with bony studs). This arrangement of body armour has led some palaeontologists to suggest that *Scelidosaurus* was a primitive type of ankylosaur (see pages 176-78). The head was small and pointed, and behind the neck was a pair of triple-spiked bony plates. Inside the mouth there were small and simple leaf-shaped teeth extending right down to the tip of the snout. At the front of the upper jaw were six, small conical teeth, so, if there was a horny beak, it was very small. The less complex jaw and teeth arrangement meant that *Scelidosaurus* would have chewed its food with a simple up-and-down jaw motion.

Name means: Lower Hind-Limb Lizard

Time: Early Jurassic (203-135 MYA)

Location: Europe: Dorset, England; North America: Arizona, USA;

Size: 4 m (13 ft)

Weight: 250 kg (550 lb)

Diet: Herbivore

Nodosaurus

Pronounced: No-doh-SORE-us

Name means: Node Lizard

Time: Late Cretaceous
(135-65 MYA)

Location: North America; Kansas,
Wyoming, USA

Size: 5.5 m (18 ft)

Weight: 2 tonnes (1³/₄ tons)

Diet: Herbivore

The typical nodosaur and the one that gave its name
to the whole family, *Nodosaurus* was first mentioned
by Marsh in 1889 but only described in some detail in
1921 by Richard Lull on the basis of partial remains.
However, a later and more unusual find in Kansas
consisted of several skeletons, all supine
(lying on their backs) that were found in
marine sediments dating from the late
Cretaceous period. It is possible that
this was a small herd of *Nodosaurus* that
died at the same time and their bodies were
washed down towards the
prehistoric sea. As they were
swept down river, the weight of
their body armour would have made them
top heavy and they would have 'flipped over'
onto their backs before eventually sinking
into the mud of the seabed, belly side up.
Its body armour was arranged from neck to tail
in bands consisting of narrow rectangular plates
that covered the ribs and alternating
with broader plates which covered the
spaces in between. Hundreds of bony
nodes studded the broad plates, which give
Nodosaurus its name. The shoulders and hips were
powerful and strong, as were the stout legs and broad
hoofed feet. The pelvis is a rather different shape to other
ornithischians: the bones of the hip were modified as
weight-bearing structures so the ilium at the top of the
hips is much more enlarged while the lower hip bones
(the pubis and ischium) are much reduced in size. Large,
powerful leg muscles were attached to the underside of
the ilium. The front legs were short and powerfully built.
Unlike ankylosaurs, nodosaurs had a narrow skull with
a more pointed snout and did not have the horn-like

projections on the rear corners of the skull. Nodosaurs also had an opening on the side of the skull, behind the eye, another feature that is absent in ankylosaurs.

Polacanthus

Pronounced: pol-a-KAN-thus

Name means: Many Spikes

Time: Early Cretaceous
(132-112 MYA)

Location: Europe: Isle of Wight,
England; North America: South
Dakota, USA

Size: 4 m (13 ft)

Weight: 2-2.5 tonnes (2 tons)

Diet: Herbivore

Polacanthus was discovered in 1865 by the Rev. William Fox on the Isle of Wight, just off the south coast of England. The skeleton consisted of the hind part of the animal, including various spines, and back and tail vertebrae, the hips and hind legs.

It appears that the front part of the skeleton was lost after being washed out to sea following a cliff fall which exposed the rear end. Consequently, the 'reconstruction' of *Polacanthus* is a matter of conjecture and debate. This debate is heightened by the fact that living at the same time in England as *Polacanthus* was another nodosaur, *Hylaeosaurus* ('Woodland Lizard') which had been discovered in 1833 in the Tilgate Forest area of Sussex, also on England's' south coast. Of this nodosaur, we have remains of the 'front end'! The 'front' and 'back' parts of these two animals do not overlap so it is impossible to compare the two skeletons directly to prove conclusively that they belonged to the same or to different animals. Furthermore, because the spines of *Polacanthus* were founded scattered near the remains of the skeleton, even their position is a matter of guesswork. It is presumed that the long dorsal (back) spines arranged in pairs may have formed a protective 'frill' around the sides of the body to protect the flanks and legs. While a shield of fused bone covered the hips, two lines of smaller vertical spines ran down to the tip of the deep, heavy tail.

Sauropelta

Pronounced: SORE-oh-PEL-ta

Sauropelta was the earliest and most primitive member of the nodosaur family to live in what is now North America. It is also the largest known member of the family estimated to have weighed around 3 tonnes (2$^{1}/_{2}$ tons). Its massive body was encased in a bony armour consisting of bands of horn-covered plates with raised keels or studs which ran transversely over the body from the neck (and were elongated into spines) to the end of the long, tapering tail which did not have a tail club. The plates were embedded into the skin to form a strong, but flexible covering over the animals' back. As a slow moving herbivore – its heavy, pillar-like legs and blunt claws would not have been capable of much more than a slow trot, and then only for a short distance. *Sauropelta* needed such protection against attack from predatory carnivores such *Deinonychus* and *Struthiomimus* against whom its best defence was simply to stand its ground, or better still 'lie' its ground: by laying down, *Sauropelta* would have guarded its most vulnerable parts (the lower flanks and underbelly). The structure of *Sauropelta's* forelimb bones suggest that it had very strong shoulder muscles which may have allowed it to bend its 'elbows' more easily than other nodosaurs.

Name means: Shielded Lizard

Time: Early-mid Cretaceous (135-65 MYA)

Location: North America: Montana, Wyoming, USA

Size: 7.6 m (25 ft)

Weight: 3 tonnes (2$^{1}/_{2}$ tons)

Diet: Herbivore

Panoplosaurus

Pronounced: pan-OP-loh-SORE-us

Name means: Fully Plated Lizard

Time: Late Cretaceous
(135-65 MYA)

Location: Location: North America:
Alberta, Canada; Montana, South
Dakota, Texas, USA

Size: 4.4 m (15 ft)

Weight: 3.5 tonnes (3 tons)

Diet: Herbivore

Although a medium-sized animal, *Panoplasaurus*, as its name 'fully plated lizard' implies was encased in a heavy body armour consisting of broad square plates with keels arranged in wide bands across the neck and shoulders, while the rest of the body was covered in smaller bony studs. Protecting the flanks, especially on the shoulders, were massive spikes which were angled to the front and side. Equally well armoured was its head: thick bony plates were so solidly fused together that the underlying skull and toothless beak on the snout were hidden. Inside this solid bony box was, however, a network of cavities and air passages with a bony palate separating the nasal system from the mouth. This allowed *Panoplosaurus* to breath and eat at the same time, chewing its vegetable food with simple ridged teeth in the cheeks. Unlike other nodosaurs, which may have lain down and relied on their body armour to protect them from attack, *Panoplosaurus* may have mounted a more active defence by directing its spiked shoulders at its attackers. Its forelegs were especially strong and suggest that *Panoplosaurus* was 'quick on its feet' and could manoeuvre its forequarters to react to its enemy's onslaught- rather like a modern charging rhinoceros.

Edmontonia

Pronounced:d-mon-TONE-ee-ah

Among the largest of the nodosaurs,
Edmontonia is also the latest and is known
from several skulls and skeletons, two of
which are complete with their armour.
Edmontonia was a heavily built nodosaur
with a bulky barrel-shaped body, thick legs (the hind
legs were longer than the forelegs) and wide, flat feet,
a short tail supporting, without a club at the end- and
a short neck carrying a low-slung, long head. It was the
armoured tank of the nodosaurs: too slow to sprint away
from danger it seems likely that *Edmontonia* lunged at
its enemies with its long forward-projecting shoulder
spikes in order to inflict crippling injuries to the legs of
theropods. Meanwhile, flank and shoulder spines helped
to protect it from attack from the sides, two collars of
bony plates shielded the back of its neck, and its wide
hips formed a solid broad base which would have made it
difficult to overturn. This heavy bodied animal browsed
through western North America feeding on low growing
plants, ripping at them with its narrow toothless but
horny beak and chewing them with rows of ridged,
leaf-shaped cheek teeth arranged along the side of
the jaw. Each tooth was about 4 cm (1½ in) long
(including the root), was flattened from side
to side and enamelled on both sides
to resist wear and tear. The
teeth were 'in-curved' so
that room was left in the
large cheek pouches to
store food. *Edmontonia's*
teeth appear to be small for
a nodosaur, but even so, they
were still larger than the teeth
of ankylosaurs.

Name means: Lizard from
Edmonton

Time: Cretaceous
(135-65 MYA)

Location: North America: Alberta,
Canada; Montana, Texas, USA

Size: 7 m (23 ft)

Weight: 4 tonnes (3½ tons)

Diet: Herbivore

Ankylosaurus

Pronounced: an-KIE-loh-SORE-us

Name means: Fused Lizard

Time: Late Cretaceous
(135-65 MYA)

Location: North America: Alberta,
Canada; Montana, USA

Size: 7-10 m (23-33 ft)

Weight: 4.5-7 tonnes (4¹/₂- 6³/₄ tons)

Diet: Herbivore

Ankylosaurus was the largest known ankylosaur and one of the last of the group to survive, right up to the end of the Cretaceous period (65 million years ago). It was massively built and is often described as a 'living tank', as its stocky body (measured about 5 m (16 ft) wide at its largest point). Its neck and head were protected by thick bands of armour plating, while the tip of its tail culminated in a great, bony club. The armour consisted of a thick, leathery skin studded with hundreds of oval bony plates and parallel rows of bony spikes. In addition, a pair of long spikes stuck out from the back of the head, while the cheekbones were drawn out into another pair of spikes protecting the face. *Ankylosaurus* had a skull about 75 cm (2 ft 5 in.) long with a broad face and blunt snout that ended in a toothless, horny beak. In contrast to the relatively simple paired tubes running from the nostrils to the back of the throat of the nodosaurs, ankylosaurs' nasal tubes followed an s-shaped course through the head, and on the side of these were additional passages (sinuses). These may have served to filter, warm and moisten the air which they breathed and allowed for an improved sense of smell, or even more making distinctive calls or noises. The backs of ankylosaurs were at least partly stiffened by bony tendons running down the spine but are most obvious towards the end of the tail where the tail club was located. Along the back, these stiffening tendons provided firm anchorage for the tail-swinging muscles, while at the end of the tail, they stopped any 'whip lash' damaging the bones. The main part of the tail had no stiffening tendons and could therefore be swung freely from side to side.

Pinacosaurus

Pronounced: pin-AK-oh-SORE-us

Name means: Plank Lizard

Time: Late Cretaceous
(135-65 MYA)

Location: Asia: Mongolia and China

Size: 5 m (16 ft 6 in.)

Weight: 3-3.5 tonnes (3 tons)

Diet: Herbivore

Pinacosaurus is one of several ankylosaurs to have been discovered in Asia. Smaller than most of its relatives at around 5 m (16 ft 6 in.) and of relatively slender build, *Pinacosaurus* was first described by Charles Gilmore in 1933 from material collected in the Gobi Desert during the American Museum of Natural History-Mongolian expeditions in the 1920s. Although lightly built, *Pinacosaurus* was still well armoured: its back and tail were covered with bony spines and the end of the tail bore a heavy bony club which could have been used as a defensive weapon, being swung with considerable force by strong tail muscles anchored to the hips. *Pinacosaurus* had a rounded beak and the top of its skull was covered with small bony plates. A recent discovery of a juvenile skull shows that these plates were at first separate, only later fusing together into a solid, heavy sheet of bone as the animal matured. Its eyes were set quite far back into the skull and it is also remarkable for having two small openings in the skull near the nostrils, the purpose of which is still unknown. In the nasal passages of *Pinacosaurus* (and found in a second Asian ankylosaur, *Saichania*), are thin curved bones which resemble the turbinal or scroll bones found in the noses of mammals. These bones are covered in membranes which filter, moisten and warm the air we breath, and it could be that *Pinacosaurus* also had this facility. The front of the skull sloped downwards to form a parrot-like horny beak. Inside its mouth were small, rather weak teeth which suggest that *Pinacosaurus* must have fed on only very soft vegetation.

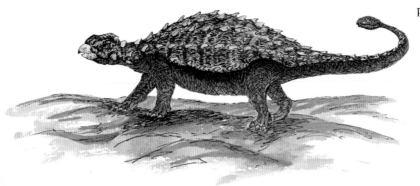

Homalocephale

Pronounced: home-ah-loh-SEFF-ah-lee

Homalocephale means 'even head' and makes reference to the fact that this pachycephalosaur did not have the high domed top to its skull that is a feature of other members of the family. Instead, it had a flat, wedge-shaped head, although the bones of the skull were immensely thickened and there were numerous dents or pits and bony knobs scattered all over it. Because the skull was thickened, this part of the animal fossilised most easily and consequently, many of the 'bone head' dinosaurs are known only from these remains. *Homalocephale* is remarkable in that in addition to its skull, other parts of its skeleton are also known. It is thought that rival male pachycephalosaurs charged at each other in 'head-butting' contests: this is something that sheep and goats do, but it can also be seen in the modern marine iguanas of the Galapagos Islands. The force of the impact was absorbed by the thick cranium which protected the brain, and large nuchal ligaments which ran from the back of the head to the neck were also large and powerful and helped to absorb a great deal of the impact. The force of the impact would also have run down the backbone so this was also strengthened with bony tendons, and the joints between individual bones in the back had special grooved surfaces to stop them from twisting around too much. The wide hips may also have been part of the 'shock absorbing' system, although other palaeontologists have suggested that this could indicate that *Homalocephale* gave birth to live young rather than lay eggs.

Name means: Even Head

Time: Late Cretaceous (135-65 MYA)

Location: Asia: Mongolia

Size: 3 m (10 ft)

Weight: 80 kg (180 lb)

Diet: Herbivore

Stegoceras

Pronounced: ste-GOS-er-as

Name means: Horny Roof

Time: Late Cretaceous
(135-65 MYA)

Location: North America: Alberta,
Canada; Montana, Wyoming USA

Size: 2 m (6 ft 6 in.)

Weight: 55 kg (120 lb)

Diet: Herbivore

A medium-sized herbivore, *Stegoceras* was first described by Lawrence Lambe in 1902 on the basis of two skull fragments found in the Belly River Formation of Alberta, Canada, and to which he gave the name 'horny roof'. The skull fragments were unusually thick and were at first thought to belong to a certopian dinosaur (see pages 187-94). In 1924 Charles Gilmore described a skull and partial skeleton found on the Red Deer River in 1920 by George Sternberg, and although incomplete, the material gave a much better picture of *Stegoceras*. Although quick on its feet, *Stegoceras* was not a particularly fast runner, as its femurs (thigh bones) were longer than the tibias (shin bones). But it had a body designed to withstand impact from head-butting – either from rival males, or perhaps in defence from predators. The skull was thickened into a dome of solid bone (protecting its small brain) and the grain of the bone was angled to the surface, enabling it to withstand the force of impact even more efficiently. During head-butting contests, the head was held face-down so that the ramming surface of the head and the neck joint were in a straight line with the horizontally held spinal column. The battering force would then be transmitted through the skull and absorbed by the backbone.

Prenocephale

Pronounced: pren-oh-Sef-a-lee

All pachycephalosaurs had a bony shelf jutting out from the back of their skulls, but in *Prenocephale*, while this was evident, it was less distinct. It did, however, have a most bulbous dome, rather like a bowling ball, surmounting the top of its skull and a row of bony bumps and spikes surrounding the back and sides of the solid skull.

This thickening of the skull in pachycephalosaurs gives them something of a passing resemblance to the ankylosaurids. In ankylosaurids, however, the thickened skulls, are created by 'plastering' new bones on the skulls while in pachycephalosaurs, it is the actual bones of the skull that have become thicker. Because this bone thickening is unique, it has made it difficult for palaeontologists to decide how the pachycephalosaurs relate to other dinosaur genera: because of their bipedal stance, some place them in the suborder of Ornithopods while others refer them to Marginocephalia. However, *Prenocephale*, like other pachycephalosaurs, is undoubtedly an ornithischian because of the existence of the tell-tale horn covered predentary beak in the lower jaw. What they ate as herbivores is uncertain, though: their small ridged teeth were not capable of chewing tough vegetation, so it is likely they survived on a mixed diet of fruit, leaves and possibly insects.

Name means: Sloping Head

Time: Late Cretaceous
(135-65 MYA)

Location: Asia: Mongolia

Size: 2.4 m (8 ft)

Weight: 75 kg (150 lb)

Diet: Herbivore

Pachycephalosaurus

Pronounced: PAK-ee-SEF-a-loh-SORE-us

Name means: Thick Headed Lizard

Time: Late Cretaceous
(135-65 MYA)

Location: North America: Montana,
South Dakota, Wyoming, USA

Size: 5 m (16 ft)

Weight: 2 tonnes (1 3/4 tons)

Diet: Herbivore

The largest member of the family found so far,
Pachycephalosaurus was also the last to exist
before the extinction of the dinosaurs at the
end of the Cretaceous period around 65 million
years ago. A giant among the 'boneheads',
Pachycephalosaurus is known in fact only from
one well preserved, 60 cm (2 ft) long skull found by
William Winckley in Montana, USA in 1940, and a few
immensely thick skull roofs! The domed head case, rather
like a huge crash helmet, was up to 25 cm (10 in.) thick.
Bony knobs projected from the rear rim of the skull dome
and short spikes projected upwards from the snout. As
well as the horny beak, *Pachycephalosaurus* had curved
fang like teeth at the front of its jaw and tiny cheek teeth
lining the sides of the jaws. Because remains other than
the skull are unknown, scientists have 'reconstructed'
Pachycephalosaurus using known skeletons of other
pachycephalosaurs, especially *Stegoceras* (see page 180)
with the body proportions and sizes estimated. The
overall picture is of a bipedal animal, about the length
of a large car, and standing about 6 ft high, with a fairly
short, thick neck, short arms with five fingered hands,
long rear legs and three toed feet, and, a sturdy body
counterbalanced by a heavy tail stiffened
by hard, bony tendons.

Stygimoloch

Pronounced: STIJ-ee-MOH-loc

Because the pachycephalosaurs are a relatively rare group, they are also quite puzzling. The first remains (a tooth from the Judith River Beds in Montana) found by Ferdinand Hayden in the 19th century was described and named by Joseph Leidy as *Troodon formosus* and suggested that it belonged to a large monitor lizard or to some extinct carnivorous reptile. It was not until the turn of the century, and later in the 1930s and 1940s that more remains were found, especially in Montana, South Dakota and Wyoming, which shed more light on the pachycephalosaurs. More recent finds in many parts of the world have turned up a number of pachycephalosaurs including the marvellously named *Stygimoloch*, or 'River of Hades [Hell Creek] Devil' which was found in the Hell Creek Formation of Montana, USA. At the moment, *Stygimoloch* is known only from parts of its skull – but what a skull it is! Not only did *Stygimoloch* have the high, domed and thickened skull characteristic of the pachycephalosaurs, but this was embellished with large, elaborate horn core which formed clusters of horns on either side of its domed head. These horns would have made it difficult for *Stygimoloch* to indulge in the ritualistic head butting contests between males that scientists believe their thick heads developed for. Instead, *Stygimolochs*' 'crown' of horns may have been sufficient to establish and maintain a position in the social hierarchy.

Name means: River of Hades [Hell Creek] Devil

Time: Late Cretaceous (135-65 MYA)

Location: North America: Montana, Wyoming, USA

Size: estimated 2-3 m (6 ft 6 in.-10ft)

Weight: unkown

Diet: Herbivore

Psittacosaurus

Pronounced: si-TAK-oh-SORE-us

Name means: Parrot Lizard

Time: Early Cretaceous
(135-65 MYA)

Location: Asia: Gorno-Altayskaya,
(Siberia); Dundgov, Ovorhangay
(Outer Mongolia); Liaoning,
Shandong, Xinjiang Uygur Zizhiqu,
(Inner Mongolia); Chaiyaphum,
Thailand

Size: 2 m (6 ft 6 in.)

Weight: 80 kg (175 lb)

Diet: Herbivore

While the ancestors of the ceratopians (which are often incorrectly called ceratopsians) is believed to be among the 'parrot dinosaurs', it is unlikely that *Psittacosaurus* ('parrot lizard') was itself the ancestor since this dinosaur had only four fingers on each hand, while the ceratopians had five. Furthermore, *Psittacosaurus* had no teeth in its beak, while the later protoceratopids (see page 186) had teeth in their upper beaks. *Psittacosaurus* was a two-legged herbivore about 2 m (6 ft 6 in.) long and resembled the 'gazelle-like' ornithopod *Hypsilophondon* (see page145) in that it could rear up on its long, thin hind legs to run from predators. However, *Psittacosaurus* had a deeper and longer body, a shorter tail and longer arms which ended in a four fingered grasping hand. Its most peculiar feature however was its skull and toothless, parrot-like beak. A thick ridge of bone on the top of the skull squared off the head at the back and served as an anchor point for very powerful muscles that worked the lower jaw. Over the course of millions of years, this bony ridge would develop into the huge bony neck frills of the later ceratopians. The cheek bones were drawn out into a pair of horn-like projections on the side of the head (the forerunners of the horny spikes on either side of the head shields of later ceratopians) and are thought to be used for fighting or for sexual display. Beneath the horn-covered part of the upper beak *Psittacosaurus* had the characteristic rostral bone which is found in all ceratopians. The cutting beak and self sharpening cheek teeth which lined the jaw suggests that *Psitticosaurus* had perhaps evolved to eat either, new forms of vegetation which needed this beak to crop it, or, it had evolved the 'parrot beak' to feed on existing vegetation that had previously been inedible by dinosaurs. Whatever its diet, *Psitticosaurus* made use of gastroliths (stomach stones) to help grind up the plant matter in its crop. Bipedal when it walked or ran, *Psittacosaurus* would have used its hands with stubby, short claws to pull down branches to its mouth.

Protoceratops

Pronounced: PROh-toh-SERRA-tops

Name means: First Horned face

Time: Late Cretaceous (135-65 MYA)

Location: Asia: Gansu (Inner Mongolia), Omnogov (Outer Mongolia)

Size: 1.8 m-2.7 m (6-9 ft)

Weight: 180 kg (400 lb)

Diet: Herbivore

The first protocertopid to be discovered, *Protoceratops* was found in Mongolia in the 1920s, with later finds revealing complete skulls and skeletons of individuals that ranged from newly emerged hatchlings to adults, as well as nests and eggs which gave an indication that *Protoceratops* probably lived in herds. The numerous remains belonged to quadrupedal herbivores with large heads, bony neck frills, sharp shearing teeth and parrot-like beaks. Although *Protoceratops* had no horns, it did have a prominent bump halfway along its snout which seems to have been larger in more mature males, suggesting it was used in ritual mating battles. Spending most of its time on all fours, *Protoceratops*' hind legs were slightly longer in comparison to the forelegs: this is usual in most land animals as the rear legs are the source of locomotion, while the forelegs act like shock absorbers as the body is propelled forwards. Although the front legs are supporting the front of the body, there are still trellis-like bones spanning the vertebrae which help stop the body from sagging. Each hind limb ended in a long foot with four toes bearing tapered, though blunt claws. The forelimbs had three, long spreading digits with the fourth and fifth digit very much reduced. Like later ceratopids, *Protoceratops* had an arched sacrum (fused sacral vertebrae) that made its tail curve downwards.

Styracosaurus

Pronounced: sty-RAK-oh-SORE-us

Perhaps not the most famous ceratopid, *Styracosaurus* was certainly one of the most spectacular of all the 'horned lizards'. While it had the neck frill of all ceratopids, *Styracosaurus* was unique in having six long spikes which had grown out from the epoccipital bones at the edge of the frill. These epoccipital bones were usually small 'knobs' of bone that gave a scalloped edge to the rim of the frill. Each of the four longest spikes on the neck frill was probably about the length of a man's arm! *Styracosaurus* also seems to have had unusually large nostrils, but the reasons for this are unknown. To lessen the overall weight carried by the neck, the bony frill had parietal openings or 'windows' covered by tough skin. *Styracosaurus* would certainly have been a formidable animal: charging head-down like a rhinoceros, its long nasal horn would have ripped into the soft underbelly of a predatory carnivore while the array of spikes protected its own vulnerable neck from onslaught by sharp teeth and claws. Standing head on to its enemy, the frill and spikes would have made *Styracosaurus* appear much larger than its 5.5 m (18 ft) and this alone may have helped deter some attackers: modern African elephants adopt a similar technique by holding their ears out at the sides of their heads to warn off other elephants.

Name means: Spiked Lizard

Time: Late Cretaceous (135-65 MYA)

Location: North America: Alberta, Canada; Montana, USA

Size: 5.5m (18 ft)

Weight: 2.5 tonnes (2¼ tons)

Diet: Herbivore

Centrosaurus

Pronounced: SEN-troh-SORE-us

Name means: Horned/Sharp Point Lizard

Time: Late Cretaceous (135-65 MYA)

Location: North America: Alberta, Canada; Montana, USA

Size: 6 m (20 ft)

Weight: 3 tonnes (2³/₄ tons)

Diet: Herbivore

A medium-sized ceratopid, *Centrosaurus* had a single horn on its snout and small spines around the back of its short neck frill. There were also two horns on the posterior (back) edge of the frill which pointed forwards and downwards. While these two 'tongues' of horn are unique to *Centrosaurus*, this horned dinosaur was typical of the short-frilled ceratopids (the Centrosaurines). But it used be known by another name: *Monoclonius* ('single stem'). Remains were first found in 1855 by Ferdinand Hayden during a geological expedition of the Upper Missouri, around the mouth of the Judith River in Montana. These remains, which included fragments of the crest skeleton, were described and named (as *Monoclonius*) by Cope in 1876. In 1904 however, Lawrence Lambe, using another frill, this time from the Red Deer River, and having the curious 'tongues' of bones which point downwards towards the frill, described and named it *Centrosaurus*. The frill itself had two window-like holes in the bone in order to reduce the weight, and their edges also served at anchor points for the powerful jaw muscles. These 'windows' would have been covered over with tough skin, as was the rest of the frill. A strong ball-and-socket joint connected the head to the neck. This joint was positioned forwards in the skull under the region of the eye, so that the weight of the frill at the back of the head was balanced by the huge horn on the snout. This mobile joint allowed *Centrosaurus* to turn its head quickly which was vital since its only weapons of defence were on its head. To strengthen the neck, some of the neck vertebrae behind the ball-and socket joint were fused together. *Centrosaurus* also had the parrot-like, toothless beak at the tip of its jaws, and teeth which are set in at the sides of the jaws to give room for cheek pouches.

Triceratops

Pronounced: try-SERRA-tops

Name means: Three Horned Face

Time: Late Cretaceous
(135-65 MYA)

Location: North America: Alberta,
Saskatchewan, Canada; Colorado,
Montana, South Dakota,
Wyoming, USA

Size: 9 m (30 ft)

Weight: 5-10 tonnes (4½- 9½ tons)

Diet: Herbivore

The most famous of all the horned dinosaurs, *Triceratops* was also the largest, the heaviest and the most abundant of the group.

Triceratops belongs to the group of 'long frilled' Chasmosaurines whose brow horns were longer than their nasal horns. Scientists estimate that *Triceratops* could reach weights of 10 tonnes (9½ tons)- heavier than a modern African bull elephant – and *Triceratops'* skull alone was over 2m (6 ft 6 in.) long. Great herds of these horned dinosaurs roamed western North America in the late Cretaceous period some 70-65 million years ago, and hundreds of well preserved specimens have been found over the years since Orthniel C. Marsh first named the creature in 1889. The massive structure of the skull and frill meant that these were more likely to be fossilised than less 'robust' dinosaur skulls: so far 50 *Triceratops'* skulls have been found. Unlike other members of its group, *Triceratops* was unique in that its neck frill was a solid piece of bone: there were no parietal openings or 'windows' in it to lighten the weight. This suggests that the main function of the frill was as a defensive shield, rather than an anchorage point for jaw muscles. It is possible that the skin over the frill was filled with blood vessels: this meant that the frill could have also been used as a heat-exchange mechanism, cooling up or warming down the body as it was angled into or away from the sun. The nasal horn was relatively short and thick, while two long brow horns, each over 1 m (3 ft 3 in.) long curved forwards and slightly outwards over a long, low face and the long snout. Using their sharp, horny beaks to snip at twigs and leaves, food was then sliced up in the mouth by rows of shearing cheek teeth. These teeth were 'self sharpening': one side of the crown was hardened by enamel, the other side wasn't. As *Triceratops* chewed, the 'softer' side of the tooth wore down quickly, leaving the hard side with a sharp cutting edge.

Chasmosaurus

Pronounced: KAZ-moh-SORE-us

Name means: Cleft Lizard

Time: Late Cretaceous
(135-65 MYA)

Location: North America; Alberta,
Canada, Texas, USA

Size: Size: 4.2 m (16 ft)

Weight: 2 tonnes (1³/₄ tons)

Diet: Herbivore

Known from a number of well preserved skulls and skeletons which were discovered along the Red Deer River in Alberta, Canada, by Lawrence Lambe and the Sternberg family, *Chasmosaurus* was one of the earliest of the long-frilled ceratopids, and smaller than many of its relatives. Its skull was quite long and narrow, with a pair of long, upwardly curving horns on its brow and a single, shorter horn on its snout. The bony frill, however, was quite enormous: it stretched from the back of the skull over the neck and shoulders. It was made lighter by two very large parietal openings that were covered with skin. These reduced the bony structure of the frill to a mere 'scaffold' which allowed the head and frill to be moved around with ease. The frill edge was embellished with epoccipital bones – triangular bony knobs and spikes. The spectacular frill was undoubtedly for display: it may have been brightly coloured, perhaps with 'eyes' as on peacock feathers,which when seen 'head on' would have warned off attackers. A brightly coloured frill may also have been the male *Chasmosaurus'* method of attracting females. Skeletally, *Chasmosaurus* is typical of a slow-moving, heavy dinosaur. Both the hip and shoulder girdles, as well as their respective legs, are very solidly constructed and are designed not for speed but for bearing weight. In the neck and back regions the vertebrae are also very strong and have extended spines to which the head-supporting muscles would be attached. The stout ribs would have supported the bulky gut as a substantial space was needed to process large quantities of vegetable matter.

Pentaceratops

Pronounced: PEN-ta-SERRA-tops

Pentaceratops may well have been a descendent of *Chasmosaurus* (see page 192) which lived earlier in late Cretaceous times. It, too, had a huge neck frill with its edges embellished by triangular bony knobs and spikes. The remains of *Pentaceratops* were found in the San Juan Basin of New Mexico and were first described in 1923 by Henry Fairfield Osborn. The name *Pentaceratops* was suggested to him by William Diller Matthew to recognise the fact that in addition to the usual three horns of the head (a straight horn on the snout and two curved brow horns) this new species 'appeared' to have five horns. The two smaller 'horns' were in fact outgrowths of the cheeks beneath and behind the eye. These cheek bones are not particularly 'horn-like', especially when compared to the nasal or brow horns, and some specimens and some other ceratopids (though not long frilled ones) have equally large cheek bones. Nevertheless, the rather fanciful name 'five horned face' has stuck! It did have a remarkably enormous head: reconstructed in 1998, the skull alone measured over 3 m (10 ft) long. To reduce the weight of the large bony neck frill, four parietal openings or windows punctured it. These may have been filled with muscles- the edges of the windows providing 'anchor points'- and would have been covered with tough skin, possibly bright coloured for sexual display.

Name means: Five Horned Face

Time: Late Cretaceous
(135-65 MYA)

Location: North America:
New Mexico, USA

Size: estimated 5-8 m (16-26 ft)
Weight: 2.5-8 tonnes (2-7$^{1}/_{2}$ tons)

Diet: Herbivore

Anchiceratops

Pronounced: AN-ki-SERRA-tops

Name means: Close Horned Face

Time: late Cretaceous
(135-65 MYA)

Location: North America: Alberta,
Canada

Size: 6 m (20 ft)

Weight: 5-6 tonnes ($4^1/_2$- $5^1/_2$ tons)

Diet: Herbivore

Also discovered in the Red Deer River formation of Alberta, Canada, and living very near to the end of the late Cretaceous period (and) the end of the Age of the Dinosaurs' *Anchiceratops* was similar in some respects to *Chasmosaurus* from which it may have descended: it has quite a long face, but it was larger, had longer horns above the eyes, and the frill was rather different. *Anchiceratops* seems a much more 'streamlined' form: its body was longer, narrower, and with a shorter tail and the tall neck frill was also quite narrow. The 'windows' in the frill were smaller than in *Chasmosaurus* and there were three pairs of enlarged epoccipital bones (bony projections) on the posterior margins but none around the sides. A further pair of triangular horny epoccipital projections pointed forwards on the top rear edge of the frill. These are much smaller than, but still reminiscent of, the curious 'tongues' of bone which project into the frill openings of *Centrosaurus* (see page 188). *Anchiceratops* had two horns which curved forward from the brows and a shorter nasal horned which pointed straight out in front. As most of the ceratopians had very similar skeletal structures, and the main distinguishing features are confined to their heads, it may be that the horn arrangements and the frill sizes and shapes (and possibly, colours) acted as species recognition signals for the various ceratopids living in North America in the late Cretaceous period.

CHAPTER 8
Reptiles of the Sea

Dinosaurs lived only on land, but sharing the Mesozoic world with them were the reptiles of the sea and air. Scientists believe that all life came from the sea and appeared about 3,500 million years ago. Only relatively recently did life come onto land – about 400 million years ago for plants and 300 million years ago for animals. Some of the first land creatures to evolve were reptiles and dinosaurs, but almost as soon as they had appeared, some reptiles returned to the seas to exploit the marine environment for food and for living. As early as 250 million years ago there were aquatic animals that had evolved from land living ancestors even before the dinosaurs walked the earth. In late Triassic times (250-203 MYA) other reptiles became adapted for life 'in the air' flying on 'wings' of skin and diversified into many forms, among them the largest flying creatures of all times.

Marine Reptiles

During the Mesozoic Era, several groups of reptiles returned to the sea and adapted to marine life. These include an ancient group of reptiles called chelonians which differ from all other reptiles in having bodies (except their heads, tail and legs) enclosed within a shell. Modern turtles, tortoises and terrapins are the only surviving members of this ancient group and have changed very little in over 200 million years. Modern crocodiles have changed very little from their prehistoric relatives which appeared in mid-Triassic times some 230 million years ago. In addition to the chelonians and crocodylia there are four distinct types of marine reptile, each of which demonstrates a different degree of adaptation to marine life. The least specialised were the placodonts of the Triassic period (250-103 MYA); the nothosaurs (also of the Triassic period); the plesiosaurs which swam in the open seas of the Jurassic (203-135 MYA) and Cretaceous periods (135-65 MYA) and, the most specialised marine reptiles, the Ichthyosaurs, which also swam in the Jurassic seas. Also in this selection of marine reptiles are mosasaurs: these were a successful but short-lived offshoot of the Family Varanidae: the monitor lizards.

ORDER CHELONIA

Even the earliest chelonians dating from the late Triassic period had a shell. They also had a solidly roofed skull with no openings in them except for the eyes and nostrils. There are two distinct suborders of chelonian which includes the 230 species of living turtles, tortoises and terrapins. The two are distinguished by the way in which the animal retracts its head into its shell: Pleurodira bend their necks sideways (a few members of this group survive today) and the Cryptodira bend their necks back vertically.

Suborder Cryptodira

Most modern turtles and tortoises belong to this group, many of whom can retract their head into their shells by lowering their heads and pulling it back vertically. The cryptodires were the most successful group of chelodians and evolved during the Jurassic period. By the end of the period, they had become extremely diverse throughout the rivers, seas and lakes of the world with new forms developing also on land.

FAMILY PROTOSTEGIDAE

(See page 201)

This family of sea turtles includes some of the most spectacular that ever lived. The protostegids developed two main features that distinguished all sea turtles from their land or river dwelling relatives. First, since there were fewer predators in the sea they did not need such heavy armour on their backs, so the shell was reduced to a lighter structure which also made them much more manoeuvrable. Secondly, the toes of the front and back limbs were more elongated and modified into broad 'flippers' for faster swimming.

ORDER CROCODYLIA

The most successful of the archosaurs or 'ruling reptiles', crocodiles, have changed very little since their relatives first appeared some 230 million years ago in the mid-Triassic period (25-203 MYA). Although modern crocodilea are more at home in water than on land, they did evolve first as small, terrestrial carnivores which could run upright on their two hind legs. All crocodiles, including the earliest ones, have the characteristic long, low and massive skull that is designed to resist the powerful 'snap' of their jaws shutting. The muscles attach at the back of the skull which allows the jaws to open wide to deal with large prey. An especially useful feature for water dwellers is the secondary plate of bone that separates the mouth from the nasal passage, allowing the crocodile to eat and breathe at the same time. The order is divided into four suborders: Suborder Sphenosuchia, the earliest known crocodiles from the mid-Triassic period; Suborder Protosucha, from the early Jurassic period; Suborder Mesosucha which also evolved in the early Jurassic, and, Suborder Eusuchia, which comprises the true crocodiles, including the 21 living species of modern crocodile (and the seven species of alligator and caiman, and the single species of gavial or gharial).

Suborder Mesosucha

(See page 202)
There are some 70 genera of mesosuchian known and these are arranged in 16 families, most of whom were fully adapted land dwellers or semi-aquatic species. However, four families were permanently aquatic. Most of the fossil crocodiles are from this Suborder Mesosucha and of the permanently aquatic species, *Metriorhynchus* is the most famous. It shared the seas with the ichthyosaurs (see page 207) and the plesiosaurs (see page 209) throughout the Jurassic period and into the Cretaceous period.

ORDER PLACODONTIA

Of all the marine reptiles, the placodonts were the least specialised of the swimmers. They appeared – and disappeared – in the Triassic period (250-203 MYA) and while during this time many types evolved, none became fully adapted to life in the open seas. They were largely confined to the shallow, coastal waters of the Tethys Sea which existed at the time between the two land masses of Laurasia in the north, and Gondwanaland in the south. Many types had turtle-like shells protecting their backs and underbellies. The order includes the families Placodontidae; Cyamodontidae; and Henodontidae.

Family Placondatidae
(See page 203)

This family of semi-aquatic reptiles were equally at home on land, walking on the sea shore, as swimming in the shallow waters of the Tethys Sea. Both areas were rich feeding grounds for the shellfish on which they lived which were crushed between their broad teeth: the warm shallow waters had encouraged the formation of coral reefs in the Triassic period and many new molluscs evolved.

Family Cyamodontidae
(See page 204)

Evolving in the mid-Triassic period and living until the end of the period, this family of placodonts had developed turtle-like shells on their backs and were more adapted to an aquatic lifestyle. Although they began to look and behave like modern turtles (see Order Chelonia, page 196), they were in fact unrelated. This 'phenomenon' is known as convergent evolution.

Family Henodontidae
(See page 205)

Evolving in the late Triassic period, these armoured placodonts developed a great bony shell that covered their backs and underbellies. They had also lost most of their teeth and instead had a horny beak like a modern turtle. In spite of their turtle-like appearance, henodonts were not related to the turtles who are members of the Chelonia order of reptiles.

Order Nothosauria

The Triassic seas saw many swimming, fish-eating reptiles. One very successful group were the nothosaurs which ranged from lizard-sized to giant, 4 m (13 ft) long creatures. They were amphibious predators with numerous sharp teeth. As their fossils have been found in marine sediments, this suggests they were sea-going creatures, but probably rested and bred on land. Their fossils show that nothosaurs were long necked with a low skull and sharp teeth for piercing slippery fish. They also had a narrow tail and broad, paddle-like limbs with webbed feet which were used for swimming.

Family Nothosauridae
(See page 206)

There are several families of nothosaurs, but this is the most well-known. Their fossil remains have been found in the marine sediments of Europe and Asia dating from the early to the late Triassic period (250-203 MYA).

ORDER ICHTHYOSAURIA

The ichthyosaurs were the most specialised of the marine reptiles: their name reflects this and means 'fish lizards'. While they ate fish and were fish-shaped (their overall body shape resembled a modern tuna) they were reptiles and breathed air. Unlike their contemporaries, the plesiosaurs (see page 209), did not rely on paddle-like flippers for swimming, but instead had a fishlike tail whose lateral (side-to-side) movements provided the propulsive force. So well adapted to marine life, the ichthyosaurs could no longer come ashore to lay eggs, but gave birth to live young, born tail first and fully able to swim, at sea.

FAMILY ICHTHYOSAURIDAE

(See page 207)

Flourishing throughout the Jurassic period and into the Cretaceous, these typical 'fish lizards' are known from some spectacular fossils – including coprolites (droppings), stomach contents, and even adult females with the bodies of their young offspring preserved inside them- making it one of the best known of all marine reptiles. They developed a streamlined body with a stabilising triangular-shaped dorsal (back) fin, short, paired paddles for steering and a large tail fin with two equal lobes for propulsion. Ball and socket joints in the caudal (tail) vertebrae allowed for powerful strokes from side to side. While some ichthyosaurs measured only about 1 m (3 ft) long others, from the early Jurassic grew to more than 20 m (65 ft) long.

ORDER PLESIOSAURIA

The great sea-going reptiles of the Mesozoic Era were the plesiosaurs. Some of these were giants, up to 14 m (46 ft) long and had adapted to marine life by evolving their limbs into long narrow flippers. Instead of there being only five or fewer bones in each finger or toe, plesiosaurs had up to ten in each. The hydrofoil-shaped flippers meant that modification to the hip and shoulder girdles, the structure of the massive collar bones and two of the three hip bones formed broad plates on the underside of the body and was unique to these marine reptiles. A dense series of ribs connected the bones to the shoulders and the hip girdle on the underside making the body more rigid and offering a strong, solid body against which the swimming flippers could move. The gastralia (belly ribs) also protected the body when the animal left the water, and using its flippers, dragged itself ashore on its belly to lay its eggs. There are two major groups, or 'super-families' of plesiosaurian which differed in the lengths of their necks: plesiosaurs had long necks and small heads, while pliosaurs had short necks and larger head. The head size is indicative of the size of prey each sought and means that the two related families did not compete for the same prey- although they did have the ichthyosaurs (see page 207) to contend with!

Super family Plesiosauroidae

(See page 212)

The early members of this super family were long-necked marine reptiles and first appeared in the early Jurassic period (203-135 MYA), flourishing throughout that period. One member of the family, *Elasmosaurus* (see page 212) was the last member to survive, living right to the end of the 'Age of the Dinosaurs' in the Cretaceous period which ended around 65 million years ago. Feeding on small fish and squid, plesiosaurs used their long necks to raise their heads high above the surface of the water to scan the waves in search of schools of fish on which to prey. The super family Plesiosauroidae contains many genera and species, forming two families: Plesidosauridae and Elasmosauridae.

Super-family Pliosauridea

(See page 213)

The short-necked, large-headed pliosaurs appeared in the early Jurassic (203-135 MYA) alongside their long necked relatives. Some like *Kronosaurus* survived into the late Cretaceous period (135-65 MYA). Pliosaurs grew to a length of around 8-10 m (25-33 ft) – although some were even bigger – but their skulls could constitute as much as one third of their entire body length. The strong jaws were powered by huge muscles allowing pliosaurs to tackle larger prey, and to take on an ichthyosaur (see page 207) and their own relatives, plesiosaurs. Having no flexible neck to help them, pliosaurs 'jumped' their prey: grabbing them with sharp, sometimes three-sided and ridged teeth. Streamlined for speed, their necks became progressively shorter: some had only 13 cervical (neck) vertebrae compared to the 28 in the even the shortest necks of the long-neck plesiosaurs.

Family Mosasauridae

(See page 214)

This family of highly successful, although short-lived marine reptiles, was an offshoot of the Family Varanidae, the monitor lizards, which are today, the largest of all land lizards. (The Family Varanidae are part of the Order Squamata, the most successful group of reptiles which today comprises the lizards and the snakes). The mosasaurs (lizards from the [River] Meuse) were fish-eating reptiles- some of whom were giants- which diversified in the Late Cretaceous period. This was a time when the ichthyosaurs (see page 207) had died out and the plesiosaurs (see page 209) were in decline. With large conical teeth and strong jaws, they preyed on large fish, turtles, plesiosaurs and other mosasaurs.

Archelon

Pronounced: Ar-KAY-lon

This giant turtle – the biggest ever known and more than twice the size of the largest modern relatives – swam in the inland sea that covered much of North America from Alberta, Canada in the north, to Texas, USA in the south, in the late Cretaceous period (135-65 MYA). Known from many fossilised skeletons in the limestone deposits of this once shallow sea way, *Archelon* was named in 1896 'ruling' or 'ancient turtle'. Instead of the heavy plated shell characteristic of fresh-water and land-living turtles who need 'armour' to protect them from predators, *Archelon's* shell was reduced to a wide, flattened shell of bony struts covered with tough skin (rather like the contemporary leatherneck turtle). The bony framework was made from the belly ribs (gastralia) that grew out from the body wall. This bony framework may well have been visible under the skin in live animals. The limbs of this massive sea creature were huge paddles which would have cut through the water in vertical strokes: the same 'vertical method' can be seen when penguins swim, flapping their 'wings' to propel them through the water. With a rather weak and toothless jaw, but having a hooked beak, *Archelon* probably fed on a diet of 'soft' jellyfish and squid.

Name means: Ancient/Ruling Turtle

Time: Late Cretaceous
(135-65 MYA)

Location: North America: Kansas,
South Dakota,Wyoming USA

Size: 4 m (13 ft)

Weight: 2.3 tonnes (2 tons)

Diet: Jellyfish, squid

Metriorhynchus

Pronounced: Met-ree-or-RINE-cus

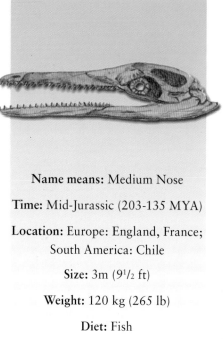

Name means: Medium Nose

Time: Mid-Jurassic (203-135 MYA)

Location: Europe: England, France;
South America: Chile

Size: 3m (9¹/₂ ft)

Weight: 120 kg (265 lb)

Diet: Fish

A sea-going crocodilian, *Metriorhynchus* (and other members of its family such as *Geosaurus*) was one of the most specialised of the aquatic crocodiles. It had dispensed with the heavy back armour of their relatives since such protection was not needed in the sea. The reduction in 'armour' also allowed their bodies to become more manoeuvrable, especially as it is believed that females would have had to haul themselves onto land to lay their eggs. *Metriorhynchus* had a streamlined shape with a long slim head, long body and thin tail. Its skin was smooth which reduced the amount of 'drag' or resistance through the water and it had a vertical, fish-like tail which it lashed from side to side to move it through the water. The tail was supported by a sharply down-turned tip of the backbone. Increasing its speed and mobility were flipper-shaped hind limbs and smaller paddle-shaped fore limbs. The long snout with nostrils set forwards suggest that *Metriorhynchus* would lay submerged in water with its nostrils above the water line ready to launch an attack. The long jaws had strong muscles attached to the rear of the skull, allowing *Metriorhynchus* to open its jaws wide and snap shut on it prey. Inside, the jaws were lined with small but razor sharp conical shaped teeth for seizing slippery fish and squid.

Placodus

Pronounced: PLAK-oh-dus

With a stocky body, short neck and sprawling limbs like
those of the early, land-living reptiles, *Placodus* was not
particularly well adapted to pachystosis – aquatic life. Its
only swimming aids were useful webs of skin between
the five toes on each foot, and the long slender tail which
was flattened from side to side. The tail may also have
had a fin along its length. The skeleton was quite massive
with three distinctive features, the chief of which was the
structure of the vertebrae of the 'trunk'. These all had
special processes which fitted exactly into corresponding
grooves on the adjacent vertebrae so they were all fixed
tightly together, making the 'trunk' rigid and immobile.
The structure of the cervical (neck) and caudal (tail)
vertebrae was quite different and they were very flexible.
A second feature was the curiously formed abdominal
ribs which turned upwards at right angles: like all the
placodonts, the underside of its body was protected
by gastralia (belly ribs) which formed a strong armour
covering the whole of the abdomen. The third feature
occurred above the back bone where there was a row of
raised bony knobs to provide at least some protection for
this otherwise defenceless animal. First described in 1830
by George Munster, *Placodus* gets its name from its flat,
blunt teeth which protruded at the front of its jaw. These
front teeth were designed to 'pluck' shellfish
off rocks, while a battery of flat
teeth arranged on the upper
and lower
jaws were
designed
for crushing
the shells.

Name means: Flat Tooth

Time: Early/Mid-Triassic
(250-203 MYA)

Location: Europe: The Alps

Size: estimated 2 m (6$^{1}/_{2}$ ft)

Weight: unknown

Diet: Shellfish, crustacean

Placochelys

Pronounced: PLAK-oh-KEE-lis

Name means: Flat Turtle

Time: Mid/Late Triassic
(250-203 MYA)

Location: Europe: Germany

Size: 3 m (9 ft)

Weight: unkown

Diet: Shellfish

Well suited to pachystosis (an underwater way of life), although they still needed to come to the surface to breathe, the rather 'newt like' body of *Placodus* (see page 203) had given way to a much broader and flatter 'turtle-like' body in *Placochelys* – a point which is emphasised by its name as the Greek word 'chelys' means 'turtle'. As slow-moving animals, many placodonts were now also vulnerable to carnivorous predators and so developed a shell as protection and covering the back of *Placochelys* was a mosaic of knobbly plates. Its tail was short and its limbs elongated and flattened to act as paddles, while the claws at the ends of its digits may have been used to 'scratch' at shellfish on rocks. While *Placochelys* no longer had the protruding front teeth like *Placodus*, it was still a specialised shellfish eater, using its very horny, but toothless, beak to pluck them off. Strong muscles worked the powerful jaws which were lined along the sides and across the palate (the roof of the mouth) with a battery of broad, flat, shell-crushing teeth.

Henodus

Pronounced: HEN-oh-dus

Henodus was unusual among placodonts in that it was able to live in the fresher, less salty waters of lagoon-like seas. Usually, changes in the level of salt in water can be stressful – even fatal – to marine animals, but shelled animals, such as turtles and *Henodus* are better equipped to cope with such changes. The body of *Henodus* was as broad as it was long – the same shape as a modern turtle. Its back and underbelly were covered in a tough casing of polygonal (many sided and irregularly shaped) bony plates which formed a defensive shell to protect it from attack from other marine species such as ichthyosaurs (see page 207) which also swam in the waters at this time. Unlike a turtle, *Henodus* had many more such plates in its shell, but like a turtle, the shell was covered in plates of horn. *Henodus* also had a strangely square-shaped snout and there were no teeth in its mouth. Instead, it is believed there was a strong horny beak at the front of the mouth which could be used to prise off shellfish from rocks: a modern sea animal that also subsists on shellfish is the walrus whose two great tusks are used for prising shellfish from rocks and it is possible that *Henodus'* beak worked the same way. Scientists also think that *Henodus'* clawed feet may also have been webbed.

Name means: Single Tooth

Time: Late Triassic (250-203 MYA)

Location: Europe: Tubingen, Germany

Size: 1 m (3 ft 3 in.)

Weight: unknown

Diet: Shellfish

Nothosaurus

Pronounced: noh-thoh-SORE-us

Name means: False Lizard

Time: Triassic (250-203 MYA)

Location: Asia: China; Mongolia; Middle East: Israel; Europe: Germany, Netherlands, Switzerland; North Africa: Tunisia

Size: 3 m (10 ft)

Weight: 80 kg (175 lb)

Diet: Fish, shrimp

The best known nothosaur, and the one which gives the family its name, is *Nothosaurus*, whose name means 'false lizard'. This nothosaur is typical of the family: its long neck, body and tail were quite streamlined and very flexible and it probably lived – as modern seals do today – fishing at sea and resting (and nesting) on land. Some fossils have impressions of webbed skin between the five toes and fingers of the feet and hands which was one of the adaptations to marine life along with knee and ankle joints that were highly flexible. Because the limb bones were not joined strongly together, and the hip and shoulders were quite weak, *Nothosaurus* would not have found it particularly easy to walk on land for long periods. It forearms were sturdier than its legs, so it appears thes   *Nothosaurus* with most of its propulsion under wa   ough the length of the spines on the caudal (tail)   suggests that this carried a fin, which would have   movement and direction. Its long snout lined w   , sharp, pointed teeth all the way to the back of the c ek region of its head, was ideally suited to catching slip y fish.

Ichthyosaurus

Pronounced: ik-THEE-oh-SORE-us

One of the best known ichthyosaurs, and giving its name to the family, *Ichthyosaurus* was a medium sized marine reptile which had a streamlined body, a long, pointed snout lined with small, sharp, conical shaped teeth, and fore flippers larger than its hind flippers. The fore flippers enclosed six greatly elongated digits- some later ichthyosaurs such as *Platypterygius* from the Cretaceous period had eight digits. The nostrils were set far back on the snout near to the eyes so it had to break the surface of the water to breathe. While the bones of the ears were huge, suggesting that *Ichthyosaurus* had extremely acute 'hearing'- that is it transmitted vibrations from the water to the inner ear- making it a .ie to judge the direction of potential prey, its main sens- for hunting was its sight. The eye sockets were ʿ   ʿ a ring of bones (the sclerotic ring) w   ꙍed to support the massive eyeball. Because .   urus' eyes were large and highly sensitive, it .   . been able to hunt at night or in poor visib·   .h as murky or very deep waters. Several hu   ꙍ complete skeletons of *Ichthyosaurus* have beer   ound since it was first described in 1818 by Cha   ꙍs Keonig and many show their bones still articulati .g with each other. Tiny bones of young were also found inside the bodies of adults: at first palaeontologists suspected *Ichthyosaurus* was a cannibal but other remains show the young emerging tail first (like modern whales) from the bodies of their parent. In addition to offspring, coprolites (droppings) and the fossilised stomach contents showing the fish-diet of ichthyosaurs have also been found. One of the most exciting fossilised remains however is of pigment cells from the smooth, thick skin which show that *Ichthyosaurus* was a dark reddish-brown colour in life.

Name means: Fish Lizard

Time: Early Jurassic (203-135 MYA)

Location: Europe: England, Germany; Greenland; North America: Alberta, Canada

Size: estimated 2 m (6 ft 6 in)

Weight: 90 kg (200 lb)

Diet: Fish

Ichthyosaurus

Plesiosaurus

Pronounced: PLEEZ-ee-oh-SORE-US

Some of the first fossilised reptiles to be seen by scientists may have been plesiosaurs: fossil specimens of *Plesiosaurus* were found over 200 years ago on the coasts of Dorset and Yorkshire in England, before the term 'dinosaur' had been invented. Many fine examples had been found by Mary Anning between 1800 and 1820 in Lyme Regis, Dorset, an area rich in fossils. The earliest member of the family, *Plesiosaurus* had already developed the main structural features that characterise these marine reptiles: it had the typical short and wide body that tapered towards the tail, with a flexible neck that was much longer than the body. Its head was relatively small, but its jaws were long and contained numerous sharp, conical shaped teeth. Its nostrils – two holes on the palate – were located further forward than the nostrils on the outside of the snout. This arrangement suggests that *Plesiosaurus* 'sniffed' the water for prey: water flowed through the snout and into the internal nostrils where scent particles were detected, and then the water left through the external nostrils. The four wide paddle-shaped flippers are thought to have been used in a combination of sculling (back and forth movements) and flying (up and down movements) making *Plesiosaurus* built for manoeuvrability rather than speed: forward strokes by the flippers on one side of the body combined with backwards strokes of the flippers on the other side would have turned *Plesiosaurs'* body on the spot. Its long neck would have then darted out to seize prey. On land however, the long neck would have made *Plesiosaurus* a clumsy beast and one that was very vulnerable to attack from hungry carnivores.

Name means: Ribbon Reptile

Time: Early Jurassic (203-135 MYA)

Location: Europe: England, Germany

Size: estimated 2.3 m (7 ft 6 in.)

Weight: 90 kg (200 lb)

Diet: Fish, squid

Cryptoclidus

Pronounced: KRIP-toh-CLY-dus

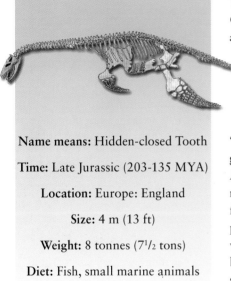

Name means: Hidden-closed Tooth

Time: Late Jurassic (203-135 MYA)

Location: Europe: England

Size: 4 m (13 ft)

Weight: 8 tonnes (7½ tons)

Diet: Fish, small marine animals

This plesiosaur is well known from fossils from England. *Cryptoclidus* had the familiar long neck made up of around 30 vertebrae – compared to the more usual seven or eight in a reptile. The small skull had a long snout with the nostrils set far back on the head. The jaws contained numerous sharp teeth, as well as a number of longer, pointed and curved teeth which interlocked when the jaw was closed to make a 'trap' for small fish or shrimp: it is this feature which gives *Cryptoclidus* its name of 'hidden-closed tooth'. Although it was a good swimmer, *Cryptoclidus* would not have been very fast or capable of pursuing its prey for long distances. It seems more likely that it caught its prey at close quarters, by shooting out its long neck: the vertebrae in the cranial end of the neck appear to have been particularly flexible. *Cryptoclidus* had a relatively short tail and had 'transformed' its limbs into flippers by greatly increasing the number of bones in each of the five digits to produce the long flexible, hydrofoil-shaped front paddles and long rear flippers which it used to propel and steer itself through the water. The gastralia (belly ribs) were moulded into bony plates that provided some protection for the underbelly when *Cryptoclidus* came ashore either to escape attack at sea from an *ichthyosaur* (see page 207) or to lay its eggs.

Muraenosaurus

Pronounced: MURE-rain-oh-ORE-us

The most successful family of plesiosaurs was the
Elasmosauridae, of which *Muraenosaurus* was
an early member. Evolving in the late Jurassic
period (203-135 MYA) and surviving well into
the Cretaceous (135-65 MYA), the elasmosaurs had the
longest necks of all the plesiosaurs. *Muraenosaurus* had a
neck that was as long as its body and tail combined and
was supported by 44 vertebrae. It is uncertain just how
flexible such long necks were, but the vertebrae at the
'head' end of the neck do indicate that this part at least
was highly flexible. There appears to have been a good
deal of lateral (side-to-side) movement possible, but in
the vertical plane (up and down), movement of the neck
appears to have been restricted. While it could hold its
head downwards, lifting its up onto the surface like a
swan would have been impossible for *Muraenosaurus*.
Perched at the end of this long neck was a tiny head,
measuring only about one-sixteenth of the total body
length. The short, stiff plesiosaur body had now also
become quite stout and rigid: the inflexibility of the body
would have meant that the flippers were more effective as
propellers.

Name means: Sea-eel lizard

Time: Late Jurassic (203-135 MYA)

Location: Europe: England; France

Size: 6 m (20 ft)

Weight: 10 tonnes (9 tons)

Diet: Fish, small marine animals

Elasmosaurus

Pronounced: eh-LAZ-moh-SORE-us

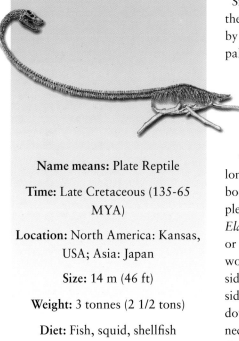

Name means: Plate Reptile

Time: Late Cretaceous (135-65 MYA)

Location: North America: Kansas, USA; Asia: Japan

Size: 14 m (46 ft)

Weight: 3 tonnes (2 1/2 tons)

Diet: Fish, squid, shellfish

"Snakes threaded through the bodies of turtles" is the description of these long necked plesiosaurs given by Dean Conybeare, a nineteenth century British palaeontologist who undertook much of the early scientific investigation into these marine reptiles.

Elasmosaurus means 'plate lizard' and is derived from the massive plate like shoulder bones that covered its chest and formed its 'arm' sockets. The huge muscles that powered the fore flippers were anchored to this plate. *Elasmosaurus* was the longest known plesiosaur: more than half its entire body length was made up of its neck. Where earlier plesiosaurs had only 28 cervical (neck) vertebrae, *Elasmosaurus* had 72- more than any other plesiosaur, or indeed, any other animal. This incredibly long neck would have allowed *Elasmosaurus* to bend it around sideways and make almost two complete circles on either side of its body. (In the vertical plane (upwards and downwards) it was only half as flexible.) Moving the neck around while submerged would have been difficult though as it would have met with considerable water resistance, and this had led some scientists to suggest that as *Elasmosaurus* paddled along, propelled by its four long paddle-shaped flippers, it held its head just out of the water in order to spot prey.

In its small head, *Elasmosaurus*' bony sclerotic rings around the eye, suggest that it had flattened eyeballs- which would have been better suited to seeing underwater and some skull have been found with ear bones. These are fused to the surrounding skull and suggest that *Elasmosaurus* was not particularly well suited to hearing sound waves transmitted through the air.

Kronosaurus

Pronounced: CRO-noh-SORE-us

The Australian *Kronosaurus* was the giant of pliosaurs.
During the Triassic (250-203 MYA) and Jurassic (203-
135 MYA) periods, the modern continent of Australia
had been dry land. But during the Cretaceous period
(135-65 MYA), the seas flooded in, and submerged vast
areas of land. The environment was warm and the waters
shallow, conditions that would have supported large
numbers of fish and other marine life. Fossilised remains,
including the stomach contents of *Kronosaurus* show that
it lived rather like a modern shark, devouring anything
that came its way. Its flat-topped skull alone measured
2.7 m (9 ft) which made it substantially larger and even
more powerful than that of the greatest land dwelling
carnivorous dinosaurs like *Tyrannosaurus Rex* (see page
82). The snout was long and triangular, and inside the
mouth were sharp pointed teeth around 25 cm (10 in)
long and 5 cm (2½ in) in diameter (although much of
the tooth was deeply embedded into the jaw). Large eyes
faced slightly forwards which suggest that *Kronosaurus*
had an overlapping field of vision. Highly manoeuvrable,
Kronosaurus had a body held stiff by tightly linked
gastralia (belly ribs). There were two pairs of flippers,
the rear ones longer than the front pair; there may have
been a fin at the top of the tail to help steer it through the
water.

Name means: Kronos [Time] Lizard

Time: Late Cretaceous
(135-65 MYA)

Location: Australia: Queensland

Size: 10m (33 ft)

Weight: 7 tonnes (6½ tons)

Diet: Marine reptiles, fish, molluscs

Tylosaurus

Pronounced: TIE-loh-SORE-us

Name means: Knob Lizard

Time: Late Cretaceous:
(135-65 MYA)

Location: North America, Japan

Size: 11 m (36 ft)

Weight: 7 tonnes (6 tons)

Diet: Turtles, fish, other masasaurs

This giant, long-skulled marine lizard was one of the later members of the mosasaur family and a fearsome predator. One of the most distinctive features of *Tylosaurus* (and that which gives it its name 'knob lizard') is the hard, bony tip of its snout which it may have used as a ramming weapon for stunning prey, or perhaps to see off rival males. The snout tip was not made of solid bone, though and some fossil remains show specimens with 'broken noses' which suggest that either they were quite fragile or that *Tylosaurus* was apt to ram at great force! It is also thought that *Tylosaurus*, like other mosasaurs, had forked tongues as their skulls show that they had the Jacobson's organ: this is a structure in the roof of the mouth found in snakes and lizards that is used to detect scent particles in the air, or in *Tylosaurus'* case, in water. In addition to large eyes and acute eyesight, it appears that *Tylosaurus* could also 'sniff out' its prey. Inside the long slim snout, were teeth on the jaws and on the palate bones. The skull bones could also move quite freely at the joints which allowed *Tylosaurus* to expand its jaws to swallow very large prey. The arms and legs of its land-living ancestors had evolved into streamlined flippers with extra long toe and finger bones making the flippers longer. These were probably not used for swimming but for steering, and the main propulsive force was delivered by the high but narrow, flexible tail which was 'waved' from side to side.

CHAPTER 9

Reptiles of the Air

The Mesozoic Era from around 250-65 million years ago is often called the 'Age of the Dinosaurs'. But the dinosaurs lived only on land. In the sea, and in the air, other reptiles also existed. The Mesozoic reptiles were among the first vertebrates (back-boned animals) to take to the air: flapping their wings or gliding on 'wings of skin' they cruised through the air across the world. None of these extraordinary flying reptiles would survive beyond the end of the Cretaceous period, their only legacy being their fossilised remains. The pterosaurs were the most important of the flying reptiles and they have been known for some time with some of the most magnificent finds coming from the Solnhofen quarries in southern Germany. In late Jurassic times, Solnhofen was covered by a lagoon filled with stagnant water, flanked by mountains to the north and the deeper waters of the Tethys Sea to the south (what is now the Mediterranean Sea). When flying reptiles (and marine reptiles) became trapped in the poisonous waters and died in the lagoon, their dead bodies floated on the surface of the water and the soft tissues decayed. The heavier parts of their bodies – their bones – sank to the bottom where they were buried along with the fine sediment that settled beneath the water at the bottom of the lagoon. Because the waters of the lagoon were oxygen-starved, no further decay of the bones was possible. The technical name for such geological occurrences (which are quite rare, with only a dozen sites known worldwide) is *lagerstratten*. The Romans first excavated the quarries at Solnhofen to make paving stones; in the 18th century, the fine grained limestone rock was found to be ideal for lithography (literally: stone-printing) which led to the rapid expansion of the quarry. This in turn led to the discoveries in the 19th century of fossil remains, not only pterosaurs, whose name appropriately means 'stone lizards', but of early birds (which appeared halfway through the Mesozoic Era), small dinosaurs and marine reptiles.

ORDER PTEROSAURIA

The pterosaurs were the first group of vertebrates to take to the skies, flying on 'wings' of skin which were attached along the length of their greatly elongated fourth fingers on each hand and rejoined the body at thigh level. These flying reptiles evolved in the Late Triassic period (250-203 MYA) and about 70 million years before the first known bird, *Archaeopteryx* appeared. The pterosaurs thrived during the Jurassic period (203-135 MYA) and survived into the early Cretaceous period (135-65 MYA) and diversified into numerous forms. Among these were the largest flying creatures of all times. Like many of their land and marine dwelling reptile relatives, the pterosaurs began their decline in the Cretaceous period and were extinct by the end of the Mesozoic Age around 65 million years ago. There are two suborders of pterosaurs: the earliest and most primitive types were the rhamphorhynchs, while the later types include the more familiar and more famous pterodactyls.

SUBORDER RHAMPHORHYNCHOIDEA

(See pages 219-33)

The Triassic period of the Mesozoic Age was a highly significant period of reptile evolution with many diverse groups such as dinosaurs, turtles and crocodiles appearing. While the fossil finds of the earliest pterosaurs have been found in late Triassic rocks (250-203 MYA), even the earliest known pterosaurs were advanced flyers. The rhamphorhynchoids were generally small animals with long tails stiffened by bony ligaments.

Peteinosaurus

SUBORDER PTERODACTYLOIDEA

(See pages 234-49)

The pterodactyls (whose name means 'wing finger') are undoubtedly the most familiar of all the flying reptiles, so famous that many erroneously call all pterosaurs 'pterodactyls'. The pterodactyls were, in fact, short-tailed pterosaurs, which were already established as a group in the Late Jurassic period (203-135 MYA) when their relatives the rhamphorhynchoids (the long-tailed pterosaurs) became extinct. The pterodactyls survived through the Cretaceous period (135-65 MYA), although only a few types survived to the end of that period. These pterosaurs had the same general structure as the rhamphorhynchoids, but their tails were shorter, their necks longer, and their skulls and beaks more elongated. They ranged in size from some of the smallest known pterosaurs to some of the largest flying vertebrates that ever lived.

Eudimorphodon

Pronounced: YOO-die-MORF-oh-don

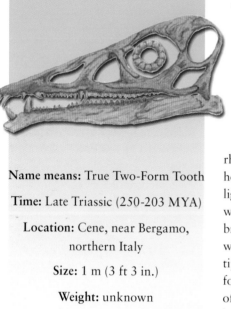

Name means: True Two-Form Tooth

Time: Late Triassic (250-203 MYA)

Location: Cene, near Bergamo, northern Italy

Size: 1 m (3 ft 3 in.)

Weight: unknown

Diet: Piscivore

About the same size as a large seagull, *Eudimorphodon* is the oldest pterosaur to have been found to date. Its remains were discovered on the western slopes of Monte Bo, in the Alpine foothills near Bergamo, Italy by Mario Pandolfi in 1973. The fossilised skeleton, which is missing its winged fingers and most of its hind legs, was discovered in a thin shale layer from the rubble of the village of Cene's former quarry.

Eudimorphodon was typical of a fully developed rhamphorhynchoid pterosaur: it had a short neck, large head and long, bony tail stiffened by a network of bony ligaments and with a diamond-shaped flap at the tip which probably acted as a rudder. The structure of its breastbone indicates that it was able to flap its wings which would have measured about 1 m (3 ft 3 in) from tip to tip. What is unique, however, are the unusual teeth found in no other pterosaur. These are not the usual row of teeth with a single cusp, but are divided into a few large front fangs and behind them, a series of smaller teeth with three to five cusps. In the upper jaw there were two more large teeth with additional cusps between the series of three and five cusped smaller teeth. In the upper jaw there were 58 teeth in all, and in the lower, 56 teeth. This makes a total of 114 teeth– all in a jaw measuring only 8 cm (3½ in) long! This type of dentition suggests that *Eudimorphodon* was piscivorous (a fish eater), although juveniles, which had slightly 'immature' dentition probably ate insects such as dragonflies.

Peteinosaurus

Pronounced: pet-INE-oh-SORE-us

Name means: Winged Reptile

Time: Late Triassic (250-135 MYA)

Location: Cene, near Bergamo, northern Italy

Wingspan: 60 cm (24 in.)

Diet: Flying insects

This pterosaur, whose remains were found in 1978 in Cene, near Bergamo, northern Italy, is one of the earliest vertebrates whose skeleton shows evidence of its ability to flap its skin covered 'wings'. The long tailed *Peteinosaurus* which lived on the shore of the late Triassic Tethys Sea was smaller than its contemporary *Eudimorphodon* (see page 218) and unlike it, *Peteinosaurus* had only single-cusped teeth which were flattened with sharp cutting edges at the front and back. At the front of the lower jaw were two large 'fangs'. Although the upper skull remains unknown, scientists believe that *Peteinosaurus* was an insectivore and in more ways, more primitive than *Eudimorphodon*. It had a light boned skeleton and a long tail stiffened by bony ligaments and its wings were relatively short, only twice as long at the hind legs. In all other pterosaurs, the wings were at least three times as long, if not longer. With a wingspan of only 60 cm (24 in), *Peteinosaurus* is considered by many scientists to be the direct ancestor of the oldest Jurassic (203-135 MYA) period pterosaur, *Dimorphodon* (see page 222).

Preondactylus

Pronounced: PRAY-on-dak-TIE-lus

Preondactylus is the third genus of pterosaur known to date. Its remains were discovered first in 1978 and consisted of three connected digital (finger) phalanges. In 1982 another skeleton was discovered in the Preone Valley in the Veneto, northern Italy by Nando Buffarini, but unfortunately, the slab of rock which contained it shattered as it was being extracted. The tiny fragments of bones embedded in the rocks were, after Buffarini had pieced the rock back together, washed away when he cleaned the rock. All that remained was the negative print of the skeleton on the surface of the rock, but a cast of silicon rubber was made to 'recreate' the pterosaur in three dimensions. Once examined it was found that this was a new species of pterosaur in the rhamphorhynchidea family and it was named 'Preone Finger', after the three flight digits found earlier which scientists believe also came from this species. This small, long-tailed genus, about the size of a pigeon, is among the earliest of the pterosaurs in the fossil records found so far. The wings were relatively short and the legs long – proportions which palaeontologists consider 'primitive' characteristics in pterosaurs. Its jaws were lined with sharp, single cusped teeth of different lengths. In 1984 one more fossil was discovered, but this time the bones were packed tight into a ball. It appears that this *Preondactylus* had fallen prey to a predatory fish that spewed out the indigestible bones as a gastric pellet which sank to the bottom of the sea and was then fossilised.

Name means: Preone Finger

Time: Late Triassic (253-203 MYA)

Location: Preone Valley, northern Italy

Wingspan: 45 cm (18 in.)

Diet: Insects, possibly fish

Dimorphodon

Pronounced: DIE-morf-oh-don

Name means: Two-Form Tooth

Time: Early Jurassic (203-135 MYA)

Location: Europe: England

Wingspan: 1.4 m (4 ft 6 in)

Diet: Piscivore

Dimorphodon is the earliest Jurassic pterosaur and was about 1 m (3 ft 3 in.) long with a wingspan of about 1.4 m (4 ft 6 in.) with a large head, typical of the rhamphorhynchs, measuring about 20 cm (8 in.) long. The skull was relatively high, and was shaped like that of a modern puffin; it had large side 'windows' consisting of eye sockets, upper and lower temporal openings, pre-orbital openings and nostrils, all separated by thin bars of bone. So, despite the size of the skull, it was quite lightweight. It had four large front teeth on each side of the upper jaw, behind which was a row of smaller teeth. In the lower jaw there were also four or five large teeth which were followed by 30 to 40 tiny, pointed teeth. This specialised dentition suggests that *Dimorphodon* was piscivorous (a fish eater). A typical long-tailed pterosaur, *Dimorphodon* had a long vertebral tail made up of over 30 caudal (tail) vertebrae: the first five or six of these were short and could move against each other, but subsequent caudal vertebrae were elongated and stiffened with bony tendons. This structure stabilised the pterosaur in flight and it was probably further assisted by a small, diamond or triangular shaped terminal tail 'vane' which acted as a drag rudder. Its short wings were also typical of early pterosaurs: the first of the four flight digit phalanges is only a little longer than the lower arm, and shorter than the second and third phalanges of the flight digit. The hind legs were relatively long and powerfully developed: the first four digits had claws, while the fifth digit was fairly long and splayed sideways. It has been suggested that *Dimorphodon* was well suited to bipedal 'birdlike' walking, its long tail balancing its head as it moved around: fossilised tracks show the marks of hind feet walking in a narrow track, with marks apparently made by the forelimbs in a wider track at each side. It would have been a rather clumsy walk, using its 'arms' rather like crutches or walking sticks, and it probably spent much of its time perched on cliffs or branches from which it launched itself into flight.

Campylognathiodes

Pronounced: CAMP-ee-lon-ATH-ee-oh-dees

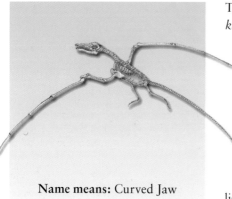

Name means: Curved Jaw

Time: Early Jurassic (203-135 MYA)

Location: Europe: Germany

Wingspan: 1- 1.75 m
(3 ft 3 in.- 5 ft 7 in.)

Diet: Piscivore

This pterosaur takes its name from the Greek words *kampylos*, meaning 'curved' and *gnathos*, meaning 'jaws' which describe the crooked ends to its jaws. So far there are two species known: *C. liasicus* with a wingspan of about 1 m (3 ft 3 in.), and the larger *C. zitelli* with a span of around 1.75 m (5 ft 7 inches). *Campylognathiodes* was a long-tailed rhamphorhynchoid pterosaur with a short head and small teeth, and a skull dominated by a large, circular eye socket. It possibly had extremely acute eyesight and may have been able to see in poor light or even perhaps at night. The end of the snout was pointed and toothed with sharp, short conical teeth set upright in the jaw. Its sternum consisted of a broad rectangular plate of bone that had a short crest (known as a cristopina) projecting forwards. In 1986 a fossil pterosaur pelvis was found in Lower Saxony, Germany: this find was of great significance as the hip sockets had survived in good condition and scientists examining the lateral and upward orientation deduced that this pterosaur at least, was not capable of bipedal walking as the upper leg bones (femora) could not be oriented vertically. A vertical orientation is vital in order for the legs to 'swing' to and fro when walking or running.

Dorygnathus

Pronounced:DOOR-ee-NAY-thus

Discovered in 1830, but named and described later in 1860, *Dorygnathus* was a long, stiff-tailed pterosaur with a relatively small wingspan of only around 1 m (3 ft 3 in.) Its skull was elongated (which gave it its name 'spear jaw') and larger than its contemporary, *Campylugnathiodes* (see page 224) with huge eye sockets and long, curved, front teeth in the upper and lower jaws which pointed forwards and which meshed alternatively when the jaws were closed. At the rear of the jaws were only very small teeth. Together, the arrangement and shape of the teeth were ideal for seizing and holding onto slippery fish. A small triangular-shaped sternum (breast bone) served as the area of attachment for the flight muscles and the flight digits (and therefore the wings) were quite short. However, the fifth digit of the foot was very long and set at an angle. The reason, and thus the function, for this is unknown: it may have been used to spread a small web of skin giving the animal more 'lift' at take-off if it landed on the surface of the sea. *Dorygnathus* appears to have been abundant in the early Jurassic period around what was once the Liassic Sea – an extensive but shallow sea that flooded broad areas of central Europe some 200 million years ago. Numerous outstanding fossilised records are from the slate quarries around Holzmaden and Ohmden in the northern foothills of the Schwabische Alb.

Name means: Spear Jaw

Time: Late-early Jurassic (203-135 MYA)

Location: Europe: Germany

Size: 2.4 m (8 ft)

Weight: 1m (3 ft 3 in.)

Diet: Piscivorous

Anurognathus

Pronounced: AN-yoor-oh-NAT-us

Name means: Without Tail and Jaw

Time: Late Jurassic (203-235 MYA)

Location: Europe: Germany

Wingspan: 50 cm (20 in.)

Diet: Insectivore

This very small pterosaur – its trunk was only 5 cm (2 in.) long – was unlike any other rhamphorhynchoid in that it had a very short tail- its name in fact means 'without tail and jaw'. The greatly reduced tail formed a kind of birdlike pygostyl – better known as the 'Parson's nose'. This strange pterosaur is known from a single fossil specimen from the Solnhofen limestone quarry in Germany which was described in 1923 by Ludwig von Ammon. It is classed with the rhamphorhynchoids, however, because it shares the general body proportions as well as certain skeletal characteristics including the short high skull, short neck and peg-shaped teeth. Its narrow head had short, strong broad jaws with teeth designed for crushing and grinding which suggest *Anurognathus* was an insectivore. It must, therefore, also have been a proficient flyer if it was to catch 'in flight' dragonflies and other insects such as wood-wasps (*Pseudosirex*) which were also preserved in the limestone deposits at Solnhofen. *Anurognathus* had wings which reached a maximum span of about 50 cm (20 in.) and were composed of a thin membrane of skin which stretched from the elongated fourth finger to the ankle. A secondary wing was supported by a pteroid bone and stretched from each wrist to the neck.

Scaphognathus

Pronounced: CA-fo-NAY-thus

Known only from two specimens preserved in the limestone of the Solnhofen quarry in Germany, *Scaphognathus* was one of the earliest pterosaur finds of all and was described as early as 1831 by the German palaeontologist August Goldfuss, but as the tail section was missing, he believed he was examining a pterodactylus, which he named *Pterodactylus crassirostris* ('thick-beaked flight finger') When a second specimen was discovered- of an immature specimen whose bones were not fully ossified but with its long, flexible tail intact- the genus was renamed *Scaphnognathus* and classified with the rhamphorhynchoids. In its general body proportions and long tail, *Scaphognathus* resembles *Rhamphorhynchus* (see page 232) but does have some interesting characteristics of its own. *Scaphognathus* had a shorter, more compact head but with a larger pre orbital fenestrae (opening in the skull in front of the eye socket). Its slender and widely spaced teeth- 18 in the upper jaw and 10 in the lower jaw- did not point forwards but were set upright into the jaw. The ends of the jaw didn't meet in a point at the end, but instead were fairly blunt, like the bow of a boat- hence its' name 'tub jaw'. It is not clear however, whether *Scaphognathus* was a fish eater or an insectivore, but its long, slender wings suggest that it could fly for long distances in the hunt for food.

Name means: Tub Jaw

Time: Late Jurassic (203-135 MYA)

Location: Europe: Germany

Wingspan: 90 cm-1 m (36 in.- 3 ft 3 in.)

Diet: Piscivore, possibly insectivore

Batrachognathus

Pronounced: ba-TRAK-oh-NATH-us

The limestone deposits of the north-western foothills of the Karatau mountains in Kazakhstan are approximately the same age as those in Sonhofen, Germany and both show a great similarity in the insect fauna (animal life) demonstrated by their fossil remains. In 1948, the remains of an incomplete and dis-articulated (the bones were apart and 'jumbled up') skeleton of a pterosaur was found. Fragments of the skull and jaw, vertebrae and ribs, and bones from the wings and hind legs could be distinguished. The shape of the jaw suggested that this pterosaur had a high, short skull about 48 mm (2 in.) long with a broad mouth, rather like a frog. In its mouth were small, peg like teeth, designed for crushing and grinding insects. It was named *Batrachognathus volans*, or 'flying frog jaw' and was likely to have been an insectivorous pterosaur which caught its prey in flight. *Batrachognathus* was a small rhamphorhynchoid pterosaur with a wingspan of around 50 cm (20 in.) and appears to have been related to *Anurognathos* (see page 226) found in Solnhofen, Germany: as the skeleton was incomplete is may be that *Batrachognathus* also had a pygostyl ('Parson's nose') rather than the more usual, long tail of rhamphorhynchoid pterosaurs.

Name means: Frog Jaw

Time: Late Jurassic (203-135 MYA)

Location: Asia: Kazakhstan

Wingspan: 50 cm (20 in.)

Diet: Insectivore

Sordes

Pronounced: sor-DAYS

Name means: Hairy Devil

Time: Late Jurassic (203-135 MYA)

Location: Asia: Kazakhstan

Wingspan: 63 cm (25 in.)

Diet: Insectivore, possible piscivorous

The Jurassic deposits in Kazakhstan, Asia have been noted for their rich fossil finds for many years, but in the 1960s a spectacular pterosaur find was made by the Russian zoologist A.G. Sharov while he was collecting fossil insects in the Karatau Mountains. The find consisted of an almost complete skeleton with imprints of the soft body parts and flight membranes. Because of the fineness of the sediment in which the fossil was contained, the rock revealed the most remarkable feature: this pterosaur, named *Sordes*, was covered in a thick fur. While traces of hair had been found in Solnhofen fossils, never had the hairs themselves been found. Here was proof at last that pterosaurs were not 'naked skin' or covered in reptilian scales, but that they were hairy. The significance of this body covering means that the pterosaurs were likely to have been warm-blooded. A typical rhamphorhynchoid pterosaur, *Sordes* was a close relative of the Solnhofen *Scaphognathus* (see page 228), sharing a similar skull and dentition, and having the short metacarpal bone and long vertebrate tail which fanned out slightly at the end to act as a rudder- but without the terminal vane as in the Solnhofen *Rhamphorhynchus* (see page 232). Long, dense and fairly thick hair covered the body- the longest body hairs were 6 mm (^{1}/4 in.)- and there was also hair on the short, broad flight membranes (which also extended between the hind legs), digits (fingers) and the skin between the foot digits (toes). The root of the tail was also covered in hair but the rest was 'naked'. A total of three specimens of skeletons of

Sordes have been found to date: the skull averages 8 cm (3¹/₄ in.) long and its wingspan averaged 60 cm (24 inches). It was probably piscivorous (fish eating) but could also have fed on insects.

Rhamphorhynchus

Pronounced: ram-FOR-ink-us

Name means: Beak Snout

Time: Late Jurassic (203-135 MYA)

Location: Europe: England, Germany, Portugal; Africa: Tanzania

Wingspan: 1 m (3 ft 3 in.)

Diet: Piscivore

Rhamphorhynchus is probably the most well known pterosaur and gives its name to the entire suborder of Rhamphorhynchoidea. Evolving in the late Triassic (250-203 MYA) and surviving to the late Jurassic (203-135 MYA), the rhamphorhynchoid pterosaurs kept their long vertebrate tails as a legacy of their land-dwelling reptilian ancestors. Because of the fine grain of the limestone of the Solnhofen quarry in Germany in which many specimens of *Rhamphorhynchus* have been magnificently preserved, we know that there was a rhomboid shaped (an off-centre diamond shaped) membrane on the end of this long tail which was used as a rudder during flight. Long-tailed pterosaurs have not been found in any later rocks, so it appears that they became extinct shortly after they had populated the shoreline and islands of the Solnhofen lagoon. Also preserved in the German limestone were *Rhamphorhynchus'* fine wing structures and membranous wings, microscopic examination of which revealed that there were very fine fibres running from the front to the back of the wings which strengthened them. *Rhamphorhynchus* was evidently a very skilful flier: it had a broad sternum (breast bone) with a forward pointing cristopina (crest), to which strong muscles were attached. The neck was short, with short, compact vertebrae, and the skull, large, elongated and pointed, with large orbital openings (eye sockets), and smaller openings in the skull in front of eye (the nostrils and pre orbital fenestrae). A pointed horny beak formed the tip of its jaw which was lined with long, slightly curved and pointed teeth directed forwards and outwards. These teeth were designed for catching slippery prey such as fish: the fossilised remains of a small fish was found inside the stomach of a *Rhamphorhynchus* found at

Solnhofen. When the jaws were closed, the 20 upper jaw teeth and 14 lower jaw
teeth meshed alternately. Several different species of *Rhamphorhynchus* have been
found in Solnhofen: the most common species is *R. muensteri*. *R. longicaudus* is
the smallest of the species with a wingspan of 40 cm (16 in.) while *R. longiceps*
is the largest, with a wingspan of 1.75 m (5 ft 8 in.). In addition to the finds in
Germany, *Rhamphorhynchus* species have also been found elsewhere in Europe
(England and Portugal) and in Tanzania, East Africa.

Pterodactylus

Pronounced: TER-oh-DAK-til-us

Name means: Wing Finger

Time: Late Jurassic (230-135 MYA)

Location: Europe: England, France and Germany; Africa: Tanzania

Wingspan: 36 cm-2.5 m (14 in- 8 ft 2 in.)

Diet: Piscivore, insectivore

Pterodactylus shows us the typical features of the pterodactyl: a short tail (with no steering or flying function), a long neck, with the head meeting the neck at right angles (rather than in a straight lines as in rhamphorhynchoids), and greatly elongated metacarpals (hand bones) which, along with the fourth finger, supported the wings. The earliest evidence of *Pterodactylus* comes once again from the fine Jurassic limestone deposits at Solnhofen in Germany, where six species have been distinguished, each adapted for a particular lifestyle and for eating a particular food – fish or insects. This is evident from the shape and length of their skulls which range from 4.2 cm (1^1/$_2$ in) long to 10.8 cm (4^1/$_4$ in.) long. The smallest of the species is *Pterodactylus elegans* with its long thin teeth found only in the front part of its jaw and a wingspan of a mere 25 cm (10 inches). The most common species is *P. kochi* with its long, narrow jaw lined with sharp, fish-eating teeth. Adults had a wingspan of about 50 cm (20 in.), but the smallest specimen ever found at Solnhofen was of a baby, and whose body measures only 2 cm (^{3}/$_4$ in.) long and its wingspan only 18 cm (7 in). Although very young when it died, this *P. kochi* was already able to fly. Larger species at Solnhofen are *P. longicollum*, whose name means 'long-necked flight finger' whose wingspan reached some 1.45 m (4 ft 9 in.) – about the same size as a modern herring gull. Of the largest species, *Pterodactylus grandis*, only individual wing and leg bones are known, but they suggest a wing span of 2.5 m (8 ft 2 in.), about the same size as a modern vulture.

Gallodactylus

Pronounced: GAL-oh-DAC-til-us

Name means: Gallic Finger

Time: Late Jurassic (203-135 MYA)

Location: Europe: Germany; southern France

Wingspan: 1.35 m (4 ft 4 in.)

Diet: Piscivore

Gallodactylus is known from finds in France and from Germany. The name 'Gallic Finger' was introduced in 1974 by the French (hence the appellation 'Gallic') palaeontologist J. Fabre for a pterosaur he examined from Var, in southern France. There were many features found to be shared with some specimens found in Germany in the 1850s and named *P. suevicus*, and these early remains were assigned to *Gallodactylus*, as were later discoveries at Solnhofen. *Gallodactylus* was one of the larger, short-tailed pterosaurs, with a wingspan of around 1.35 m (4 ft 4 in.), In general appearance it resembled *Pterodactylus* (see page 234) but it did have a number of distinct features. Its elongated beak, with a small number of forward-pointing, narrow teeth confined to the front end of the long, slender jaws, was ideal for catching and holding fish. Its skull was about 15 cm (6 in.) long with a large nasopreorbital opening which reduced the weight of the skull. Most significant, however, was the short, horny, medial (mid-line) crest at the rear of its head that ended in a point. This may have been used for signalling or as a 'cut water'- to stop the head from moving as it dived into water to hunt fish.

Germanodactylus

Pronounced: Jer-MAN-oh-DAK-til-us

Germanodactylus ('German Finger') was a short tailed pterosaur found first in Solnhofen in 1925, but named in 1964 by the German-trained Chinese palaeontologist Dr. Yang Zhong-jian (who is known familiarly as Dr. C.C. Young). There have been very few finds of this genus which is represented by two species: *Germanodactylus cristatus* (from Solnhofen), and the smaller of the two species with a wingspan of around 98 cm (3 ft 2 in.) and *Germanodactylus rhamphastinus* (found in Daiting, Bavaria, southern Germany, with a wingspan of around 1.08 m (3 ft 5 in.) making it the larger of the two). Both however, were characterised by having long, thin bony crests on the mid-line of their skulls, starting at the nostrils and extending above the openings of the eye sockets. This was probably covered with a horny carina or 'keel' and may have been used for signalling or as a 'cut water'. Inside their jaws was a long row of powerful, short teeth. It has been suggested that *Germanodactylus*, which lived on the shores of the Solnhofen lagoon, may have used its strong finger claws to climb trees and may also have hung 'bat-like' from branches by turning its feet backwards to provide a strong grip.

Name means: German Finger

Time: Late Jurassic (203-135 MYA)

Location: Europe: Germany; France

Size: 1.08 m (3 ft 5 in.)

Diet: Piscivore

Ctenochasma

Pronounced: STEN-oh-KAS-mah

Name means: Comb Jaw

Time: Late Jurassic (203-135 MYA)

Location: Europe: Germany

Wingspan: 1.2 m (3 ft 9 in.)

Diet: Piscivore

Although the late Jurassic skies over Germany appear to have teemed with pterodactyloid pterosaurs, *Ctensochasma* ('Comb Jaw') is a rare specimen. It was first described in 1851 by Hermann von Meyer (1801-69) although his specimen, from the Hanover area of Lower Saxony, consisted only of the front section of the lower jaw with numerous tightly packed and strong teeth. Meyer named his find *Ctenochasma roemeri* in honour of the palaeontologist F. A. Roemer. The first specimen to be found in the limestone at Solnhofen – a fragment of upper jaw – was also in the 1850s. Later, more complete skeletons were found and were named *Ctenochasma gracile* by Albert Oppel. *Ctenochasma's* name was chosen on account of its long jaws, which were bent slightly upwards and equipped with a total of 260 long, inwardly curved and slender, teeth which made it a perfect 'filter feeder'. Rather than feed in flight, *Ctensochasma* would have waded in the shallow water and swept its jaw from side to side to strain small marine animals from the water. It was not until 1981 that another specimen came to light – this time with a porous bony crest on its skull. This species was named *Ctenochasma procristata*. The largest of the six specimens known so far had a skull around 20 cm (8 in.) and a wingspan of at least 1.2 m (3 ft 9 inches). Because of its strange dentition, which is significantly different from other pterodactyloid pterosaurs, palaeontologists place *Ctenochasma* – along with another pterosaur, *Gnathosaurus* (see page 239), in a family of it own known as the Ctenochasmatidae.

Gnathosaurus

Pronounced: NATH-Oh-sor-us

Gnathosaurus is another extremely rare specimen of pterodactyloid pterosaurs from Solnhofen in Germany: only fragments of two specimens are known. The first find consisted of a remnant of lower jaw discovered in 1832 but mistaken for a piece of crocodile jaw. Later however, Hermann von Meyer assigned it the name of *Gnathosaurus subulatus*: 'subulatus' is the Latin for 'awl-like' and describes the shape of the teeth von Meyer found in this 'Jaw Reptile'. It was not until a second find in 1951 – a skull about 28 cm (11 in.) long – that it was proved that *Gnathosaurus* was not a land-dwelling dinosaur, but in fact was a pterosaur, a flying reptile – even though the rest of its skeleton has not been found. *Gnathosaurus* was a large pterosaur with a wingspan of around 1.7 m (5 ft 6 in). While its teeth were fewer than *Ctenoschasma's*, (see page 238) and they were much more powerful and less densely arranged in its jaw (*Gnathosaurus* had only 130 teeth), palaeontologists assume that *Gnathosaurus* was also a 'filter-feeder'. *Gnathosaurus* had teeth extending well towards the rear of its jaw, with the longest teeth at the front which was shaped like a spoon. Like *Ctenochasma*, *Gnathosaurus* also had a low crest of bone on its skull. Because of it strange dentition, *Gnathosaurus* is placed with *Ctenoschasma* in the family known as Ctenochasmatidae.

Name means: Jaw Reptile

Time: Late Jurassic (203-135 MYA)

Location: Europe: Germany

Wingspan: 1.7 m (5 ft 6 in.)

Diet: Piscivore

Orinthocheirus

Pronounced: OR-in-THOH-kiy-rus

Name means: Bird Hand

Time: Cretaceous (135-65 MYA)

Location: Worldwide

Wingspan: 2.5 m (8 ft 2 in.)

Diet: Piscivore

Described by Henry Govier Seeley in 1869 from fossil material found in the Cambridge area of the east of England, *Ornithicheirus* was one of the most numerous pterosaurs of the Cretaceous period (135-65 MYA): a total of 36 species have been distinguished. In 1914 R.W Hooley reordered the material and reduced the number of different species to five different groups, which he named on the basis of their jaw bones. Because of the fragmentary nature of the largely incomplete skeletal remains, there is still much controversy about what belongs to this genus of pterosaurs, with many other fragmentary remains from Europe, Africa, South America, Australia and New Zealand all ascribed to it. As a result, the generic name *Orinthocheirus* has become something of a 'waste bin' and palaeontologists are working on clearer definitions. So far, they have suggested that *Orinthicheirus* was a medium-sized, short-tailed pterosaur with a wingspan of around 2.5 m (8 ft 2 in.) which lived world wide. It had a long, slender skull and the jaws were lined with numerous sharp, pointed teeth which extended to the very front of the jaw, indicating that it was likely to have been piscivorous. It is also highly probable that *Orinthocheirus* had a bony crest on its snout.

Dsungaripterus

Pronounced: D'SUNG-ah-RIP-ter-us

The first pterosaur *Dsungaripterus* to be discovered in China, was found by Dr Yang Zhong-jian (C.C. Young) in the 1960s. The fossil material consisted of front sections of the skull and lower jaw, and a large part of the rest of the skeleton. In 1973, a second find of complete skulls, a sternum (breast bone) and pelvic bones was made in the Junggar basin near Wuerho, Xingjian Province, China. *Dsungaripterus* was a fairly large pterosaur with a wingspan of some 3-3.5 m (9 ft 8 in. - 11 ft 5 in.) and a skull up to 50 cm (1 ft 6 in.) long, but its most striking feature was the toothless tip of its jaws which were bent slightly upwards, and acted like a pair of giant forceps. Further back along both the upper and lower jaws were blunt knobs which appear to have been used as crushing tools. Palaeontologists believe that *Dsungaripterus* used the upturned tip of the jaw to pluck bivalves, snails and crustacea from rocks or out of crannies along the seashore, and their shells were then crushed by the bony knobs. A second feature of *Dsungaripterus* was its cranial crest on its skull. This was an elongated crest on the snout along the mid line which extended over the eyes with a short crest over the back of the head. The eye socket was quite small with the largest 'hole' in the skull being the nasopreorbital opening. Like a bird, *Dsungaripterus* had a series of fused front dorsal (back) vertebrae (called a notarium) and fused sacral vertebrae (called a synsacrum).

Name means: Junggar Wing

Time: Cretaceous (135-65 MYA)

Location: Asia: China

Size: 3 m (9 ft 8 in.)

Diet: Piscivore

Phobetor

Pronounced: foh-BET-or

Name means: The Frightening One

Time: Early Cretaceous

Location: Asia: Mongolia

Wingspan: 1.5 m (4 ft 9 in.)

Diet: Piscivore

At the beginning of the Cretaceous period, shallow seas began to divide the southern continents (although South America and Africa were still attached to each other) and the Atlantic Ocean began to form. The northern and southern continents were now separated and the sea dividing Asia from Europe was growing. By the late Cretaceous times, the continents were in pretty much their more familiar positions, with South America and Africa drifting apart, and India moving eastwards across the Indian Ocean. Australia and Antarctica had also detached themselves from what had been Gondwana. These changes affected the climate and the further development of plant and animal life: this period saw the first deciduous trees and flowering plants. While dinosaurs still dominated the land, and birds were becoming more numerous, the short-tailed pterosaurs dominated the air and were to be found on all the continents except Antarctica.

Discovered in 1982 in Zagan Zabsk in western Mongolia, *Phobetor* was a close relative of the Chinese pterosaur, *Dsungaripterus* (see page 241), but only about half its size. The first remains consisted of bones from the wing and hind legs thought at first to belong to a species of small *Dsungaripterus* and were named *D. parvus*. But later, skulls were also discovered and it was clear that there were many differences between this pterosaur and the Chinese one that it was renamed *Phobetor* ('The Frightening One'). It had similar bony crest structure along its head, along with a toothless point to its jaw, but *Phobetor's* jaws were much straighter and they contained real, conical shaped teeth, rather than the bony crushing knobs of *Dsungarpiterus*.

Nyctosaurus

Pronounced:NIK-toh-SORE-us

In his book *The Lost World* (1912) Sir Arthur Conan Doyle, the creator of Sherlock Holmes, told of pterosaurs still alive in South America! Living throughout the world (except Antarctica), in reality, the last of the pterosaurs in fact survived until the end of the Mesozoic Age around 65 million years ago, and it would be as late as 1953 when the first exciting pterosaur remains would be discovered on the continent by L.I. Price in Brazil. The first fossil was part of a humerus (arm bone): the complete bone would have been about 16.5 cm long (6¹/₂ in.) which would have made this a large pterosaur with a wingspan of around 3.5 m (11 ft 5 inches). The humerus found in Brazil was seen to correspond with bones already discovered in Kanas, USA and named *Nyctosaurus gracilis* by O.C. Marsh in 1876, but it was much larger. *Nyctosaurus* was a toothless pterodactyloid pterosaur a short-tailed pterosaur (which differed from its giant contemporary *Pteranodon* (see page 248) by being smaller and having no bony crest on the back of its head. The Brazilian find was named *Nyctosaurus lamegoi*, in honour of A.R. Lamego who was the divisional director of geology and mineralogy of the Department of Mineral Production in Rio de Janeiro. If future finds of this species are found, it could turn out that the Brazilian pterosaur is completely different from its North American cousin, and be a completely new genus.

Name means: Naked Reptile

Time: Cretaceous (135-65 MYA)

Location: North America: Kansas, USA; South America: Brazil

Wingspan: 3.5 m (11 ft 5 in.)

Diet: Piscivore

Anhanguera

Pronounced: an-hang-GERR-ah

Name means: Old Devil

Time: Cretaceous (135-65 MYA)

Location: South America: Brazil

Wingspan: 4.15 m (13 ft 6 in.)

Diet: Possible Piscivore

In north-eastern Brazil, on the slopes of the Araripe Plateau (Chapado do Araripe) and bordering the states of Piaui, Ceará and Pernambuco, is the Santana Formation, a layer of rock about 200 m (656 ft) thick which was formed about 115 million years ago. From Santana come unique fossil preservations and strange, new pterosaurs. *Anhanguera* - 'old devil'- is one of the most well known pterosaurs from the Santana Formation and takes its name from the local Tupi Indian culture. This new pterosaur genus was described first in 1985 by D.A. Campos and A.W.A Kellner. It had a slender skull about 50 cm (1 ft 6 in.) long with a medial crest along its snout which was an outgrowth of the upper jaw bone. A similar, though smaller crest may have appeared on the lower side of the lower jaw. Its jaw was toothed and it was probably a fish eater, so its crest may well have acted as a cut water, stabilising the head as it dived into the water in the hunt for fish. The proportions of this pterosaur are quite unusual: it had a wingspan of more than 4 m (13 ft) and the skull was twice as long as its body. The pectoral girdle was large and strong, while the pelvis was quite small. This meant that the hind legs of *Anhanguera* could not have been brought into a vertical position under the body. Instead they would have been slightly 'splayed' at the sides, making bird-like bipedal walking near impossible. It seems more likely that *Anhanguera* 'walked' on all fours.

Cearadactylus

Pronounced: SEE-ar-a-DAK-til-us

Another new genus of pterosaurs was established in 1985
based on finds from the Santana Formation of north-
eastern Brazil: *Cearadactylus* (Ceará [one of the Brazilian
States which borders the formation] Finger). The finds
consist so far, of an incomplete skull, the overall
length of which (when 'reconstructed') would be
around 57 cm (1 ft 9 inches). Using this skull length,
palaeontologists estimate that *Cearadactylus* would
have had an enormous wingspan of some 5.5 m (18 ft).
An outstanding feature of the skull is the very powerful
teeth: the front teeth are much longer and stronger than
the back teeth. When the snout was closed there was a
gap in the front area. The long front teeth, set into jaws
which broaden out into a spoon shape at the end, rather
like the jaws of the modern gavial crocodile, suggest a
pterosaur with a very strong, 'fish-grip'. Until further
fossil remains are found, palaeontologists can only
assume certain features about a number of the varied
pterosaurs which lived in this region. It is possible that
when further finds are made, we will discover that some
of them may be related to North American and European
forms.

Name means: Ceará-Finger

Time: Cretaceous (135-65 MYA)

Location: South America: Brazil

Wingspan: 5.5 m (18 ft)

Diet: Piscivorous

Pterodaustro

Pronounced: TER-oh-DOW-stroh

Name means: South Wing

Time: Cretaceous (135-65 MYA)

Location: South America: Argentina

Wingspan: 1.33 m (4 ft 4 in.)

Diet: Piscivore

Nicknamed the 'flamingo pterosaur', *Pterodaustro* is one of the most unusual pterosaurs to be found to date. Discovered in 1969 and named by dinosaur hunter extraordinaire Dr. Jose Bonaparte, *Pterodaustro* was found in early Cretaceous rocks in the province of San Luis in Argentina. A short-tailed pterosaur, *Pterodaustro* had the most remarkable 'elastic' teeth: the skull was very elongated and the front parts of the jaws were bent upwards. In the lower jaw was a groove into which were set a vast number of long, tightly packed teeth, which were more like bristles. Around 24 of these bristles are embedded into 1 cm of jaw: in a jaw 20 cm (8 in) long, that works out at some 500 teeth in each half of the jaw! This made *Pterodaustro's* lower jaw a very effective sieve for filtering small marine organisms from the water: a feeding method similar to that used by blue whales. However, the collected food was then chopped up into smaller bits by blunt, short teeth in the upper jaw. This filter device suggests that *Pterodaustro* did not feed on the wing, but instead had to wade into the water to feed. Its skull was only 23.5 cm 9¼ in.) long, but its wingspan was 1.33 m (4 ft 4 inches). Although *Ctenochasma* (see page 238) found in Solnhofen in Germany was also a filter feeder, it had considerably fewer teeth and for this reason, palaeontologists place the remarkable *Pterodaustro* in a family of its own, the Pterodaustridae.

Quetzalcoatlus

Pronounced: KWETZ-al-CO-AT-lus

Pteranodon sternbergi (see page 248) held the record for
being the largest flying animal ever, until 1971 when an
even larger pterosaur fossil was found in late Cretaceous
rocks in Big Bend National Park, Texas, USA. It was
given the name *Quetzalcoatlus*, after the
Aztec god Quetzalcoatl, who was worshipped
in the formed of a giant winged snake.
Quetzalcoatlus is the last known pterosaur to
have survived to the very end of the Cretaceous period,
but unlike other pterosaurs, its remains were not found in
marine sediment, but in river bedrock which suggests that
while it may have plucked fish from rivers, it may also
have fed on carrion (the carcasses of dead animals). Only
fragments of this immense pterosaur have been found to
date, but the finds suggest a creature with enormously
long and narrow wings . Some palaeontologists
estimate the wingspan between 11 m and 12 m (36-
39 ft): among living birds, the Royal Albatross has the
biggest wingspan, reaching a relative small 3 m (10 ft).
Quetzalcoatlus had an estimated total body weight of 65
kg (142 lb). It also had an extremely long, though rather
inflexible neck, a slender, pointed, and toothless jaw, and
a head topped by a long bony crest. It was probably more
of an accomplished glider than a flyer, soaring high above
the ground on rising thermals. Like a modern vulture,
its keen eyesight would have spotted carrion from great
distances. When it landed it would have probed the dead
beast's body cavity with its long neck
and toothless jaws.

Name means: Quetzalcoatl

Time: Late Cretaceous
(135-65 MYA)

Location: North America: Texas,
USA

Wingspan: 11-12 m (36-39 ft)

Diet: Piscivore, possibly also fed on
carrion

Pteranodon

Pronounced: ter-AN-oh-don

Name means: Toothless Flier

Time: Cretaceous (135-65 MYA)

Location: North America: Kansas, USA

Wingspan: 7 m (23 ft)

Diet: Piscivorous

The first fossil remains of North American pterosaurs were described by O.C. Marsh in 1871. In subsequent years, explorations of the Smoky Hill River in West Kansas (which in those days was still Cheyenne territory) yielded great success and the remains of Cretaceous reptiles were collected in great quantities. The first remains of a pterosaur consisted of half a metacarpal bone from which Marsh estimated that this giant pterosaur had a wingspan of around 6 m (20 ft). Further finds yielded skulls which Marsh discovered were toothless and had a long crest at the rear of the head. None of Marsh's finds of skull were attached to any other bones of the skeleton save for the neck vertebrae which made it difficult to 'match up' skeletons with heads. Nevertheless he did distinguish various species of *Pteranodon* based on the different head crests. *P. ingens* had a skull 1.70 m long (5 ft 9 in.) of which almost half was the crest which extended back to reach as far as the base of the tail. *P. sternbergi* had a jaw that was longer than *P. ingens* and an estimated wingspan of over 9 m (30 ft). It also had a high, upright crest which rose steeply and was broader at the top. *Pteranodon sternbergi* was the largest of the species and was only exceeded in size by the azhdarchids such as *Quetzalcoatlus* (see page 247). But unlike *Quetzalcoatlus*, *Pteranodons* had rather short necks with very strong cervical (neck) vertebrae. They always had crests on the backs of their heads, but never on their snout or lower jaw. All their bones were thin-walled and hollow with small air vents which possibly allowed the penetration of air sacs which were connected to the lungs. The vertebrae also had lateral openings in order to lighten their construction. In order to keep air-borne for long periods, *Pteranodon* needed to keep the body structure as lightweight as possible in order to sustain

flying and soaring as it ranged far out over the seas to hunt. The strata of
West Kansas where the finds of *Pteranodon* have been made, are the deposits
of the 'mid continental sea way', an extended sea which ran through the
North American continent in the Cretaceous period, separating it into eastern
and western halves. The fossil finds of *Pteranodon* were found some 160 km
(100 miles) from what was then the coast and suggest that they flew great
distances from their nesting sites on the coast.

GLOSSARY

Age of Reptiles Alternative name for the Mesozoic Era.

Ammonites Distant relatives of octopus and squid; evolved in the Palaeozoic Era with a flat, spiral shell. Flourished during the Mesozoic Era.

Amphibian Moist-skinned animals that live in both water and land.

Ankylosaurs 'Rounded reptiles': A group of low, heavy, armoured dinosaurs.

Apatosaurus Giant sauropod dinosaur once known as Brontosaurus ('Thunder lizard').

Archaeopteryx The earliest recorded bird from the Jurassic period.

Archosaurs The group of reptiles from which dinosaurs evolved. Today, the crocodile is the only living archosaur, but, the descendants of the early archosaurs are birds.

Arthropod An invertebrate animal with a jointed body and limbs. Insects, spiders and lobsters are all arthropods.

Biped/bipedal Walking on the two hind legs only.

Brachiopods Marine invertebrates with a bivalve shell with a pair of tentacles inside the shell which they use to direct microscopic food to their mouths.

Brontosaurus The dinosaur now known as Apatosaurus.

Carnivore A meat or flesh eating animal.

Carnosaurs Lizard-hipped, carnivorous dinosaurs, the largest of which was Tyrannosaurus

Ceratopsians Horned dinosaurs, the last group of dinosaurs to develop.

Club moss A plant related to the fern; first appeared in the Devonian period and grew to great sizes in the Carboniferous period.

Coelyoposis One of the earliest known dinosaurs of the Triassic period.

Coprolite Fossilised dung.

Cotylosaurs A group of early reptiles of the late Palaeozoic Era and Triassic Period; often known as 'stem reptiles' as they gave rise to all other reptiles.

Cretaceous period The third and final period of the Mesozoic Age, during which time the dinosaurs became extinct.

Diapsids A reptile group with two skull openings behind each eye socket.

Dicynodonts 'Two dog teeth': the first herbivorous mammal-like reptiles of the Permian period with a single pair of tusk-like teeth in the upper jaw.

Dinosaur 'Terrible Lizard': used to refer to any now extinct reptile that lived on earth from 225- 65 million years ago. Dinosaurs divided into two main groups: Lizard-hipped (saurischians) and bird-hipped (ornithiscians) according to the structure of their pelvic bones.

Gastroliths 'Stomach stones': stones swallowed to help grind up food in the stomach.

Ginkgo The southeast Asian 'Maidenhair' tree.

Gondwana The major land mass that made up the southern part of the super-continent Pangaea during the Triassic period. It included present day Africa, Australia, India, Antarctica and South America.

Hadrosaurs 'Duck-billed' dinosaurs. Bipedal dinosaurs of the Cretaceous period which lived on the northern continents. Had wide, toothless beaks and are grouped according to their various head crests (see Hadrosaurines and Lambeosaurines).

Herbivore Plant eating animal.

Ichnology The study of footprints preserved in rocks.

Ichthyosaurs A group of marine reptiles of late Triassic period which resembled modern dolphins in appearance.

Iguanodonts 'Iguana toothed' herbivorous dinosaurs.

Insectivores Insect eating animals.

Invertebrates Animals without a backbone.

Ischium One of the two lower hipbones of the dinosaur (the other was the pubis) Pointing downwards and backwards from the hip socket, the ischium anchored the muscles that powered the hind legs.

Jurassic period The second period of the Mesozoic Era.

Lambeosaurines A hadrosaur (duck-billed dinosaur) with large tubular crests on their heads

Laurasia The 'Northern Continent' in the Triassic period comprising North America, Europe and Asia and which was separated from Gondwana by the sea, Tethys.

Lobe-finned fish Lobe fins take their name from the fact that their fins are carried on short, scale-covered legs. They were the first land-living vertebrates: they had lungs and could breathe air. (See Rhipidistians).

Mammal Any class of higher vertebrates including humans which give birth to live offspring which they feed on milk secreted from mammary glands.

Mesozoic Era The Age of Middle Life, made up of three periods: the Triassic, Jurassic and Cretaceous. The dinosaurs evolved and became extinct in this era, from about 248-65 million years ago.

Mosasaurs Giant sea-going reptiles of the late Cretaceous period.

Nothosaurs A group of marine reptiles that flourished in the Triassic period and had back fins and webbed feet.

Ornithiscians 'Bird-hipped' dinosaurs: one of the two main groups of dinosaurs which are distinguished by the structure of their pelvic girdles.

Ornithopods Herbivorous 'bird-hipped' dinosaurs.

Palaeontology The scientific study of flora (plants) and fauna (animals) that existed in former geological periods.

Pangaea The single land mass or super-continent which stretched from pole to pole in the Triassic period.

Placodonts 'Plated teeth': Triassic period aquatic reptiles: some had 'paddle-like' limbs to propel them, while others had webbed digits and waggled their tails to create a forward motion through the water.

Plesiosaurs Long-necked marine reptiles which swam with flipper-shaped limbs.

Pliosaurs Short-necked plesiosaurs (see above).

Prosauropods Early, herbivorous saurischian dinosaurs.

Pterosaurs 'Winged lizards': Mesozoic 'skin-winged' flying reptiles.

Quadruped/quadrupedal Walking on all fours.

Reptile Cold-blooded vertebrates including lizards, snakes, turtles, crocodiles and dinosaurs.

Rhipidistians A group of Devonian period carnivorous lobe-finned fish (see above) which gave rise to the amphibians.

Saurischians 'Lizard hipped': one major grouping of dinosaurs based on hip structure in which the pubis is long and points forwards and downwards from the hip socket.

Sauropodomorphs Large herbivorous quadrupedal saurischian dinosaurs.

Stegosaurs 'Plated/Roof lizard' Quadrupedal, herbivorous ornithischian dinosaurs with two rows of bony plates and/or spines along the neck, back and tail.

Synapsids A reptile group characterised by a single opening low down on the skull behind the eyes.

Thecodonts 'Socket teeth'. A mixed group of archosaurs (see above) which were the ancestors of dinosaurs and pterosaurs.

Theropods 'Beast feet': the predatory, carnivourous saurischian (lizard-hipped) dinosaurs, armed with sharp teeth and claws.

Triassic period The first period of the Mesozoic Era.

Vertebrates Animals with an internal backbone.

Resources
Museums, Galleries and Sites

United Kingdom

Natural History Museum, Cromwell Road, London SW7
www.nhm.ac.uk

Oxford University Museum of Natural History, Parks Road, Oxford
www.oum.ox.ac.uk

Sedgwick Museum, Downing Street, Cambridge
www.sedgwick.esc.cam.ac.uk

Hunterian Museum, University of Glasgow, University Avenue, Glasgow
www.hunterian.gla.ac.uk

The Dinosaur Museum, Icen Way, Dorchester, Dorset, DT1 1EW

Crystal Palace Park, Sydenham, London SE20

Continental Europe

Institut Royal des Sciences Naturelles de Belgique Rue Vautier 29, B-1040, Brussels, Belgium
www.kbinirsnb.be/general/eng/main_e.htm

National Museum of Natural History, Institute of Palaeontology, Rue de Buffon 8, F-75005, Paris

Musee Parc des Dinosaures, Beziers, France
www.musee-parc-dinosaures.com/anglais/index.htm

USA

Academy of Natural Sciences, 19th & The Parkway, Logan Square, Philadelphia, Pennsylvania 19103.

American Museum of Natural History, Central Park West/79th St, New York, NY 10024
www.amnh.org

Carnegie Museum of Natural History, 4400 Forbes Avenue, Pittsburgh, Pennsylvania, 15213
www.clpgh.org/cmnh

Smithsonian Museum of Natural History, 10th Street & Constitution Avenue, Washington, DC
www.mnh.si.edu

Field Museum of Natural History, 1400 Lake Shore Drive, Chicago, Illinois
www.fmnh.org

Peabody Museum of Natural History, Yale University, 170 Whitney Avenue, New Haven, CT.

Los Angeles County Museum of Natural History, 900 Exposition Blvd, Los Angeles, California
www.lam.mus.ca.us

Dinosaur National Monument Quarry, PO Box 128, Jensen, Utah 84035
www.nps.gov/dino/dinos.htm

Utah Museum of Natural History, University of Utah, Salt Lake City, Utah, 84112

Canada

The Royal Tyrrell Museum of Palaeontology, PO box 7500, Drumheller, Alberta
www.tyrrellmuseum.com

Royal Ontario Museum, Toronto, Ontario, M5S 2C6

National Museum of Natural Sciences, Ottawa, Ontario, KA1 0M8
www.nature.ca/nature_e.cfm

Dinosaur Provincial Park, Patricia, Alberta – excavation in progress

Mexico

Natural History Museum, Mexico City, Mexico

South America

Museo Argentinos de Ciencias Naturales Av. Angel Gallardo 470, 1404 Buenos Aires, Argentina

Museum of La Plata University, La Plata, Argentina

Australia

Australian Museum, College Street , Sydney, New South Wales 2000

Queensland Museum, Gregory Terrace, Fortitude Valley, Queensland, 4006
www.Qmuseum.quld.gov.au

Museum of Victoria, 328 Swanston Street, Melbourne, Victoria 3000

South Africa

Bernard Price Museum of Palaeontology, University of Witswatersand, Jan Smuts Avenue, Johannesburg, 2001

South African Museum, PO Box 61, Cape Town, South Africa, 8000

WEBSITES:

www.bbc.co.uk/dinosaurs
Dinosaurs brought to life by computers by the BBC

www.discovery.com/exp/fossilzone/fossilzone.htm
High tech animation courtesy of the Discovery Channel

www.dinodata.net
Dino facts and figures

www. nhm.com.ac.uk
Stroll through London's Natural History Museum and get up to date information on the latest research, discoveries, and sites

www.dinosauria.com
Images and discussion group

www.nationalgeographic.com/dinorama
Includes models and animations

For younger palaeontologists:

www.goldenbooks.com/dino
Animation, time travel and dinosaurs for children

www.imax.com/t-rex
Travel back in a time machine to meet Tyrannosaurus Rex!

www.projectexploration.org
Join a team of young palaeontologists as they search for fossils in Montana

www.EnchantedLearning.com/subjects/dinosaurs
The best prehistoric and dinosaur jokes!

BIBLIOGRAPHY:

For younger readers:

Steve Parker *1000 Things You Should Know About Dinosaurs* Miles Kelly Publishing, 2002

Dr. Michael Benton *Discovering Dinosaurs* ZigZag Books, 2002

Dr. Michael Benton *Dinosaurs and other prehistoric animals* Kingfisher, 2001

Dougal Dixon *Snapping Turtle Guides: Dinosaurs* Ticktock Publishing, 2001

Selected Bibliography:

J. Augusta and Z. Burian *Prehistoric Reptiles and Birds* Paul Hamlyn, 1963

J. Augusta and Z. Burian *Prehistoric Sea Monsters* Paul Hamlyn, 1964

Deborah Cadbury *The Dinosaur Hunters* Fourth Estate, 2001

Neil Clark and William Lindsay *Dinosaurs* Dorling Kindersley Pocket Books, 1997

Professor Barry Cox, Professor R.J.G Savage, Professor Brian Gardiner and Dougal Dixon *Macmillan Illustrated Encyclopedia of Dinosaurs and Prehistoric Animals* Macmillan, 1988

Encyclopedia of Dinosaurs and Prehistoric Life, Dorling Kindersley, in Association with the American Museum of Natural History, Dorling Kindersley, 2001

David Lambert *The Ultimate Dinosaur Book* Dorling Kindersley, in association with The Natural History Museum, London. 1993

D. Norman *The Illustrated Encyclopedia of Dinosaurs* Salamander, 1985

Dr. David Norman & Dr. Peter Wellnhofer *The Illustrated Encyclopedia of Dinosaurs* Salamander Books, 2000

Hazel Richardson *Dinosaurs and Prehistoric Life* Dorling Kindersley, 2003

M. Tweedie *The World of Dinosaurs* Wiedenfeld and Nicholson, 1977

J.N Wilford *The Riddle of the Dinosaurs* Faber, 1985

Credits & acknowledgements

Special thanks to the staff- and to all the 'experts'– most of whom averaged 12 years old –- at the Natural History Museum, London, for their enthusiasm and knowledge of dinosaurs, and for their recommendations regarding books and websites. Thanks also to Vic Swift at the British Library, London.

Picture credits
Pictures pp 7, 8, 9, 19, 26, 41 © Getty Images